D0191045

QUOTES

"An extraordinary and deeply moving account of a woman who lost her husband, Michael Zaslow, to Lou Gehrig's disease. She has become a prime mover in the battle to eliminate ALS. She's a brave and caring woman."

—MIKE WALLACE, CBS CORRESPONDENT

"Obviously I knew how the book would end, but as I read I was completely mesmerized. Susan Hufford writes so beautifully and poetically I almost felt like I was reading a great mystery. The book simply took my breath away. I applaud Hufford for her truth and honesty and humor and for her passion to show the world that there was a man in that ravaged body, and he had, and continues to have—a powerful soul. This book must be read!

—AMY FERRIS, AUTHOR & COLUMNIST

"Susan Hufford has been a consistent and determined champion on behalf of ALS victims since the diagnosis of her late husband, Michael Zaslow. I urge you to buy this amazing book!"

—ALEC BALDWIN, ACTOR, ACTIVIST

"Michael Zaslow was a giant talent who took on the killer disease ALS with passion and grit. ZAZ and his beloved wife Susan have written exquisitely of their biggest drama ever. This is a piercing story of courage, betrayal, terror and love. Don't Miss It!"

—DONNA HANOVER, JOURNALIST AND FORMER FIRST LADY
OF NEW YORK

Not That Man Anymore is a moving and inspiring look at the battle against ALS through the eyes of a couple on the front lines. Susan Hufford and Michael Zaslow have given us a beautiful narrative in which a loving husband and wife alternate their voices as together they establish a diagnosis, search for treatment, and display their determination to help others. For clinicians and scientists, this book provides a valuable reminder of the urgency of their work. For patients and families, it provides a window into the strategy of coping. And for every reader, *Not That Man Anymore* is a rare and revealing view into the strength of the human spirit."

—ROBERT BOWSER, M.D., Ph.D. UNIVERSITY OF PITTSBURG

NOT THAT MAN ANYMORE

Other Books By Susan Hufford:

Reflections
Going All the Way
Miracles
Trial of Innocence

Grateful acknowledgment is given for excerpts from:
T.S. Eliot's *Four Quartets*
Jean-Dominique Bauby's *The Diving Bell and the Butterfly*
Shakespeare's *King Lear*

NOT THAT MAN ANYMORE

(A MESSAGE FROM MICHAEL)

Michael Zaslow & Susan Hufford

AMADOR COUNTY LIBRARY
530 SUTTER STREET
JACKSON, CA 95642

iUniverse, Inc.
New York Lincoln Shanghai

NOT THAT MAN ANYMORE
(A MESSAGE FROM MICHAEL)

Copyright © 2005 by Susan Hufford

All rights reserved. No part of this book may be used or reproduced by any means, graphic, electronic, or mechanical, including photocopying, recording, taping or by any information storage retrieval system without the written permission of the publisher except in the case of brief quotations embodied in critical articles and reviews.

iUniverse books may be ordered through booksellers or by contacting:

iUniverse
2021 Pine Lake Road, Suite 100
Lincoln, NE 68512
www.iuniverse.com
1-800-Authors (1-800-288-4677)

ISBN-13: 978-0-595-34050-7 (pbk)
ISBN-13: 978-0-595-78837-8 (ebk)
ISBN-10: 0-595-34050-4 (pbk)
ISBN-10: 0-595-78837-8 (ebk)

Printed in the United States of America

This book is dedicated with deepest love to our daughters, Marika and Helena. Their presence in our life is *proof* of the divine wisdom, compassion, and goodness inherent in this journey called Life.

It is also humbly dedicated to all PALS everywhere and to their families, present and future—until there is a cure.

This dynamic, precarious, mysterious thing that
we know as…life, is constantly altering,
changing. It is not a "fixed nugget," but an
unfolding narrative, not an immutable tale, but a
transitory tale of ambiguity and contingency,
a celebration of adventure and change and difference.

The negativity and hopelessness that surrounds
Amyotrophic Lateral Sclerosis (ALS) offends my sense of logic. Of course
there will be a cure.
Michael Zaslow, September, 1998

Contents

AUTHOR'S NOTE

I have made every effort to protect individuals and institutions in this book by changing certain names, locations, and details. My goal has always been to tell this story as candidly and truthfully as I can.

FOREWORD

It is with both great honor and regret that I have been asked to write the foreword for this book. As one of Michael Zaslow's treating neurologists, I was privileged to share in Michael's fighting spirit and optimism as he battled ALS (Amyotrophic Lateral Sclerosis). Michael's intent was to use his celebrity status to raise awareness and accelerate the pace of ALS research. This was in 1998 and for the first time there was finally a glimmer of hope that a breakthrough was on the horizon. There were several tantalizing new prospects including the possibility that stem cells could be used to halt the progression of the disease. There was the emerging recognition by ALS researchers that in addition to pursuing the single "magic bullet" approach to treatment, a combinational approach to treatment should be a top priority. Furthermore, there were new scientists from various highly esteemed institutions who were making it a point to share data in a collective effort to fight this fatal disease.

At the time it seemed that with so much brain power focused on a single effort, a breakthrough in ALS was imminent. But the pace of research paled in comparison to the pace of the disease and Michael died before seeing the fruits of his labor.

So, where are we now, almost seven years after Michael's own battle with ALS was lost? In some ways it seems we are closer to that breakthrough and, in other ways, still far away. Thanks to Michael, more research dollars are devoted to ALS and there is a renewed sense of urgency amongst scientists to study the disease. When I was in my training, the prevailing attitude regarding ALS was "diagnose and adios." Little was offered to patients other than options regarding life support. Today there are numerous clinical studies and basic scientific research exploring the genetic and metabolic factors involved in the pathological cascade of ALS. There is a cautious, but nevertheless renewed, optimism that a cure may be on the way. But the clock keeps ticking and ALS is an impatient, merciless disorder. It is more virulent than HIV and the majority of cancers. It quickly robs patients first of their dignity and then of their lives. Only by fixing our gaze unwaveringly on this killer will we find the cure that eluded Michael and so many other patients. We all owe Michael a deep debt of gratitude for showing us the way. I deeply regret that he won't be here to see it when it happens.

Dr. Jay Lombard
Director, Brain Behavior Center, Rockland County, New York

INTRODUCTION

July 1, 1999, Roxbury, Connecticut

As I attempt to complete the book my husband began when he first noticed the vocal slurring which led to the unthinkable diagnosis of ALS, I am struck by a memory from only two years earlier. This indelible image is of Michael in tennis whites, red-faced and sweaty, pumping like crazy to bike up our steep driveway. He was proud of himself for having played two sets of tennis, for having persevered, for continuing to live the life he had taken for granted.

Michael was determined to write about his journey with Amyotrophic Lateral Sclerosis, more familiarly known as ALS or Lou Gehrig's disease. Although this so-called orphan's disease strikes about the same number of people as Multiple Sclerosis, it has become a metaphor for hopeless. A cruel neurological disease that fractures families emotionally, physically, and financially, ALS robs men and women of their ability to walk, talk, and finally to breathe while their minds remain totally unaffected.

From the day he was diagnosed, Michael said, "Yes!" to every opportunity to raise funds for or to create awareness about ALS. He started writing a book. When the disease weakened his right hand, we felt lucky because he was left-handed. Soon his left hand faltered, his script became an indecipherable wavy line. Doggedly he pecked away at the computer. We made plans to spend more time at our country home in Roxbury so that he could work on the book.

It never happened. Without warning, on a sunny, crystal cold December Sunday, Michael stopped breathing. It was barely a year after his diagnosis, unexpected, even for ALS. When I arrived home from our daughter, Helena's violin recital, two ambulances were angled onto the sidewalk outside of our New York apartment building. In an instant I grasped the significance of the inexplicable flow of tears I had been powerless to control throughout the

1

entire recital. I started running as fast as I could and when the elevator man informed me the ambulances were for my husband, I snarled, "I know!"

Our apartment was a chaotic jumble of medics and police. Michael lay face up on our rug. In an attempt to revive him, someone had ripped open the front of his favorite T-shirt. A Father's Day present from Marika and Helena, the shirt featured the image of a fiercely majestic silver wolf that had always reminded me of Michael.

Michael and I had been unable to have a conversation for over two years. The loss of our abundant sharing of thoughts, ideas, opinions, and jokes, was devastating. Like that of Beatrice and Benedict, from the very beginning our love affair had been defined by a torrent of words. We had stayed up until 7 AM talking…after our very first date! We gabbed incessantly. When Michael lost his voice the silence drove a wedge between us.

After his death, I began talking to him, in my head. How could I be faithful to his vision for a book about his journey with ALS? How could I even begin to convey the moment-to-moment losses, the uncertainty, fear, or the satisfaction he found in being able to make a difference for people with disabilities and misunderstood, under-funded diseases? I was reluctant to assume his voice, though after twenty-seven years, we often read each other's thoughts, to a humorous, and occasionally scary, degree. For all my love, my insight and good intentions, could I really presume to know what it was like to live with ALS?

For the first time in over two years, Michael and I had conversations unencumbered by my sense of guilt because I could talk, his occasional anger at me for doing so, and the ever-present yellow legal pads and frustrating, augmented-voice computers which were his only means of communicating. Talking to a departed loved one is not unusual. I knew it was considered a healthy form of grieving. Whatever it was, those mental dialogues were our first real discourses in ages, and, in some strange way, they were a relief.

So, in my mind we talked, seemingly making up for lost time. The day of his memorial service at Riverside Chapel, as I was resting on our bed, I told him: "It's not really you. It's me talking for you. It's my imagination making up things I want you to say because I can't bear that you aren't here."

"I'm here. I'm with you," Michael assured me.

"Prove it." I challenged him.

"I will." His mischievous tone of voice suggested he was grinning like the Cheshire cat he could be. "Speak at the memorial service."

"No way," I recoiled. "I don't speak in public. That's your bit. You know I don't even like big parties. I curl up in a corner and leaf through magazines or I latch onto one person until one of us gets bored or one of us has to pee. I can't speak in front of large groups."

"There are things that must be said. You have to do it."

"How can you prove it's *you* talking and not me? *I need proof!*"

"You'll know it's me because you won't be nervous."

I did not believe him, but I sat down at the computer and began to write. I asked Bob Krimmer, a fellow-actor and friend to accompany me to the podium so he could read my words if I faltered.

But I wasn't nervous...not even a little bit. You might say I was in shock. And you would be right. But this first "message" from Michael, together with other messages, have convinced me it was more than shock.

Months later, poring through scraps of paper, old e-mails, stacks of medical records, the brief draft Michael had labored over, I asked for another message. I hadn't a clue where to begin finishing a book he had barely begun.

Then, I received a message. As I was walking with our dog, Lily, on Welton Road, a wooded, rutted dirt road near our house in Connecticut, I was struck by patches of light. These myriad designs, some large and lacy, others barely dots and freckles formed a constantly changing patchwork. The patterns created by light filtering through leaves transported me into the world of an Impressionistic painting. Those paintings were a part of our life together. We loved them and, whenever we were in Paris, we headed straight to the Musée d'Orsay to visit our old friends. With each reunion, we were bewitched and fascinated by the use of light, which endowed every-day objects and scenes with a deeper, mysterious reality.

The light, the variety of form, the shadows, the indescribably beautiful, complex, shifting, playful shapes and images on that Connecticut dirt road clarified how I should proceed with the book. I had received another message from Michael.

Many people's words, not just Michael's and mine, make up this book. Contributors include angels, both seen and unseen, as well as the people in our lives during the illness—our daughters, Marika and Helena, friends, colleagues, doctors, and Michael's loyal fans. Their perspectives, like the light shimmering through oak, maple, and beech leaves help illuminate Michael's journey, just as reflected light transforms a dirt road into a ribbon of dancing shapes.

All diseases infect more than just the person with the illness. Michael's battle was excruciating, but it was also inspiring. Whenever I walk on Welton Road, it is clear to me that the book is writing itself in his absence. Or, perchance, it is being celestially dictated from some other dimension many of us can neither fathom nor accept. The messages, as you will see, continue to come.

At Michael's memorial service, I asked William Baldwin to read a section from T. S. Eliot's *Four Quartets*, which we recited as part of our wedding vows in 1975. As the journey continues, Eliot's words resonate with an even more profound meaning.

> *We shall not cease from exploration*
> *And the end of our exploring*
> *Will be to arrive where we started*
> *And know the place for the first time.*
> *Through the unknown, remembered gate*
> *When the last of earth left to discover*
> *Is that which was the beginning;*
> *At the source of the longest river*
> *The voice of the hidden waterfall*
> *And the children in the apple-tree*
> *Not known, because not looked for*
> *But heard, half-heard, in the stillness*
> *Between two waves of the sea.*
> *Quick now, here, now, always—*
> *A condition of complete simplicity*
> *(Costing not less than everything)*
> *And all shall be well*
> *All manner of thing shall be well*
> *When the tongues of flame are in-folded*
> *Into the crowned knot of fire*
> *And the fire and the rose are one.*

1

NOTHING IS IMPOSSIBLE!

Someone once asked me what it was like when I first realized my husband had a fatal illness. There are countless accounts of couples coming to grips with "the worst," sharing their grief, planning for the inevitable. Maybe we should have done that...but we didn't. There was no gestalt, no singular moment, but an avalanche of moments and with each one we cried, "No! No, this is not going to get US. So it's ALS. Michael will beat it. We will find a cure. Nothing, no nothing is impossible! We are going to win! Denial? Or survival?

—Susan Hufford

"I'm not that man anymore." In September 1996, the moment I first noticed something was wrong with my voice was captured on videotape forever. I repeated the phrase in the sanctity of my dressing room, surrounded by photographs of my darling daughters, Marika and Helena. The walls were covered with their artwork. My mirror was a collage of their faces from infancy.

"I'm not that man anymore. Mananymore. Nanymore." My tongue would not negotiate that simple phrase. My voice sounded unfamiliar. Not me anymore. I tried the phrase on Maureen Garrett, the actress who played Holly, and a friend of long standing. She said she couldn't hear any difference in my speech and neither did anyone else. It was only on that one line. I felt the kind of uncertain trepidation I hadn't experienced since my early years in television.

For the previous six months, I had faced the most difficult challenge I had ever endured as an actor. I, or rather, Roger—the character I had played on The Guiding Light on and off for over a quarter of a century—had pretended to go mad while actually unraveling completely off the spool. That was my take on it, at least, since the only way I, the actor, could justify Roger's lunatic behavior as scripted, was by deciding he must be losing his mind!

He (Roger) had poisoned his gorgeous young wife with a fictional substance the writers referred to as "lonotrat." The writers offered absolutely no other motivation than money. Roger was rotten, Roger was slippery, but one thing Roger never was, was simple minded. He was far too complex a character…convoluted, yes, even sick…but simple, never. This was not the Roger I had lived with for decades, and I made the writer and executive producer aware of my concern about the logic of the character.

My opposition came to no avail. I was working every day, despite a clause in my contract stipulating I was to work no more than four days a week. I digested as much as forty pages of dialogue and then emptied my brain of those forty pages to make room for the next batch. Never had I worked so hard and never had I labored in such an illogical story line. But I was being handsomely paid to justify Roger's apparent dementia so I just shut up and worked.

Three months earlier, in June of 1996, I had also been learning lines for my role as Henry Higgins in My Fair Lady, *in which I was to appear at the Pittsburgh Civic Light Opera. Higgins quite literally does not shut up for over two hours.*

My last week at the studio, I had fifty pages of dialogue daily to be spit out at a feverish pitch as Roger's descent into madness accelerated. Finally, Friday rolled around. The writers were well aware that I was to begin My Fair Lady *rehearsals that evening. Despite the four-show-a-week limit in my contract, they scheduled me for a fifth day Friday morning and handed me the largest volume of dialogue I had seen in my twenty-seven year experience. Lamentably, I had acquired the reputation of an actor who was a quick study, a label I had come to deem a curse rather than a compliment.*

The scenes took place in a courtroom where Roger, representing himself, called himself to the stand as a witness. In an eight-page monologue, Roger pleaded his sanity to the judge. I had no one else with whom to trade dialogue. I had only Roger (and the writers) to blame. He ended his testimony by screaming us both hoarse and plunging an ink pen he had been fiddling with into the witness stand!

The cast and crew burst into applause, I said my goodbyes and left the sound stage to shed my Roger clothes and makeup. I had packed the night before, and a car was waiting to rush me to La Guardia. I was through being a split personality between Roger and Henry Higgins. And myself? I didn't really have time to think about that.

*   *   *

When Michael flew off to Pittsburgh, he had no apparent symptoms. He was thrilled to be playing Henry Higgins and with his usual diligence had been studying the role for months. Marika and Helena and I had listened to *Fair Lady* tapes in the car as we drove back and forth to Connecticut, all of us singing along. Any one of us could have played Henry at a moment's notice. I thought Michael was the ideal Henry, both irritatingly perfectionistic and utterly brilliant.

Yet there was something different about Michael, and even then I was aware of some vague change, which I believed was stress-related. From the time of his first rehearsal, our nightly phone calls had a rough, unsettling edge. I'd lived through decades of Michael's rehearsals and knew how finicky and fretful he could get, but this time he was constantly agitated and unable to enjoy an experience he had been looking forward to for the past six months. At first, I figured his anxiety stemmed from the pressure of so many words and of not having performed in a musical in a number of years. But when Marika and Helena and I visited him before the opening, I found him uncharacteristically frazzled and insecure.

*   *   *

I was not prepared for the palatial proportions of Pittsburgh's Benadum Opera House, nor the marquee, which blazed my name. It had never occurred to me to covet the role of Henry Higgins because the character as created by Rex Harrison was perfection and I was certainly not his type. But I had come to love Henry and could tap into the unrelentingly high standards he set for himself. The obsessive perfectionism was something with which I was all too familiar.

Opening night was packed. Susan, Marika, and Helena were out front, and I was giddy with happiness at being back in the theater, singing. I did have one miserable moment when my body mike went out on me just before a fast change into black tie and mourning coat. In the midst of my change, a technician burst into my dressing room and, overriding my protests, insisted on changing the mike. My temper was about to go over the top but the technician's determination prevailed and I took off. I ran wildly back to the stage with my dresser and the soundman trailing in a vain attempt to render me less disheveled. I arrived on stage just barely under the wire, which, I soon realized was poking out this way and that from my unbuttoned vest. I was fighting mad. A perfectionist does not like to appear in public with his wires hanging out.

Still, it somehow turned out to be a perfect opening night. Experience had taught me to resist the urge to dash out first thing in the morning and buy newspapers so I could read the reviews. When I had arrived in New York at the age of twenty-five and found getting an acting job far easier than finding an affordable apartment, I landed the role of a Liverpudlian rock drummer in the national tour of the British import There's A Girl in My Soup. *Receiving exit applause after my two short scenes, I began shamelessly playing to the audience and lapping up their laughter like an attention-starved toddler. The night after we opened, at the Dupont Theatre in Wilmington, Delaware, I zipped out at the first hint of daylight in a sweat of anticipation to read my brilliant notices, forgetting completely how the others had fared or how the show had done. With my exit applause echoing in my ears, I had torn open the paper and stood on the corner, gobbling up what was a very bad review for the show and its stars. But where, I wondered, was the mention of moi? The reviewer had saved the last paragraph for me and me alone: "But worst of all in every way, was Michael Zaslow." One never forgets a review like that.*

So my rave notices in My Fair Lady *were hearsay, since I religiously avoided reading reviews. But my hunger to work in the theater was full-blown, and I was determined to spend more time there. The two-week run flew by and I was back in New York pre- and post-taping* Guiding Light *shows before we headed for Martha's Vineyard for a well-deserved week of rest and relaxation.*

✳   ✳   ✳

Our week in the Vineyard was just about perfect. The weather was cloudless and sunny, except for one night when the fog rolled in to Edgartown so thick that we could scarcely see our hands stretched out in front of us. I had spent hours on the telephone with a quixotic real estate agent and we were not disappointed in the gray, shingled cottage he procured for our stay. Our abode was located at the end of a two-mile dirt road and offered an unparalleled, uninterrupted vista of water and a view of a horizon that was timeless and unmarred by human improvements. There was a tiny beach, a dock with a good enough canoe, and there was even a small guesthouse for Milt, Michael's Dad.

Michael rose early and biked while I logged a record-breaking fifty miles of race-walking during the week. We shared books, lounging in bed reading out loud to each other the way we did when we first met in 1971. One night,

Michael short-sheeted the bed! We laughed, high on life, love, two wonderful daughters, and our hard-won good fortune. How amazing that we, two neurotic only children, had created such a life! We posed for a photograph on the deck with the ocean behind us, holding hands and grinning. How lucky were we? We cooked lobster almost every night and drank in the stars. Time was a wonderful thing to have and, for once, we had plenty of it. Just having it was more than enough.

2

A NERVOUS BREAKDOWN

I remember the scene where I first noticed something was wrong. He, I mean Roger, the character Michael played on our show, was going into an insane asylum. Michael had a line saying he was "not that man anymore." He was frantic. Scared. He kept saying something was wrong with his voice. I said, "It's nothing. You're fine." But I really thought he, Michael, was having a nervous breakdown.

—Maureen Garrett, friend, actor

"Not that man anymore." After our fun week in the Vineyard we were back in New York and I no longer felt so lucky. I joked with Maureen Garrett that maybe the loquacious Higgins had done me in, and I thought longingly of my weeks on stage in Pittsburgh. Daytime television had been very good to me. I felt very protective of my alter ego Roger, but at times I felt trapped. Despite the salary, the schedule was often daunting, and usually there was so much dialogue to learn that I'd been unable to find time for theater projects, as many daytime actors do.

I tried the dreaded line on Susan when I got home, and when she said she heard "something," I was both relieved and scared. I repeated the line again and again until she was ready to boot me out. I could affect no change in the subtle, but to my ear, garbled sound.

*   *   *

Michael and I were the only people who detected any change in his speech. That is how slight it was. Our friends couldn't hear anything different, and neither could his costar Maureen Garrett or any of the other cast members. Why was Michael making such a big deal about such a tiny flaw? Wasn't this just an extreme example of the perfectionism, which everyone who knew him was familiar with? We teased him about this new tick, as if it was part of his charm.

But this particular idiosyncrasy wasn't funny anymore. Maybe he was falling apart. He worried constantly about his father, Milton, who had declined both physically and mentally since his wife Edith's death a year earlier. Milton was losing touch with reality and, at times, it seemed so was Michael.

I shared my concerns with close friends. His best friend Stephen Yates and tennis partner Pete Gurney were worried about the same thing. I tried to persuade Michael to go back into therapy to explore not only the vocal symptom, but his self-reproach for ostensibly not living up to his potential. If he was unhappy on the show, he should quit, I told him. If he wanted to do theater, we would adjust our lives. We would manage. We were not people who needed a certain lifestyle to be happy. We needed only ourselves and each other. We had two brilliant, beautiful, good daughters. We were lucky.

*   *   *

After that first terrifying episode, I encountered phrases that grew increasingly difficult. I consulted a speech therapist with the hope of figuring out what was going on. That was where I first encountered the word dysarthria, *stemming from the Greek word that means "crooked speech".*

The irony was all too obvious. I had just played the role of the obsessive speech pathologist Henry Higgins, and, lo and behold, I had developed a speech problem. I spun around in the psychological conundrum, searching for some hidden meaning that would lead me out of the maze. But the maze grew more twisted and harder to navigate each day.

It was true that I had been dealing with more than the usual amount of stress. Little more than a year before the speech problems began, I had lost my dear mother. She went the way she wanted to go, which came as no surprise to anyone who knew Edith Zaslow. Mom lived her life as a force of nature—full blown, always at the blustery peak of emotion. On Mother's Day, a rose in one hand given to her by her adoring husband, and a martini in the other, Edith was felled by an aneurysm to the brain. Her final words were: "No! No, not the hospital!"

An intrepid fighter for the rights of others, Edith feared nothing so much as lying helpless in some hospital, "non-compos mentis," as she put it, with nobody to unplug the respirator.

As soon as Dad telephoned me in New York, I flew to San Diego and took a taxi-cab to the Del Mar Beach Club, where my parents had spent seventeen idyllic years situated high on a bluff overlooking the Pacific Ocean. Mom kept figuratively pinch-ing herself to believe that Little Edith, after a lifetime of struggle, could have had such good fortune. Her own father had committed suicide when she was three, and three years later, her mother and a boyfriend, under the guise of a family picnic, had literally deposited Mom and her older sister, Hilda, at a home for children in Wilton, Connecticut.

Edith's mother, Dora Bernstein, was a skilled seamstress in New York's garment district and when Edith was old enough she followed her mother's lead and entered the needle trade. Naturally skillful and fast, Edith performed what was called "piece-work." This type of work was high in the pecking order, and Mom was paid according to how much she produced instead of according to how many hours she labored. Although the garment business was her trade, my mother's true passion, from start to finish, was in the class struggle. Everywhere Mom looked she saw injustice, and she didn't have to look far to see it in the sweatshops in which she her-self toiled. Edith became one of the early organizers of the ILGWU, or International Ladies Garment Workers Union. She organized and led strikes for better working conditions and for a genuine living wage. One of her (and my) most prized memen-toes was a photograph of her and my godmother, Mary Donovan, grinning trium-phantly through the bars of their jail cell. They had been incarcerated for lying down in an alley in an attempt to block delivery trucks and to stop the so-called scabs workers who were crossing picket lines to go to work.

My father, Milton Zaslow, was the youngest of three brothers born to Russian immigrants Etta and Saul Zaslow. Like Edith, Milton was also a spokesman for the underdog and an uncompromising fighter for justice. He met my mother through the socialist movement and fell in love with her tremendous spirit. Dad, a founding leader of the Socialist Worker's Party, once ran for governor of New York on the party ticket.

I, Michael Joel Zaslow, more often called Mickey by the family, was born in 1942 in San Pedro, California, where my father worked in the shipbuilding trade and also organized unions. When I was still a toddler, my family moved briefly to Chicago for more union organizing, then to New York City and back to Los Angeles, where I completed high school and attended UCLA. When my parents were finally able to retire, they were shocked by the California lifestyle they had realized through a combination of enterprise, perseverance, and plain good luck.

Though not religious, my parents were deeply thankful for what they had. Almost every sunset, Dad would make two perfect martinis, and he and my mother would walk out to the bluff overlooking the Pacific. There, drinking in the grandeur and serenity, they would toast each other and me, their only child.

3

HOW CAN A VOICE JUST DISAPPEAR?

How did Michael lose his voice? How can a voice just disappear? Could it happen to me? I used to like how he would smell our dinner and come in and ask for some. He was funny. Boy did he like to eat! When he couldn't walk anymore, he would still smell cookies and ride in on his red motor chair. I miss him.

—*Rachel Pollan (age 5), friend and neighbor*

Edith and Milt's only child…that was me. Since adulthood (whenever that occurs), I have been striving to please them. I guess I succeeded, to a degree. In May 1994, exactly one year before my mother's death, I won the Emmy for Best Lead Actor on a Daytime Serial.

"Look, Mom and Dad, I am the best!" Finally, I had a major trophy, something tangible to show them.

That year, I agonized over whether or not to prepare an acceptance speech for my Emmy. After all, I had prepared a speech the previous year, only to end up wadding up the speech and depositing it in my tuxedo pocket when my name hadn't been announced. Susan and I had crept through the bowels of the Marriott Hotel like thieves, just to avoid facing the press and disappointed fans. We laughed about it later, but it was a jaunt I did not look forward to repeating. I was afraid of jinxing myself if I wrote another speech. When my name was called as the Emmy winner, I was glad I had taken Susan's advice and written something "just in case."

I was ecstatic both for myself and Susan, but even more so for Marika and Helena, who wouldn't have to write another consolation note and tape it to our front door. But I was happiest of all for my parents, and I saved the last sentence of my

14

acceptance speech for them: "But most of all, I thank my parents, who taught me how to love."

My elation at finally being a worthy son was short-lived. Maybe winning the Emmy upped the ante. Proving myself became a kind of addiction, and I threw myself into as many worthy causes as I could manage, all on top of my regular job responsibilities and fathering my beloved daughters. I was deeply committed to the work of The Creative Coalition, an advocacy organization of people in the arts, and served on their board of directors. I also served on the national board of our union, the American Federation of Radio and Television Artists. "Look, Mom and Dad, isn't your sonny boy a chip off the proverbial block?" I was seemingly unable to turn down any request to appear for a worthy cause. Meanwhile, my cantankerous Uncle Danny was near death in an upstate nursing home. I was Danny's sole responsible relative and so, every other week, I hired someone to drive our car up to visit him while I sat in the back seat memorizing lines. In addition, my father, who struggled valiantly after Mom's death, was exhibiting troublesome symptoms that required my constant surveillance.

The logical explanation for the change in my speech was that I, like my mother, had suffered a slight stroke. I telephoned our internist and friend Dr. A, who prescribed the necessary tests. The answer was conclusive: there was no evidence of a stroke.

Susan was relieved. I was not.

I sought the top speech therapist, Dr. B. There was a three-month waiting list, but thanks to Roger, I found a fan in Dr. B's assistant who bumped me to the head of the list. Dr. B put me through a battery of tests, the most memorable of which was a high-tech test that consisted of me reading my next day's script into a microphone and watching as the machine graphed my speech pattern. We devised ways of skirting the problem, often rewriting difficult phrases. After a few weeks, Dr. B suggested I change my career from acting to directing. That was my last consultation with Dr. B.

I found a new speech therapist, and we went to work, drilling my lines and rewording problematic phrases. So it went, the occasional lapse in perfect diction being my only symptom. Still, no one at the studio noticed! I even asked one of our directors if he had detected any change in my speech or heard a buzz in the control room pertaining to my problem. He assured me he hadn't and promised to alert me if he did. Incidentally, I am probably the only person in history who has a videotaped record of this dysarthria from its onset.

*   *   *

At times, I suspected Michael was intoning certain words on purpose, as if he were preparing for a part and had chosen this vocal device for the character. I'd seen him throw himself into roles before, unconsciously allowing the character to spill over. The slurring and nasality were extremely subtle, occurring infrequently, but he was always still listening. I felt as if he could no longer hear what I or Marika and Helena were saying. He was always listening to himself.

*   *   *

The tension between Susan and I mounted, but I couldn't stop asking if she heard what I heard. Her answer was always the same—it was stress. I was never satisfied. I never stopped.

She was right about me never being able to stop. There was an AFTRA board meeting, a Creative Coalition Retreat coming up on the 28th, and on October 15, I'd agreed to be the master of ceremonies for Sarah and Jim Brady's annual gun control fund-raiser in Washington, D.C. There was a St. Jude's Benefit in New York and our chimney in Connecticut had to be cleaned. I made a note to try to schedule that for October 5. There was Marika's birthday party on September 24 and Helena's on October 23.

*   *   *

When Uncle Danny died, there was not only the house in Woodstock, but all of Danny's paintings, in addition to the time-consuming entanglements that go with probate and settling an estate. Michael had a strong sentimental attachment to the house, but there was no way he could deal with it and he was determined to sell it before winter, even if it meant taking a loss. There was Jose, our elevator man who had ended up in prison and was being held for an unreasonably high bail. Over the years, he had become like part of our family. Michael and I both spent hours talking on the phone and writing letters trying to wrest Jose from a judicial quagmire. Throughout, Michael was extremely vigilant of his speech, testing himself constantly: "I'm not that man anymore. Mananymore."

Something was suddenly threatening our happiness, unsettling all that I had come to trust and believe in: *us*. I sometimes dreaded being with him because everything revolved around him and the almost imperceptible change in his speech. The optimistic Michael whom I loved and upon whom I relied was turning into a negative hypochondriac. Or so I thought. "…Not that man any more?" This was definitely not the man I knew.

*   *   *

Was I, like the character I had played for so many years on The Guiding Light, *losing my mind? But Roger was only pretending to lose his mind, and what was happening to me felt all too real. I retreated into our bedroom, stretched out on the bed and took out tomorrow's script. I read out loud and listened intently to each word, each syllable. I called and made an additional appointment with my new speech therapist and then telephoned Dad in California to see if his medical reports were back yet. Finally, I allowed myself to do what I really wanted to do, which was work on the speech I was scheduled to give for Sarah and Handgun Control Dinner Benefit.*

Susan and I took the afternoon air shuttle to Washington and were met by a car from Sarah Brady's office. The car took us straight to a television studio where I did an interview for the CBS affiliate. Then it was back to the Marriott Hotel where, in a matter of hours, I would be standing in front of a packed political house. The dreaded word "anybody" was in the speech. I tried it out on Susan as the car crept through the thick, five o'clock traffic.

"Thank you, Sarah and Jim," I rehearsed my speech. "When Sarah asked me to give the closing speech at this event last fall, I was honored and delighted. When she asked me to MC the event this fall, I was intimidated." I stopped.

Susan reassured me, and I continued. "To write and deliver a short speech was one thing, but to MC?" I said. "Well, I demurred politely. But has anybody ever tried saying no to Sarah?"

"Did you hear it?"

"I heard a little tiny bit on 'anybody,'" she answered. "Nobody else will notice."

"Anybody, any body, any buddy," I repeated the word under my breath, inside my head, hoping the difference I heard would go away, hoping that I was just being my usual overly critical self.

The car dropped us at the hotel, and we went up to our room. We'd been looking forward to the trip and the time alone, including a leisurely lunch tomorrow after a visit to the National Gallery. Pat Alexander, who had worked for us when the chil-

dren were younger, was staying with Marika and Helena. We had the entire evening and all day tomorrow to have fun.

"Handgun violence is but one of the daunting symptoms that plague our nation. America is the world leader by far in weapons production and sales, which, in fact, is directly related to the unparalleled level of violence at home. Every day 135,000 children take guns to school..."

The phone rang and I continued practicing my speech as Susan answered it.

"The benchmark of a society must be the degree to which it nurtures, educates, and protects its citizens, especially its children. It seems self-evident that each baby, each child, depending on how he or she is treated, will grow up to either help or hurt the world. As parents, we look for ways to protect our children, to try to keep them out of harm's way."

Suddenly, Susan exploded on the phone. Pat, who had not missed a day in all the years of working for us, had left a message saying she couldn't stay with the children. It was not life threatening, but she had to go to the hospital for immediate evaluation.

"They'll be fine with Diane and Richard next door."

"They say they can't stay alone."

That was ridiculous. They were always lobbying to stay without a babysitter. I took the phone and listened as they bemoaned their vulnerability.

"I don't believe this..." my wife cried, although I have purposefully omitted her more colorful exclamations. "My purse is gone! My glasses are in my purse. I can't wear sunglasses at night in Washington!"

At that moment, neither of us could see any humor in the situation, and plans for a romantic interlude fell by the wayside. After solving the babysitter problem and making calls regarding the whereabouts of Susan's glasses, we threw on our clothes and went down to the benefit.

"The United States is at or near the bottom in critical indicators of infant mortality, low birth weight, and children living in poverty. In the last two categories, we are dead last among industrialized nations."

I somehow made it through my opening remarks without making a fool of myself. Thanks to the brilliant singing of both Barbara Cook and Rosemary Clooney and the return of Susan's purse, which was found in the car, we were both feeling better. We laughed because, without glasses, Susan was so near-sighted she couldn't find me in the crowded ballroom. It felt like a happy ending. At least it would be once I got through the closing remarks.

On my cue, I walked to the podium and faced the audience, which included dig-nitaries such as Senator Ted Kennedy. I sailed through my final speech and headed for my conclusion.

"We need to implement economic reform, put a stop to the money flow which has addicted so many of our politicians and subverts the very democracy which we all cherish and sometimes mourn. As Ralph Waldo Emerson said: 'Only that good prof-its, which we can taste with all doors open, and which serves all men.' I'd like to close with my favorite Emerson quote:

'It is for man to tame the chaos, to scatter the seeds of science and song, that climate, corn, animals, and men may be milder, and the germs of love and benefit be multiplied.'"

4

AS THE BALL DROPPED

We celebrated Christmas in Connecticut, just like always, and on New Year's Eve, we went down to Ric and Susan's house for a party with my godfather. There was this game that one of Dad's therapists suggested where each person chooses a positive phrase to shout at midnight. So at 11:58 PM on December 31, 1997, we all made a circle in the middle of the living room with the fire in the fireplace casting a glow. Dad sat in the middle and the look on his face revealed that he believed our ritual would help cure his speech problem. We all held hands, and as the ball dropped on the muted TV, we yelled out what we wished for my Dad: "You will get better! Miracles happen. You're good and you deserve the best! You can do it!" I didn't shout real loud at first, but then Dad turned his head and looked straight at me. I knew his look meant, "Please! For me." I gave it everything I had. I went for it. I looked around at everyone and couldn't believe how much hope and faith I felt in that room. And so, we instilled even more hope in him than I think he knew was possible—more than I thought, at least. He cried that night. I did too.

—*Marika Hufford-Zaslow, daughter*

Michael was a Jewish Christmas maven who geared up in November by practicing the piano so he could accompany friends in a rousing "Good King Wenceslas." In years past, our home had rollicked with verses of the most obscure carols, which Michael had sung repeatedly with a loud, boisterous, energetic voice. That December 23, after Michael's internist, Dr. A, telephoned to report one more round of tests and blood work had come back normal, Michael started his exuberant caroling!

What a relief. Was it my imagination or had his voice improved since the telephone call?

True to our tendencies to run late, it was dusk when we all climbed into the Jeep to set out on a search for the perfect Christmas tree. Eleven-year-old

Helena laid claim to a fifty-foot spruce, and with good news ticking through our minds, we trudged through the crunchy snow. We each had our own idea of the perfect tree, and so we split up to pursue our own individual ideals. Our approach was not an expedient one, and so darkness had fallen by the time we had reached a reasonable accord.

Michael loved to chop down his own tree. Like a religious convert, this city-kid-turned-country-gentleman was as proud of the wood he cut for his neatly stacked woodpile as he was of his Emmy Award! Watching him swing the ax that evening, I told myself we were fine. The MRIs were normal. We had our lives back.

The cold snapped out the tension, we huddled in the wagon as the tree farmer drove us back to the barn. Once there, we sipped hot cider and paid for our Douglas fir, which was considerably shorter than fifty feet but, even so, managed to satisfy even Helena.

*   *   *

What could be better than Christmas in Connecticut? We went to dinner with friends. Susan and the girls baked enough Christmas cookies for a battalion. A couple of times, I even cajoled Marika and Helena into playing The Bach Violin Double, *while I accompanied them on piano. Something was amiss with the performance, however. My right hand was slow. The piece had always been a challenge, but well worth the hours of practice to have the great pleasure of playing with my darlings. I tried to steer my mind away from these details. After all, as Susan annoyingly reminded me at every opportunity, the MRI results had been normal.*

I was short-tempered. I could take no comfort from the last tests. No one understood, least of all me. Everyone discounted what I felt. The holiday season and its overwhelming theme of merriment and togetherness only served to make me feel lonelier and lonelier. It was impossible to ignore what everyone else could not hear.

Before coming to Connecticut, I had visited another highly recommended neurologist, Dr. C. He reviewed the growing stack of medical data and simply scratched his head, unable to shed any light on my condition. Shouldn't I, as Susan reiterated, be satisfied with that?

I remember clearly when and where I first heard the dreaded initials. Several days after Christmas, I was working out at the Mayflower Inn's health club, just down the road from our home. Over time I'd made the acquaintance of the guy on the neighboring treadmill, a doctor with whom I'd been confiding the existence of the slur in my speech and a vague and subtle yet persistent feeling of loss and dread. This mental and physical sensation hovered over me every waking minute. Since there was no diagnosis, my treadmill companion suggested I press my latest neurologist for "his best guess."

"Why would you want him to guess?" Susan was appalled. "He said he didn't know. Sometimes I think you want it to be something horrible."

"You can be really mean." Her lack of empathy infuriated me. I thought of leaving.

"I don't want to be mean."

I did not believe her. I needed to get away...from her and, honestly, from everyone.

"The doctors keep telling you everything is normal," she told me. "Maybe the best you could do is accept what they say. Maybe if you stop worrying, it'll get better. When you're more relaxed, I don't hear the slurring."

I reached for the phone.

"You're sure you want him to guess?"

I did. I never, for a minute, suspected that this phone call would forever change my life.

"Well, Mike, like I said, I don't know," the doctor told me. "I don't know for sure or I'd tell you, wouldn't I?"

"But if you had to guess..." I pressed.

"Well...If I had to put my nickel down on some diagnosis I'd say it was ALS."

"What's that?" I asked. "ALS?"

"It's Lou Gehrig's disease."

*   *   *

When Michael told me Dr. C had guessed as to the nature of Michael's condition, I was no longer frustrated with Michael. I was instead furious with the neurologist.

"Did he really say he'd put his 'nickel' on ALS? His *nickel?*" I had some fuzzy idea of what ALS was. I knew it wasn't good.

"I pressured him." Michael, who was usually more generous than I, was willing to give Dr. C the benefit of the doubt.

"So what?" I cried. "He's the professional! The healer! You're the one with the problem who's seeking some solution, some reassurance. What kind of doctor guesses?"

I wished we could take back the phone call, but all I could do was try to convince Michael that any doctor who would casually toss out a diagnosis at

Christmastime over the telephone could not be taken seriously. ALS...there was something repellant in the initials. I didn't even know what they stood for. Anyway, I knew it wasn't true. Whatever ALS was, Michael didn't have it.

I reached out for him, and we held each other. At least it was a relief not to be angry at each other. Within an hour, there was a telephone call from his father's doctors at Scripps Hospital in San Diego. Milton had pancreatic cancer.

*   *   *

The noose seemed to tighten around my neck...literally. Sometimes I felt as if I could not breathe. Lately, Susan and I spent most of the time angry at someone, something, at each other.

Marika and Helena's godfather, Beau, found reams of information on the Internet regarding pancreatic cancer. None of it was good. I, in turn, checked the Internet for information on ALS. No treatment. No cure. No treatment? I went over to Susan's side. I was consumed by rage at the guessing Dr. C. The next day I called Dr. D, one of the top neurologists at a major facility, and made an appointment.

*   *   *

Over the years, Michael and I had accompanied each other to far too many doctor's offices and hospitals. Between his fertility problems and my fertility problems, we joked that if we had a biological child, we would name her Blue Cross. Then there were Michael's five knee operations dating from the first months of our courtship, culminating in a six-hour surgery five years earlier. I had been at Michael's side throughout these ordeals, just as he had been at mine. But because his vocal problem seemed so very minor, I had not felt it necessary to be present at any previous medical appointments.

"All this looks fine," Dr. D, reputedly a rising neurological star, told us. He had a friendly manner and a boyish appearance, while still projecting a sensitive knowledgeable maturity. Michael and I exchanged a hopeful glance. This was not a guessing doctor. Here was someone whom we could really trust.

"The swallowing is normal. All your times are completely within normal range."

"Then what's going on?" Michael asked.

"Excuse me a moment," Dr. D answered his phone and we waited while he talked to someone about plowing the snow out of his driveway.

"Sorry," he apologized when he returned to us.

"You're sure I didn't have a stroke?" Michael asked.

"It doesn't appear to have been a stroke. We can't say for sure. How's your sleep?"

"Not good," I interjected. "Maybe because the studio gives him so much dialogue to learn every time he's on."

"I keep waking up," Michael explained. "I feel like I can't breathe."

"Forty pages is a lot to learn," Dr. D said. "That could be part of what's going on."

I scrutinized the doctor for some trace of veiled concern. Michael settled back in his chair, and the hawk-like look left his face. After a moment he tensed, compelled to repeat a question he had asked several times since we had arrived.

"Could stress be responsible for my vocal troubles?" Michael asked.

"It definitely could be. It's hard to say at this point."

"What do you mean, 'at this point?' At what point will I know what's happening to me? When I'm asleep, I wake all of a sudden feeling like I can't breathe. Maybe it's sleep apnea. Is there a way to test for that, to see if I stop breathing at night?"

"We could arrange for a test," Dr. D jotted notes. "You'd be hooked up to a monitor at home. We could do that if you like. You have to relax a little, Michael."

I felt encouraged by Dr. D's manner, which conveyed no sense of urgency or ambiguity.

"Maybe I should talk to the producer…stop trying to hide this, whatever it is."

I shook my head, no, as Dr. D nodded, yes.

"Whatever you can do to reduce the stress," Dr. D said.

Never one to avoid speaking his mind, Michael vocalized his deepest concern.

"Dr. C said if he had to make a stab at a diagnosis it would be ALS."

Dr. D's response was emphatic and ever so slightly critical: "There is absolutely *nothing* to indicate that you have ALS."

As we left the building and emerged onto slushy Madison Avenue, I felt like I had been released from prison. As much as I had told myself that Michael was fine, my body finally seemed to be accepting this truth. I pounded Michael's arm, trying to drum my relief into him.

"Let's celebrate!" I exclaimed. "I don't want to say I told you so, but I told you so! He said it's absolutely not ALS. You've got to stop making yourself go nuts with worry."

"I want to believe it," Michael replied.

"You've got to! Why believe the worst when every doctor except one says that, based on your normal tests, a lot of scary stuff has been eliminated? We'll get to the bottom of this, and it is going to be all right. I promise you."

*   *   *

I felt hopeful. I was glad Susan had come along. How beautiful is that sense of relief? Even for a moment. We had such a good life, and it was going to be even better for having gone through this scare. We found a parking meter right outside of Eli's, and this was another good omen. Over breakfast, we discussed plans to close up Dad's house in Solana Beach and our intentions to move him into the Esplanade, an upscale senior residence located just three blocks up the street from our apartment on West End Avenue. I told myself things would be a lot easier with Dad nearby.

My relationship with Guiding Light's *producer had not always been an easy or pleasant one. Back when I played David Rinaldi on ABC's* One Life to Live, *we had had several heated confrontations. The most serious one had occurred in 1984, and stemmed from my desire to implement my out clause so that I could play the role of Shostakovich in* The Master Class *at the Kennedy Center in Washington, D.C. This producer was not known to be a favorite among daytime actors, but when he replaced Jill Farren Phelps as producer of* The Guiding Light, *I determined to lay the past to rest and to concentrate on the positive. It was rumored that as a reformed alcoholic, he had learned to control his temper, his inflated ego, and his habit of hitting on women. Despite his rocky reputation with actors, he also got results in terms of cost efficiency and ratings.*

Susan challenged my decision to confide in my producer, but I couldn't stand the anxiety of not knowing when I would stumble over some simple word. I lived in fear that the show would have to stop taping because of me.

After I revealed my problem, the producer hugged me. He claimed he had noticed I was having "a little trouble," and he promised to do anything he could do to help.

My agent and good friend, Marilyn Szatmary, had negotiated one of the best contracts in daytime. I was costing the show a lot of money. Maybe if I had cut back on the number of shows in my guarantee, I would have felt less pressure. Maybe then the problem would go away. It was unheard of for an actor to make such an offer to management, however. By reducing my guarantee from four to two shows a week, I was offering them the chance to cut my salary in half. Still, I did not hesitate.

"Michael, you and I go way back. If you need to work less, we can arrange that. We'll do whatever we can."

"It will save you a bundle."

"But that's not the point is it? What's important is you."

5

THE FITTEST MAN IN THE WORLD

I saw Michael during the illness and also when he was perfectly well. He seemed the fittest man in the world. We both were bikers. I used to park mine on the street, but Michael carried his up to my office on the seventh floor. He appeared one day, after not having been to see me for some time, and said he was having trouble pronouncing certain words. He said them and I told him: "I think you're barking up the wrong tree." He kind of insisted and said the words again. Since we had worked in the past on his tendency to perfectionism, I, in a sense, led him down the garden path and said, "I don't think this is a problem, Michael." Susan came in for a session one time, and I think we both told him he was full of hot air. And, you know, he was generous. He never seemed resentful that I hadn't heard it. And he went on this odyssey to find out what was going on.

—Fred Eberstadt, psychotherapist

From the moment Milton came east and moved down the block into the Esplanade, the pressure escalated. Michael's speech spiraled downward. When he wasn't worried about his dad, he was angry at himself for not being the perfect son and for not spending more time with Milton. The demands of work, children, overseeing his dad's medical care, and continuing to solve the mystery of his condition dominated our lives.

Two weeks after his arrival, Milton was unable to walk safely. I interviewed home health aides and we hired someone to stay with him. What we had thought would simplify our lives, however, became more complex each day, as the aides we hired either did not show up on time or quit. Michael and I were both on the phone negotiating with agencies for aides, sorting through insurance conundrums or scheduling doctor's appointments for both Milton and Michael.

Michael had viewed the move as a chance to be closer to the dad he idolized, but within weeks of his move east it was no longer safe to include Milton when we went to Connecticut on weekends. At night, he would wander around in a fugue-like state. Once, Michael found Milton lying fully clothed in the bathtub at 3 AM.

Just as Milton's body wandered aimlessly, so did his mind. In the middle of a conversation, he might address his departed wife or some other unseen person. Such behavior coming from a super-rational, political pragmatist was bizarre and surreal, as I often felt our own lives were becoming.

Most of us struggle to accept the fact that our parents are growing old and fragile, but it was especially hard for Michael. Milt was still his hero, "Brando" handsome and intellectually superior. He even heard his father's singing voice as better than his own. Michael was demoralized by Milt's rapid decline from an articulate, tennis-playing dad in his seventies to a shuffling, disoriented old man.

Sometimes we were able to laugh. Sometimes Milton himself was even amused by the incongruity of his visions, which in moments of clarity he viewed with detachment. We took to calling him "Pops" and tried to love him enough and accept whatever was happening.

*   *   *

Dad seemed to be giving up. I was annoyed at him and more annoyed at myself for my reaction. Childhood is a common experience but the quality of childhood is what separates us. I'm reminded of Craig Cornelia's son "The Kid Inside." The kid in the song had a supportive and loving father. Well I did too, though the grade I most remember was an A-. I brought home that A- with pride, to which my father responded, "How come not an A?" I'm told he said it with a smile, but I clearly remember those words. How accurate this memory is, like so many others sifted through time, I can't say. Had I brought home an A, would Dad's rejoinder have been, "Why not an A+?" I'll never know. I may have missed some subtext, but I heard my father loud and clear.

＊ ＊ ＊

As inexcusable Francophiles, we had always intended to visit the tiny French island of St. Barthelemy. St.Barths was not only one of the most beautiful Caribbean havens, but by far the most expensive. Although we were feeling less than flush, in an act of willed, conscious optimism in March of 1997, we flew to St. Barths and stayed at the luxurious Hotel Guanahani.

We settled in a bougainvillea-covered bungalow with a patio overlooking the azure sea. Marika and Helena, to their great delight, had their own bungalow next to ours. The Guanahani lived up to its reputation in every way. It was mind-bogglingly *cher* and worth every penny! Even Marika and Helena, who at fourteen and eleven, were oblivious to economic realities, were impressed by the price of a soda. In addition to being a vacation, the Guanahani was also an educational experience.

Michael and I negotiated a deal. He would only grill me about his speech between one and three in the afternoon. It became a game. I would see a glint in his eye, realize he wanted to ask if I'd heard anything, and then we would both laugh. He seemed relieved, as if he was off the hook. After only a day, we agreed that he sounded more like himself.

We lounged beside the pool, read under palm trees, and traversed ribbon-slim, curvy roads to explore a deserted beach where Michael and Helena bodysurfed until they were dizzy. Michael and I hit the tennis courts daily, and found plenty of alone time, while Marika and Helena reveled in their independence, their separate room and their abilities to sign for Cokes. Most evenings, we were all in the swimming pool horsing around until past dark. Escaping from New York, I honestly thought our lives were back on track. We were looking forward to flying to St. Thomas the next day to visit Michael's godsister, Maria Hodge, and her family.

Our last evening on St. Barths, we sat with our daughters and the Feldmans, another New York family, under a star-sprinkled sky with the picture-perfect, blue Caribbean sea below. Throughout dinner on the Guanahani Patio Restaurant, Michael seemed distracted, quieter than his usual loquacious self. I tried to catch his eye, but he was remote, as if he'd already left our island paradise and returned to the frenzied life in New York. I knew he was worrying about his speech. I could feel myself getting irritated. It was precisely this fixation on his speech that made it worse.

Finally, Michael perked up at the Feldman's description of a boat trip in Turkey. As we left the restaurant, he was his bon vivant self, already planning for our next vacation—to Turkey!

Then, without warning, Michael fell. One minute he was laughing and talking about Turkish ruins, and the next he lay face down in his own blood. An electrical current shot through my body. I knew he was gone. How could it be?

"Daddy! Daddy!" Helena wailed. Waiters in white jackets flocked to the scene. Nearly everyone else was swarming around us. Almost like *déjà vu*, I felt sucked into the vortex of a nightmare that seemed chillingly familiar. I threw myself down next to Michael. He wasn't moving. I screamed his name, as I ran to the bar for ice.

He was dead. How could that be? How could he die just like that? How could it be? I was aware that my thoughts were irrational, but they reverberated in my mind. Our wonderful life was over. Beyond words, there was a visceral certainty that I had lost him.

I demanded ice, but it seemed everyone was moving in slow motion. I grew furious, and wanted to smash the bartender, fix it, *unhappen* it. Instead, I yelled at the bartender to hurry.

I returned to Michael's side with the ice which was wrapped in a napkin. As I placed it on his nose, I saw his head move. His eyes opened as his hand moved to his nose, which was bleeding profusely. He pulled himself to a sitting position and looked at me sheepishly as he took the ice. He was alive! My eyes told me he was going to be fine but the *déjà vu* nightmare feeling would not go away. I struggled to fit his fall in somewhere. It defied logic. I thought of the dazed, preoccupied expression he had worn all evening, how he had scarcely joined in the conversation. He had brought the fall on himself with his preoccupation with his speech. I concluded he had not been paying attention and so he had tripped.

I was ashamed of my anger, but it was better than the nightmare feeling, so I latched onto it. Meanwhile, Michael held the ice to his nose and insisted he was fine. He kept looking at me, I knew he was trying to communicate. I looked away.

The hotel personnel, no doubt concerned about legal implications, watched nervously as we helped Michael to his feet and examined the steps to see what might have caused his fall. Someone rushed up to tell us a doctor was on the way.

*   *   *

I felt stupid. I didn't have a clue as to what had happened, but I knew I'd ruined a perfectly good evening. Helena could not stop sobbing. She clung to me as I walked down those same steps, proving that, yes, I could still walk. What could have prompted my accident? I had not even indulged in a glass of wine with dinner. No one could detect any irregularity that might have caused me to fall.

We walked back to our rooms, trying to console Helena. I had to work in three days. If my nose was broken, what kind of medical care could I expect? The doctor who arrived promptly allayed my fears. She was professional and knowledgeable. Best of all, she informed me my nose was not broken! There was a nasty cut and I knew I could count on a whopping bruise and plenty of discoloration. Our Caribbean vacation ended abruptly. That troubling incident was not to be the last of my mishaps, however. The next evening, at the home of our friends Maria and Larry Hodge in St. Thomas, a carton of orange juice flew out of my hands and splattered to the floor. The world I had always trusted had grown inexplicably dangerous and unreliable.

6

I HAD TO ACT LIKE
NOTHING WAS WRONG

People at the studio were saying he had a brain tumor. That it was affecting his behavior. If they changed anything in the script, he was crazed. Michael, who was always on top of everything, every camera angle, every detail. To see him floundering was horrible. I remember his last scene. He just couldn't do it. And I had to act like nothing was wrong. I couldn't do anything to help him.

—Maureen Garrett, actor, friend

The horror of Michael's fall in St. Barths would not leave me. At some level, I wonder if I knew that whatever *it* was, it was all-consuming and that it would change our lives forever. I wonder if Michael also knew, months, perhaps, even years before the first symptom appeared.

ALS is a diagnosis by default, by process of elimination of other less-horrific neurological diseases. Many people with ALS (known as PALS) go from doctor to doctor for months, sometimes years, before a diagnosis is confirmed. By then, it is estimated that 20%–60% of the PALS' motor neurons have already died. The PALS are sent home with the standard two-to-five years life expectancy.

After the incident in St. Barths, I recalled an earlier incident at a seaside hotel in Delaware, well before there was a problem with his speech. Michael had sprung from the bed as we were making love. In a panic, he claimed he was dying. He had found a malignant tumor on his thigh. He had been monitoring it and knew it was growing. He asked me to feel it, but I couldn't feel a thing. He was angry that I wasn't paying enough attention and kept insisting that if he could feel it I should be able to feel it too.

I shut my eyes and moved my fingers over the spot on Michael's thigh. I had only seen him in such a state once before, after a knee surgery when the morphine they gave him triggered a full-blown panic attack. I tried joking around to bring him out of his sense of foreboding. Hadn't he been saying for years that he would die young? Didn't I keep telling him it was already too late for that?

We lay silently for a while, before he asked me to examine the spot again. I acquiesced by focusing all my concentration on the area. Still, I found nothing. His worries unrelieved, Michael visited the doctor the following week, while the girls and I waited in the parking lot outside the office. Despite my protests, I was nervous. Finally, Michael loped out grinning. He had been given a clean bill of health! But there was *something* and I have come to believe that Michael sensed it. Even then.

*   *   *

Returning from our vacation, I could not shake the thought that I was going to lose my job. Despite Susan's reassurances that I was popular with fans, not to mention the recent Emmy Award, I was convinced that the wheels for my departure had been set in motion. At that time, I was slated to work four consecutive shows, followed by a week off. Nobody ever gave the character of Roger a week off, let alone right when he had just come back from a vacation.

*   *   *

When Michael told me he believed he was going to be fired, I was not in the least afraid that he would lose his job. I was deeply shaken and fearful that he was losing touch with reality. I made a hysterical telephone call to a psychiatrist friend. He was on vacation, but I was able to I track him down at some motel. I didn't know where else to turn. He gave me the name of a colleague who specialized in depression, and I made an appointment.

Meanwhile, I tried to convince Michael that he would not be fired. My words rolled off him. I stuffed the terror from St. Barths deep inside. I still could not find a logical explanation for his fall and I could not explain my prior absolute certainty that he had died, except as one of my over-the-top reactions. My only pressing concern was that Michael's pessimistic predictions might create a self-fulfilling prophecy.

In bed that night, Michael groaned and thrashed around. He stalked through our apartment and returned to bed for only a few minutes, before rising restlessly to pace around some more. Long before dawn, he said sleep was out of the question, so he was going to go to the studio.

*   *   *

I was suspicious when the producer called me to his office after my first morning back. I'd worked so hard on the script and really thought it hadn't gone badly. I stopped by my dressing room on my way and picked up the box of Cuban cigars I had purchased for him in St. Barths. I tried to calm myself by recalling Helena's shock at their price. I figured I could joke with him about her reaction to lighten the heaviness I felt.

I didn't have a chance to make any jokes. The producer greeted me, closed the door to his office, and told me I might be replaced. He added quickly that I was "irreplaceable."

I thought that my legs were going to give out on me as they had in St. Barths. I'm not sure what I said to him then. I must have reassured him that I was working hard with my speech therapist, and that he would see a change. I left the studio and went home to study the next three scripts, to get them all "perfect."

I didn't sleep for the next three nights. The night before what turned out to be my last show, I got up around 2 AM and wrote the producer a note. I reminded him that I had several times beseeched him to write my speech impairment into Roger's story. I reminded him about Charita Bauer, the talented and loved Guiding Light *star who had cancer, which necessitated the amputation of one of her legs. The writers successfully incorporated her disability into the storyline and the fans were grateful. I argued that the daytime genre was famous for including actors' health problems into their characterizations and storylines.*

I was a sleep-deprived zombie when I arrived at the studio to do my fourth consecutive show. The schedule would have proved daunting under the best of circumstances. Every time I opened my mouth I struggled with revulsion at the sound that came out of me.

After the final taping, I was summoned to the producer's office again. This time the executive in charge of the show was there as well. This was the same executive who, when she had been hired in September, would continually stop by my dressing room asking me for suggestions about how to improve the show and telling me I was the "linchpin" of Guiding Light. *It occurred to me that she had not stopped by my dressing room once since I revealed I was having a speech problem.*

"Michael, we're sorry." I think this is what they said. They must have phrased my dismissal with some tone of empathy, but I am not sure because I was so exhausted. The whole scene seemed like a dream. They were going to replace me, and there was no mention of any type of financial settlement. After a long silence, I realized it was going to be my duty to bring up this unwelcome subject. The executive decreed they wanted to be generous, so they decided to pay me a holding fee.

A holding fee? This figure was not even a tenth of my usual salary.

"And of course we ask that you say nothing to the press," they told me. "For your own good."

I left the studio without even going back to my dressing room. When I got home, Helena was practicing the violin and Marika was already in her room doing her homework. Susan was starting dinner, and I asked her to go for a walk with me down by the river.

*   *   *

He wandered into the kitchen as I was placing a garlic-stuffed chicken into the oven. I was feeling good for having prepared the food early so we could eat at a reasonable hour. Because of our unpredictable schedules and our children's good natures, we too often found ourselves sitting down to dinner at 8:30, or sometimes later. That night was to be the start of my new "early dinner" regime and I was determined not to go off course. Michael hung in the doorway a moment before he asked me to come out for a walk with him.

"It's such a pretty evening. We won't be long."

I found myself complying without a word. Outside in the spring dusk we walked to Riverside Park, entered the dank underpass at 72nd Street, and continued silently towards the promenade that parallels the Hudson River. We held hands and I was glad that I, for once, had been flexible enough to abandon my agenda.

We were within sight of the 79th Street Boat Basin when he told me. He had been let go from the show. He just said it. Flatly.

I put my arms around him. He was stone quiet and that scared me more than anything, more than the speech problem, more than the loss of a job. My Michael did not accept injustice without a fight.

We sat down on a bench and held hands as we looked out over the smooth-rolling river on which a handful of modest boats bobbed up and down.

"You didn't get furious?" He shook his head meekly and the feeling that this was "not that man anymore" came over me again.

"Should we tell Marika and Helena?"

I was stunned by his question. How could we not tell them?

"How can we keep it from them?" It was a rhetorical question on my part, but he seemed to consider it. I added, "It's nothing to be ashamed of."

"I don't want them to worry," he said.

"They can handle it." It was Michael I was worried about.

"They loved going down to the studio with me," he shook his head regretfully.

"It's going to be all right," I responded, then angrily: "Those assholes! How can they do this to you? You'll see. We'll figure it out; we'll call AFTRA. They can't do this to you!"

"I'm out of a job."

"Don't think about that!"

"I feel so stupid."

"You didn't do anything wrong. It's not your fault!"

*   *   *

It was all my fault. I had failed. Failed the show, my fellow actors and, worst of all, my dearest daughters. I tried to take Susan's words to heart. Her anger, I knew, was appropriate. Where was mine though?

We returned to the apartment and called Marika and Helena into the living room. I told them flat-out that I would not be working on Guiding Light *anymore. They listened carefully and did not seem worried.*

"Well Daddy, you weren't always sure you liked that job anyway," Marika responded. "Now you can find something you like better." As usual, she was able to impart more wisdom and clarity than most adults.

Helena, on the other hand, was a rollicking ball of fury. She zeroed in on the expensive Cuban cigars I had purchased for the producer in St. Barths.

"I think you should go right down to the studio and take back those cigars!"

We all laughed. Helena was right.

7

NOBODY WANTS TO CALL ANYTHING PSYCHOSOMATIC

Nobody wants to call anything psychosomatic. It's an insult, and, if you, as doctor, if you want to hold onto your practice, or as a person, want to hold on to your friends, you just don't go there. It is a treacherous area. As a physician I face all kinds of complaints for which there is no definite disease as an explanation. Considering what he was going through at the time with his father, it seemed not an irrational thing to say it was psychosomatic. He was having a bit of difficulty with his speech, but it didn't sound like so much. But then he lost his job. I remember very well the day I came over to his home. I was worried—we all were—that the pressures in his life were taking a toll. We walked down by the river. I carefully broached the subject that this could be psychosomatic, and, of course, he didn't like it. I would not have liked it myself.

—Ivan Strausz, MD, friend

I took Dad to Sloane Kettering Hospital and waited three hours in the Urgent Care Unit. I then conversed with Dr. Lewis before heading home. I'd felt really good until all of that. Then, I went with Dad to Dr. Beer's, whose office is handily located on the ground floor of our apartment building. Dr. Beer and I discussed plans for Dad.

I tried to rescue the day, but it was painful being with Dad. I brought up our great rafting trip on the Snake River and he talked about his panic in the middle of the night. I suggested he try to concentrate on his breathing whenever he started to feel panicked. I'm beginning to try that technique myself, although it's not always effective.

This morning, I woke at 5:40, just as light was forming outside, and, unfortunately, I felt a sense of deep despair. To combat my steady companion, Panic, I did one-and-a-half loops of the park on my bike, and I ran into Penney, the healer who is Susan B's friend. I really like Penney. She's not pretentious or grandiose like some healers. When I got home, I called my therapist, Fred Eberstadt and told him I could no longer afford to come to therapy. Until I know what's going on with my health, and what's going on with a possible settlement, our financial future feels shaky.

My speech was garbled when I spoke to Penney, and I'm trying not to draw conclusions from this. I will somehow contact Andrew Weil, a respected bona fide doctor. He holds holistic and spiritual proclivities, and I think he is my best shot for a doctor who can help me help myself. And I am going to go back to Dr. Z for cranial massage.

✳　　　✳　　　✳

As usual, Michael stayed busy. He worked out at the gym for hours, rode his bike, met with more specialists about his speech, and tried to stay on top of his dad's medical situation which looked bleaker every day. Another doctor confirmed that Michael did not have ALS. He took no comfort from this "good news."

It was difficult for me to understand the depth of my husband's hopelessness regarding his professional future. He was still the gorgeous, intriguing man with whom I had fallen in love. It was only natural that he was demoralized by his employer's callous dismissal but Michael was a fighter. Quick to rebound, negativity was normally not a facet of his character. I had never known him to take "no" for an answer. Once, when I had stupidly allowed my passport to expire and realized it only hours before a scheduled flight, he took me in tow and performed the impossible. Minutes before the Immigration Office at Rockefeller Center closed Michael cut through red tape with his charm and determination and twenty minutes later we left with my new passport tucked safely in my purse. He had a knack for feats like securing a dinner reservation at a booked-up, four-star restaurant or getting the table with the best view. He relished the challenge of getting what he wanted and usually he succeeded.

Now, although he was constantly on the move physically, he seemed emotionally and mentally stuck. Even with our dwindling financial income, it made no sense to discontinue psychotherapy. That therapy, I believed, would help lead us out of this nightmare. I contacted Edy Nathan, a colleague I knew to be compassionate and inventive. She generously agreed to see Michael.

*   *   *

Susan and I went up to our Roxbury house. Alone. But even though I felt more relaxed, I still had to take an Ambien at 2:30 AM and woke up worried about my hands and about the piano. Pieces that should not be difficult are now a challenge. Could I have arthritis? Or something else? The nameless. Is there a connection? In any case, I was determined to continue playing my beautiful new Yamaha.

I made coffee for Susan, cut her melon, and fed our crew of animals. Willy, our senior silver Persian cat, loved the big can of Friskies and kept coming back for more. He stared up at me hopefully, asking me to lift him up on the counter where he can dine out of reach from our Springer Spaniel puppy, Lily. Willy returns again and again for his food, seemingly never completely satiated. It was so good to be up early. I am determined now to recover completely, or at least to the best of my abilities!

I then sat down and played the piano! My beautiful, beautiful piano! I wrote this little snippet:

> *Two girls who used to be so small*
> *Are wearing Mommy's shoes in no time at all*
> *Wearing Mommy's robe–*
> *Parading down the hall*
> *In no time at all.*

*   *   *

For over twenty years, I had practiced Nichiren Buddhism, overcoming tremendous obstacles and creating a life overflowing with value and happiness. I dug my heels in and chanted long hours in order to stay positive. I determined to turn whatever poison came my way into medicine. I continued to paint, if not a rosy future, an interesting and productive one. I argued that even in the worst case scenario which I was convinced was only that Michael would not be able to work as an actor, he would still be a dynamic multi-talented man. If acting was out, he could always direct or write. We had earned a decent living writing scripts together in the past, and we could do it again. Michael had graduated Phi Beta Kappa from the University of California with a major in political science. There was no reason he could not go to law school and use the passion he felt for justice to help others. It was not difficult to imagine him entering politics, running for office, and winning! I envisioned limitless possibilities and hammered away trying to ignite his enthusiasm for our future.

And I meant it. I really believed the Buddhist position that what appears to be an obstacle is actually an opportunity in disguise. We had only to push our way through and come out the other side. The Ohio cheerleader in me would not let up, but I still felt I was getting nowhere.

Michael was a rational, logical man, now his actions sprang from panic. Despite his constant worry about our finances, he began seeing a healer who charged $500 a visit. I had always leaned more toward esoteric, non-conventional paths than Michael, and I was certainly in favor of any treatment that made him feel better, but the healer's exorbitant fee signaled fakery and exploitation. Initially, I kept my opinion to myself because I wanted a miracle cure for Michael as much as he did.

*   *   *

The healer had a huge apartment overlooking the Hudson River in Washington Heights. I would arrive, undress, and sit in a tub full of tepid water while he sprinkled herbs and liquids into the water. He would do this while chanting incantations and waving his arms. I, who had been raised by Trotskyite atheists, sat there trying to suspend my disbelief as he shuffled in and out of the room throughout our hourly sessions. I felt foolish, but I attended the sessions on the chance that I could get my life back. The healer promised, in no uncertain terms, that what I was going through would be resolved and that I would progress towards a state of enlightenment. He said my special nature and my destiny were the causes of my current tests.

I returned home after each session with little packets of herbs and a mimeographed sheet of words to repeat. I could not help myself. What he was doing made no sense to me. I did not even like him that much.

*   *   *

The healing sessions made Michael feel ashamed, and he became more depressed. He continued to see his therapist, Fred Eberstadt, who suggested medication, so he tried Zoloft for a brief period. When that didn't work, he tried several other antidepressants and sleeping medications. He wrenched his back, which left him in such pain he was unable to sleep, let alone exercise. Without a job, he was disconnected, even from himself. The remnants of his former life were still in his dressing room, but he did not return to claim them. It was as if he had left himself there, and that he, Michael Zaslow, was missing. "Not that man anymore."

I had the reoccurring sensation that he was disappearing on me, that he was a star who had passed through my life and was now growing dimmer and dimmer as he orbited out of our universe, on and on into space. I kept trying, but I could not reverse his course.

8

IT SEEMS HE CAN'T GET HIS VOICE WORKING

I was nervous watching. I hope he's not sick with a palsy, but it seems he can't get his voice working. I'm worried about Mr. Zaslow.

*   *   *

I'm worried about him too. **Guiding Light** *wouldn't be the same without Rotten Roger. Please get well, Michael. A lot of people really care about you.*

*   *   *

I guess I'm not very observant, because I didn't realize anything was wrong with Michael Zaslow—until Friday's episode. I felt so bad for him—it was all I could do not to burst into tears.

—*e-mails posted by* Guiding Light *fans Jane, Betsy, and Tangie*

Because the show was pre-taped, my fans were not yet aware I was gone. Through the magic of the Internet, which had suddenly taken on a greater importance in my life, I was aware of the fans' concern about me. I had taken an oath of silence to my producers, and so could do nothing except take comfort from their messages on the Internet.

I heard from some of my friends at work, but guessed maybe others were hesitant to contact me now that I was persona non grata. The ones who did stay in touch, Ron Raines, Jay Hammer, and Maureen Garret kept me updated. Jay left funny, encouraging messages almost every day. Nobody can know how much I appreciated every call I got. I felt ex-communicated, disowned by my Springfield family. My friends who stayed in touch all expressed one sentiment—shock. They were dismayed

42

that I was not there and that, for the first time, someone else besides me had been hired to play Roger.

I have always believed that my profession is one of the noblest and most generous, that actors are a rarity in a world too often based on greed. The note I received from my replacement, Dennis Parlotto, confirmed my belief. He wrote: "I want you to know that I am wishing you a speedy recovery and I am wanting you to return to the role you have created and played so powerfully for over two decades. I will do my best to fill in for you, but I am hoping you are quickly back in your rightful place."

*   *   *

If only Michael's employers had displayed the same grace and understanding as Dennis Parlotto. There were no phone calls, however, no friendly get-well notes, nothing. For the first time since Michael broke into daytime television over twenty-five years ago, he was not invited to attend the Emmy Awards. His employers wanted to make certain he was out of the picture.

Was this the way to treat family members who suffer an impairment? Do unto others as they do unto you, unless it's going to cost money? We fantasized showing up anyway, like the thirteenth fairy in *Sleeping Beauty*. We knew that so much anger was toxic, but at times it was the only recourse to too much pain.

*   *   *

I once said to Susan, when this thing was cranking up, that I was grateful for the experience and wouldn't trade it for anything in the world. I guess I meant I was grateful, contingent on moving through it to good health. She, mouth agape, was disbelieving and angry. How could I be thankful for a turn of events that had turned our lives inside out? That perspective was one of a person who believed, despite plenty of evidence to the contrary, that everything could be rationally addressed, that solutions would appear if one applied oneself in a positive manner. It seems our positions are now reversed. Just today, Susan said it would be good if I could look on all this, hard as it is, as an opportunity.

Last night, I had a laying on of hands session with Susan B. She was so empathetic and she talked quite soulfully about what she was receiving. With her encouragement, I talked to my friend Mickey, the child whom I was and am. I felt anew how we are all connected. "Identify, won't you identify, past time to identify with me."

I used to write in those blank books or ringed notebooks—lyrics, thoughts, observations, and quotes. All my life, I had my book and pen in hand, but for some reason, I stopped. I didn't have enough time, and had too many obligations. Now I'm going to focus on myself once again. I told Mickey that I loved him and I know he needs to be fed. I told him I haven't taken very good care of him, but that's going to change. I've been so afraid of being alone with you, Mickey. Why? Because you're needy? Because you're terrified? I want to embrace you and your fear. I will learn, and you will also teach me.

Susan B's friend, Penney the healer, said the same thing when I ran into her yesterday in the park. She saw me as having been essentially stuck and saw this experience as akin to a rebirth.

I can dig that. Perhaps I can be the paradigm, the positive example I've always dreamed of being. The possibilities and future have broadened. Maybe? Maybe not. Breath and Believe!

*   *   *

For the first time in twenty-two years, our wedding anniversary, June 7, arrived, without us making plans to celebrate. I said it was because of the expense involved, but we both knew otherwise. Most of the time I was bitter, resentful, angry, and confused. I didn't even feel like working in my garden. I kept wondering how this could have happened to us? Whatever was stealing Michael's voice was also stealing our love, and I felt powerless to stop it.

I found myself straining to understand what he said. I became so anxious when he opened his mouth that my mind fuzzed out. Maybe I was going deaf. Marika and Helena could understand him so much better than I could. Almost everyone understood him better than me. Sometimes I would pretend I'd understood him when I didn't have a clue what he said. I dreaded asking him to repeat himself. When I did, it was like I'd stuck a knife in his heart. And so I began to avoid him. And he avoided me.

*   *   *

Our twenty-second wedding anniversary started with a dream around 7 AM of our old Saab. This husk presently sits in the driveway with a dead battery and one unhinged door. In my dream, I had foolishly sold my sweet connection to our youth and now I had a chance to buy it back all restored, buffed, and clean. It was in a parking lot much like the one at Montefiore Hospital where I drive in ascending cir-

cles until I find a space. The car deal is complicated by a rival force, possibly my old buddy Tim who did himself in at a young age with too much Jack Daniels and cocaine. This rival force is very dark and threatening. I try to protect the Saab by hiding it in an out-of-the-way garage. I engage in all sorts of sneaky things to throw Tim off my trail, because I know if he finds the car he will mutilate it and that would be unbearable. I survive countless chases and evasions with the help of benign forces and allies, and do indeed buy back my heart—my beautiful, red 1974 Saab.

In waking reality, I have an emerging cold and a slight fever. I feel flushed and achy, especially in my right knee. At least we are in Connecticut, though, and we were able to grill out for the first time this season. We feasted on yummy chicken with mustard marinade, zucchini, red peppers, and potatoes. After dinner, we rented the videotape of Emma *and all had a good time. I slept in the guest room again, so I wouldn't disturb Susan with my hacking and snuffling.*

*   *   *

Michael's new speech therapist, Dr. Stephen Blaustein, referred him to Etoile LeBlanc, director of the Center for Craniofacial Disorders at Montefiore Medical Center. Etoile's report confirmed his seven-month history of "mild dysarthria of unknown etiology" and "poor coordination of respiratory support for speaking tasks." According to Etoile, "Mr. Zaslow has made marked progress in a very short period of time within the goals established for him. Mr. Zaslow has proven to be an effective communicator when implementing the skills he has learned as strategies. Based on the improvement made thus far, it is felt that he will only continue to progress in his ability to improve his communication skills to the level of speaking ability."

Etoile's report looked good on paper but Michael was demoralized. He felt grotesque and didn't want to be around people. It didn't help when I told him that I still saw the same handsome man I married. I did not add that while I saw the man I had always loved, I often felt his mind seemed to have been taken over by a stranger. Nothing I said or did made a difference.

Marika and Helena's violin recitals had always been a cause for celebration, but as we packed the car to drive back into the city, Michael's mood was foul and he grumbled about having to give up a sunny Sunday in the country. He even threatened not to come to Marika's after-recital party. There were tears and misunderstandings all around. Marika was angry and hurt, and we all felt like we were being deserted.

*   *   *

I had difficulty getting back to sleep after I awoke at 2:30 AM, and, two hours later, I chewed a sliver of an Ambien pill. It was starting to get light. I fell back to sleep, but I have felt mopey this morning. Despite my efforts the same sadness and dread that shattered my sleep accompanies me wherever I go and colors whatever I do. No one can help.

What am I going to do about Marika's party after the recitals? Perhaps I will go to a play or movie and dine by myself with a book or my writing. I cannot bear to think of my hyper-nasal slurring voice sounding out like a walrus' ridiculous blare at our dinner table.

When I speak, I don't feel like myself. Who is that? Whose voice is that anyway? And the choices I'm making, such as going to that healer? Who is behind such irrational choices? I, Michael Zaslow don't make choices like that. I must resist! I definitely cannot continue taking the rhino's horn medicine powder. Did I really choose to take a substance derived from the brutal slaughter of endangered creatures? And if not me...then who?

9

ALWAYS SO HOPEFUL

I was working at Isabella's restaurant when Michael came in with his dad. I was so excited to see him. I wasn't aware of what was happening with Michael's health and, at first, he wasn't really talking, just nodding. Then he spoke and I noticed there was this little bit of a slur. He said, "Don't be alarmed. I'm not really sure what it is, but we're working on it." I remember thinking, "This seems so odd." It sounded a little bit like when someone is deaf and they can't make consonants. Then, six months later, the first time he came over to our house with the talking machine, he again told us not to worry. That was the first time I was scared. But I was also hopeful, because Michael was always so hopeful.

—Alizon Hull, friend, opera singer

I took Dad and Margaret Dullea to an ambitious lunch at Isabella's. Our dear Alizon was waiting tables, which is what she has to do to support herself while she studies for the opera. How many years ago was she the devilish, red-haired cherub for whom I composed Alizon? It was terrific to see her, except we couldn't hear each other, and I was forced, as the person in the middle, to act as interpreter, a role for which I am currently not exactly suited for at the present time. Margaret is amazing, going on ninety-something, positive and eager. Dad talks very softly and I got a little frustrated. It was an ordeal of sorts.

After returning Dad and Margaret to the Esplanade, I picked the girls up at Trinity, drove them home, and then headed up to Montefiore Hospital. I was scheduled to be fitted for an obturator, a device designed to help improve my speech. I feel I'm really in secure hands at that hospital up there. Three hours later, I was back home.

I didn't feel as badly as the day before when I had been so low I did not even want to get up. I just wanted to lie around, so I decided to go back on the Zoloft.

47

I did push-ups and sit-ups with Lily, who was particularly enthusiastic about the sit-ups. I was so excited that my strength, contrary to my expectation, seemed to be at full power. I did one hundred push-ups in three sets, after I had already taken Lily on a brisk walk along the Hudson River to the garden where the irises, tulips, and daffodils are in full bloom. I love this spring, the silence in the garden, and the flowers with their aromas! Despite a rough night, by the time I finished exercising and yoga breathing, I felt much better.

Between rainstorms, I biked over to see Dad at the Esplanade. He and Kofi, the young man from Guana who we recently hired, were laughing as I gave Dad the black power salute, crying, "Power to the people!"

I felt like I was on a roll, so I biked through Central Park around 5:30 PM. Every flower seemed magical, and every tree seemed pumped full of lustrous color. I marveled at the bright fuchsia, the azaleas, and the wisteria arbors. I chanted on a bench by Bowling Green, while looking out at Sheep's Meadow. I had dinner with Susan at Pannevino Café, and we took in the opening performance of the New York City Ballet's Sleeping Beauty. *The show was magnificent! We had intended to leave early, but could not tear ourselves away.*

Here are my present symptoms as I see them: Gigantic appetite, combined with unexplained weight loss. Is something parasitic going on? Could it be related to the diverticulitis, which I've been prone to for the past ten years?

Depression is a constant battle, but why wouldn't it be? I'm a guy without a job, no prospects, and an undiagnosed illness. The instances of choking when I drink liquids has not grown worse, but maybe I'm adapting. I do believe my quality of speech has worsened since my working days. Also, my nose has become extremely sensitive! This nose persists in shutting down at the slightest whiff of smoke, cooking oil, or even perfume. One of the worst symptoms is not being able to fall asleep, night or day, unless I take an Ambien. That goes for naps also. And here's a new one: When I lie on my left side with my left ear on the pillow, I hear my heart beat accompanied occasionally by a sort of hum, which parrots my heart and changes pitch, occasionally alternating a whole tone.

*   *   *

Michael was most afraid that he would never work again as an actor. The American Federation of Television and Radio Artists (AFTRA) reassured us we would receive a financial settlement for the remainder of Michael's contract, but there were no guarantees. We tightened our belts.

Unfortunately, I was not as much help in the financial arena as I would have liked to have been. Like most writers, my income was not predictable or reliable. I had just gone into partnership with another psychotherapist and taken an office across the street from our apartment. My practice was still in its infancy, however, and my concern about Michael, his dad, and my own father, who had recently broken his hip in Ohio and was taken kicking and screaming to a nursing home, made it hard to focus or to find the time to build up the practice.

Although Michael continued to see his former psychotherapist, I wasn't sure that was helping. I too returned to therapy to attempt to deal with my anger, with a growing sense of powerlessness, and with my fear that the life I loved was disintegrating.

Michael was breaking apart and, in my panic, I called a mutual friend who was a psychiatrist and got the names of people who specialized in depression. The distance between Michael and I was growing greater. My sense that he was moving farther and farther away from me was becoming a reality. He was literally disappearing, losing a great deal of weight.

We decided to go organic and loaded up on vitamins. I mixed countless smoothies laced with ice cream and weight-gain powders, as part of my battle with his weight loss. Feeding Michael was one thing I could successfully do. It was the one clear path on which I could give him something tangible, something that could, for a moment at least, give him pleasure.

*　　*　　*

I indulged my lifelong love affair with chocolate chip cookies, but what had once been a pleasure, in the face of my unexplained weight loss, often felt like just another battle. Our nightly reading consisted mostly of books by Dr. Andrew Weil and various other books from the health food store. That is where I spent so much time searching for any kind of a lead.

Then, we received an incredible piece of good news. My EMG was again normal! After dropping the girls off at school, I drove to the neurological institute and, by 9 AM, I was enduring the electrical impulses and needles of another EMG. I'd been given the first one in February, and had not known what was at stake. This time, however, I was aware of the full deal. I gave thanks to the godhead who resides inside us all that the test results proved, as Dr. D said, "unremarkable." He added that he would expect some abnormality by now if I had ALS or Bulbar Palsy! How incredible! I was a completely healthy fellow, except for the speech problem!

Still bouncing from my good news, I had lunch with Susan and Phillip at Pier 72 and we pondered the possibility that I had Lyme disease. Susan had been sleuthing along these lines for some time, supporting her hypothesis with evidence of an undiagnosed illness I had in the early eighties. Phillip, though not a neurologist, was a top physician in his field and a man whose judgment I trusted. He thought the possibility of Lyme disease was definitely worth investigating, so I immediately scheduled a spinal tap for next week. Oh, won't that be grand?

After lunch, I returned to Trinity to pick up Marika and Helena. I then dropped Marika off to buy a Mother's Day gift, and drove Helena down to the School for Strings for her violin lesson. I actually accompanied Helena on La Folia, *no easy feat, and the practice went well. She plays the heck out of that virtuoso piece. What a thrill!*

While Helena had her string quartet session, I zipped over to the chiropractor's office. I got in a quick cranial session and returned to the school in time to spring Helena so she could get to Chelsea Piers for Ellie's party.

It was a terrific day. The time with Helena was quality, fun for both of us. While Helena enjoyed the remains of Ellie's party, I sat on a bench looking at the river and felt more peaceful and positive than I had in months. Then, I went back to 54th Street to pick up Marika from her violin lesson. The next duty was to pack the cats, Lily, and all of us, plus Marika's friend, Hannah, back into the car and drive up to Roxbury.

It had been a long day, but I felt great. I stretched out contentedly on our bed, while Susan threw together some dinner. Closing my eyes, I listened to Helena practicing La Folia *in the other room. Amazing what a little positive news can do!*

The next day, for the first time in months, I was able to go to sleep without the aid of drugs, and slept solidly until 5:30 AM. I continued to doze on and off for more than an hour, and I know I fell asleep again, because I dreamt of a conversation with the producer in his office. In my dream I told him if he was searching for the right thing to do, he need only think how he would like to be treated if our roles were reversed.

The following day, my physical and mental state plummeted like mercury in the Antarctic. My voice sounded hollow, and the elation over my recent test results seemed a distant memory. Still, I practiced my speech therapy and took Helena to Costco to buy a basketball. We returned home and drove over to Shepaug School, where we shot some hoops in the drenching rain.

After everyone left to go back to New York, I began to feel more like myself. It's easier being alone, in a way, because I don't have to speak. The sound of my voice is the constant reminder that something strange is happening. When I'm alone, I can imagine my old familiar twang.

For the first time since my dismissal from the show, I feel like I'm moving forward and taking care of business. Stephen Yates and I drove to Woodstock, where I was able to finally go through the contents of Uncle Danny's house. Stevie took an old pine chest and I returned to Roxbury with the rest of Danny's paintings and the old dictionary stand and dictionary. We'll have to deal with the rest of the furniture later, but at least I made a start.

Returning to Roxbury, I seeded the lawn, spread straw, and got some more morning glory seeds to supplement the ones Susan already planted in the large pot. I also visited New Morning Organic Foods and picked up more gingko, blue cohash, and evening primrose, to name a few. Steve and I sanded and stained the oak table and, tomorrow, I will apply the polyurethane. Now that Steve has taken off for the city, Lily and I are relaxing on the patio, catching the last rays of the sun. I love it here. I'm feeling like very a relaxed man. I slept again without drugs.

The next day, however, was dismal. I had to call and make the appointment for the spinal tap. Even though I'd had another decent night's sleep, without drugs I found I could hardly talk on the phone. I stuck to my routine, however, and shopped for dinner, which didn't materialize because Susan's not feeling well and decided not to drive up. I'm sorry about that, but also I'm glad because I don't have to talk. What bliss to just exist, just me and Lily.

The straw I put down to cover the grass seed was blown away by the westerly gale force winds, but it's okay because I'm here on the patio breathing in the last light of the day. Bonnie Raitt is singing in the background, and I've just finished the third coat on the table. I had a great talk with Teresa Hargrave, who gave me two good contacts for healing. She told me of Norman Shealy, an MD and former neurological surgeon who was one of the first to break with the medical establishment and veer off into the realm of alternative medicine. He has an institute in Missouri, and I'm definitely going to consult with him.

It is supposed to thunderstorm tonight. I hope it does. King Lear's words kept resounding in my mind.

"Blow winds and crack your cheeks! Blow! Blow!"

Rain on the sunflower seeds that I just planted. Tomorrow's my spinal tap! Come on, Baby! Some more good news, maybe? I'm still sleeping unaided!

10

A HUMAN APPROACH

I met Michael in Riverside Park, when he was still walking, when he could still talk. He had more fear in the beginning than he did in the end. See, he went in with a human approach. We all do when we're hit with something that we just don't understand and which seems to pull our lives apart. Our bodies are disintegrating and we're not aware of how to put ourselves back together again. It's a total fear in the beginning, usually. Unless there's denial.

—Penney Leyshorn, healer

Through our friends Michael Collyer and Susan Bruin, Michael met Penney Leyshorn, a self-proclaimed healer who lived in our neighborhood. Penney's offer to treat Michael for no fee was appealing financially and ethically, especially in light of his costly excursions with other healers.

Don't get me wrong. We don't believe healers deserve less income than other workers. Michael was beyond generous and fair with money. He raised his voice teacher's fee three times. At the same time, nobody could drive a harder bargain than Michael. He was a tough negotiator on his own behalf, and one of his union's most committed and valuable forces at contract time. With money, as in all things, he was a humanistic pragmatist. But if the top orthopedist in the city charged $300 a visit, how could the spiritually inclined charge twice as much?

There was something soothing in Penney's quiet, serious manner. I cannot say for sure what transpired in their weekly sessions, but I do know Michael was always more peaceful and positive when she left. When Michael was in the advanced stages of ALS, she emerged silently after a session and put her arms around my shoulders.

"You need each other," she told me. "Just lie next to him…and maybe make faces at him."

I was stunned. How could she have known I had always been a face-maker? Many times I used clowning to break a deadlock between us. There was little clowning being done at this stage, however, and no screwy faces being made. Laughter, the bedrock of our life, had all but disappeared.

*   *   *

Penney the healer said I would have deep and memorable dreams after our session yesterday and, sure enough, last night was one dream after the other. I had good sessions with both Fred and Penney, and left feeling strong and positive.

Mark Hodge stopped by, and we walked down to Riverside Park, where Susan and Lily were romping in the middle of the track with the local dog group. Then, Helena, Mark, Susan, and I went out to dinner at Café Popolo. Helena bounced her new basketball throughout until we confiscated it for the sake of the other diners.

The next day, Stevie drove with me to Roxbury and, on the way up, we stopped at Fairway North to shop. We played tennis, grilled out, and assembled the new lawn mower. Later, we watched the girls' violin recital tape and I got all teary. The next day, tennis doubles at Pete Gurney's was a real high point. Then, it was home to make dinner for Susan and Helena, who are driving up from the city.

On Father's Day, Ric and Susan came over for a grill-out, which proved very enjoyable and relaxed, despite my coughing. I was exhausted by my combined efforts at eating, coughing, laughing, and trying to make myself understood. Dad is doing terribly. I called him to wish him a happy Father's Day, but there was no contact, only the repulsive sound of 'me' struggling to articulate words, which felt empty, and his disjointed response. It is so exhausting.

The following morning dawned as splendid as any June day, another day to rejoice in being alive. From the terrace, I watched Susan water the magical, anarchic garden in the woods. The peonies have popped, some of the rhododendrons are fading, but the laurels are in their glory.

Banter is a thing of the past, but witticisms and bon mots still occur to me all the time. I feel claustrophobic, as if I'm trapped in an irremovable astronaut's helmet. I sound like a creature from the nether reaches of hell, like that in T.S. Eliot's Hollow Men. *If I could, I would remain mute, as I did most of yesterday.*

I hate obsessing about my health, but this cough worries me and I think I'd better see Dr. A. Helena is so concerned about my cough. She is always asking me if I'm all right. I assure her I am, though clearly I am not. Marika trusts us more. She believes that if we were dealing with something potentially grave, we would tell her. There is still no diagnosis, but we won't fill her head with imaginings.

We are still hitting the uvula with the speaking device at Montefiore Hospital. Will this ever produce results? I am going to try to stay positive about trying to solve the technical difficulties and, once that is accomplished, the effectiveness of this approach. I had an earlier appointment with Dr. D. He is disturbed by the progression and about to give a provisional diagnosis of Bulbar Palsy. He will probably prescribe drugs to slow the condition's advances. He thinks this speech device is a good idea, and he wants me to repeat the barium swallowing test and the MRI. He still sees no evidence of ALS. It seems quite unlikely I have that.

I had another dream about the conversation in which Beau said I was determined to have an incurable illness. His judgmental attitude pains me even when I sleep.

The more I read of Bauby's book, The Diving Bell and the Butterfly, *the clearer I see my condition. This dynamic, precarious, mysterious thing that we know of as a life is constantly altering, changing. It is not a fixed nugget, but an unfolding narrative. It's not an immutable tale, but a transitory tale of ambiguity and contingency, a celebration of adventure and change and difference.*

11

YET ANOTHER
SPECULATION

Yes, it is an invasion of your privacy for me to be writing you with yet another speculation, but at least this one seems to incorporate some of the symptoms that have not only been noticed but that have also been traditionally misdiagnosed as something else. Attached is a printout about Lyme disease. However, the best doctors in the country initially dismiss the obscure in search of the obvious. I wish you the best, and again apologize for any intrusive impact this letter may have on you.

—Pam Cain, Fan

*   *   *

You have many symptoms of Lyme disease caused by a deer tick bite. Lyme disease is curable with antibiotics. Vocal cord and muscle paralysis are also caused by Lyme, so if you have not tested for Lyme, I would suggest it. Not all people with Lyme disease will show positive. If you don't show positive, maybe your doctor will be willing to treat you with intravenous antibiotics for two months or more to see if your symptoms improve. If you can't find a doctor, please feel free to write or call.

—Eugenia Berg Taylor, Fan

His fans continued to lighten his load with letters, e-mails, get-well cards and well-meaning advice. Huge packets of mail arrived daily. A significant number of them included information about Lyme disease.

We spent long hours on the phone or online, gathering information on Lyme disease. We were struck by the similarities to Michael's symptoms—slowed articulation, thick speech, difficulty in swallowing, poor muscle coordination, weakness, and even mood disturbances such as irritability, bursts of crying, and temper flares.

Every day hurt feelings and misunderstandings sprang from Michael's new habit of smiling or laughing at something serious. I knew that that emotional lability was a symptom of Lyme disease, but it was hard to accept Michael's explanation that he could not control his reactions. Marika and Helena could certainly not understand why their Daddy would suddenly smile, or even laugh, when they were upset about something.

The possibility that Michael might have advanced Lyme disease did not come out of left field. One Sunday in the summer of 1985, I and Marika, then age three, left Michael in Roxbury to drive back to the city. He was supposed to begin rehearsal the next day for a production of *Anyone Can Whistle* at the Berkshire Theater Festival in Massachusetts. He planned to drive our old Saab up there that evening. We arrived in the city and found a message from him on the answering machine. He had not gone to Stockbridge, but had driven to nearby New Milford Hospital, where he was immediately put in the intensive care unit with an undiagnosed illness.

I can only imagine how much pain he was in to head for a hospital instead of a theater. His symptoms included a blinding headache, a dangerously high fever and quite suddenly acutely stiff joints. These are all symptoms we now identify with Lyme disease.

Michael was put on antibiotics. He remained in the hospital for a week, after which he was placed on intravenous antibiotics for several weeks. His symptoms disappeared, and we returned to our normal lives. I could not stop wondering if "something" that had occurred over ten years ago might have remained dormant and was now responsible for his present condition.

*   *   *

When I told Dr. D about my undiagnosed illness, he seemed annoyed by my attempt to find an explanation for what was wrong with me. He had no suggestions about what I could do to improve my rapidly deteriorating speech so that I could get back to work and earn money to support my family. He flatly refused to prescribe intravenous antibiotics, on the chance that I had Lyme disease. When I conveyed my growing sense of desperation and willingness to try anything, especially antibiotics, which I had been told posed no direct threat to my health, he abruptly ended the conversation.

That weekend, when we were all in Connecticut, Susan and I sat on our patio reviewing the stacks of data on Lyme disease. She was convinced that we were on the right track. At first I resisted her optimism, but I was beginning to grow excited about actually beginning a course of treatment. Somehow, we would track down a medical person out there who would support us and start me on antibiotics. I left numerous messages for Dr. D, the young rising star from one of the top neurological institutions in the world. He did not return my calls.

Presumably I had crossed the line of acceptable behavior for a patient and was infringing on his authority by acting on my own behalf. Dr. A, my internist who was helping co-ordinate my expanding dossier of medical tests, also left messages for Dr. D. His calls were not returned either.

*   *   *

Our *raison d'etre* was to track down a doctor who would prescribe antibiotics. Michael was becoming more obsessively critical of his voice. He especially hated struggling to be understood on the telephone, so I made most of the calls. Two names surfaced as innovative Lyme specialists—Dr. Patricia Coyle at Stony Brook, and Dr. Joseph Bourascano in East Hampton. I began to track them down immediately, but before I could make contact, Michael sniffed out a physician in Greenwich Village who worked with AIDS patients. Dr. F agreed to prescribe a two-week round of Rocephin. Although our research suggested that a two-week regime was a very short period for treating advanced Lyme disease, we were ecstatic. At last we had secured a treatment! It felt like we were finally winning.

*   *   *

I'm back at Montefiore yet again in Dr. E's office for another fitting of the interim obturator, which I'm assured will greatly improve my speech. I can't help wondering why I am alone in this process. Why aren't other people with some form of Bulbar Palsy being fitted for an obturator? At least Dr. E thinks, as we do, that the more aggressive we are in tracking down and eliminating the cause of my problems, the better off we are. Also, he agrees there is no real drawback to taking antibiotics. One is forced to wonder what exactly were the other doctors' aversions to prescribing antibiotics?

*   *   *

The big day finally arrived! We are like kids at Christmas. Michael got up early and took the subway down to Greenwich Village. When he came home, he waved his bandaged arm triumphantly. He had gotten the antibiotics! I was convinced he would be healed.

*   *   *

I have the hepborn lock in my arm, having had the first dose of the antibiotic of choice for Lyme disease. Hope springs eternal! Sitting on our patio in Roxbury, admiring our view of the hills to the west, I can finally believe I am on the road to recovery.

Our next-door neighbors are going to have their wedding in their yard. Since Lily was requested not to be present, I locked her in the house where she sulked and rolled her spaniel eyes. Around evening time, I strapped my bike on the car and drove to Welton Road and accompanied Lily on a refreshing jaunt. We then came home, and I shot myself full of more antibiotics and had a good dinner. I feel really good about my leg. It's actually improving! This is the first physical malady that has actually shown some improvement. I was beginning to worry about that prick Dr. C's pronouncement about ALS. I have to stay vigilant and remind myself that my right leg is my bum leg. Even though my symptoms seem to be confined to my right side, below my neck, they only seem to be affecting my leg, hip, and knee. Finally something health related to celebrate!

I wonder about letting my former producer know that I am hurt and worried about my family and that I am contemplating asking publicly why a $35 billion company can't honor the contract of a former employee previously touted as a family member.

*   *   *

When we were in the city, Michael's days were as packed as they had been before all this began. He was on the road, working out, going to this doctor or that, practically commuting back and forth to Montefiore Hospital for another adjustment on the obturator. I couldn't imagine how he endured the endless fittings. The thing resembled some medieval retainer with wires that looked as if they gouged into the tender area around the uvula. With each modification, Michael came home and demonstrated to me how much his speech had improved. I never actually heard a significant difference, but sometimes I said I did. It was enough to see him determined and committed to this course of action. I was deeply grateful to the team at Montefiore.

*   *   *

Yet again, I'm at Montefiore in Dr. E's chair, feeling more hopeless than I've felt lately. It seems like it's all a trial on ME rather than on them. This obturator is proving to be an experiment, which was not how it was initially presented to me. I know how hard they are working, but it's so sad. I'm weeping inside all the time, and occasionally my despair bursts forth in public, which mortifies me.

My father is in the hospital, and did not seem to recognize me. Maybe he hasn't actually recognized me my whole life. I remember when Mom ran off to Florida and he decided to go after her, leaving me behind. I was thirteen then, and pretended it was great being alone, so independent, so responsible that both parents could do as they wished. I decorated the Christmas tree by myself that year and made happy. At thirteen, maybe it was easier to fake it.

The next appointment, Dr. E and Dr. G jubilantly declared that the obturator "provisionally works." Even so, we went over to Etoile's and they scoped around with it. I gagged and swallowed. I guess I'll come back tomorrow to be fitted with a more refined version and take it home. Oh joy!

*   *   *

I wasn't sure if I knew what was real anymore. Sleep had always been a challenge for me, but now it was even more problematic as I listened to Michael thrash around in bed. There was no way to talk about it because talk itself was not only too difficult but an insidious reminder of our predicament.

Was Michael's speech improved by the torturous-looking obturator? I no longer trusted my judgment, but I didn't think so. I wanted to be positive and encouraging. The process was painful and the mechanical device was so rigid and unwieldy. I couldn't imagine sticking it down my throat. When Michael came home and described the tedious and endless fittings at Montefiore, I struggled not to gag. How did he endure it day after day?

Once the obturator was ostensibly fixed we spent most of the time in Roxbury. Marika and Helena went to a day camp in New Milford and, for the first time in years, we had time alone. We once would have loved such a carefree schedule, so much time. Now, time was our adversary. What we needed most of all was distraction. I began lobbying for a trip, anything to take Michael's mind off his dad, his voice, his joblessness. The future.

*   *   *

Today is Dad's birthday. I tried lying down in bed with Susan last night. I coughed, though, little single dry death rattles, so I moved into the guest room. Susan hasn't been sleeping well and is miserable. Fred thinks a support group would be helpful for her, and I'd like one too. Imagine—a group of guys all talking like me!

My thoughts were very grim while waiting on the interminable toll line from Montefiore to Manhattan. High over Harlem River, I thought: "I wouldn't mind if just my car section of the bridge gave way." Oh, I'd mind, maybe for three seconds, but that would be it. I was, and am, feeling thoroughly spent. This time last year, I was winding up my story on the show and starting rehearsals in Pittsburgh for My Fair Lady.

Kofi, the young man who cares for Dad, told me it would "be good if you could see more of your father." Right. What does he know? What does anybody know? After once again waiting for hours, I have yet another version of the obturator and it does indeed cut the hyper-nasality. I'm drooling and gagging, though, and Dad is giving up. I'm taking the palatal lift in and out and infusing myself with antibiotics and driving while too tired to keep my eyes open.

12

A WRONG NUMBER OR A
PRANK CALL

I always admired Michael from the very first time we met. We were cast members together in the out-of-town tryout for Butterflies Are Free. *Michael was so dynamic, always full of joy. He was a fabulous actor, sang beautifully and played a mean piano and guitar. I remember a wonderful day off when we all raced sailboats on the lake near the Falmouth Playhouse in Massachusetts, where we were performing. We were like crazed four year olds, ramming into each other's boats, tipping them over, collapsing afterwards, weak from exhaustion from the laughter. We always affectionately called Michael our Communist. He was as passionate about politics as he was about the theater. You could not find a guy more committed to helping others. He was a terrific influence on those of us self-centered actors all wrapped up in our budding careers.*

I'll never forget the day he called to tell us about his ALS. I couldn't understand it was Michael on the phone. I suspected a wrong number or a prank call. I hung up. He tried two more times, not daunted by my failure to recognize him. When he finally got through to me, the blood drained out of my body. I simply couldn't believe this horrific disease was destroying the body of one of the most vital men I'd ever known. His body, yes, but not his soul! Michael had the purest one of those. He'd called us himself, wanting only to get the word out that there was a problem to be solved and wanting us to climb on board.

I never saw Michael again. I know he would say "Don't waste time wallowing, get out there and do something!" I see those intense, laughing eyes, hear that mellifluous voice, his big laugh, and his insistence that we continue his work in trying to make the world a better place.

—Blythe Danner, actor, activist, friend

It feels so good to be alone with only my pen and notebook as company. I believe I'm starting to love and care for myself perhaps for the first time. I am awake before everyone else, and sit at the kitchen counter sipping green tea at Andrew Weil's sug-

gestion. I nibble on toasted olive bread smeared with organic peanut butter and apricot jam. My vitamins are at the ready, and my Gary Null's mixture is at hand to wash them down. I've already popped my Biaxin, which I finally agreed to take for this lingering cough. There is a very thrilled woodpecker hoarding the birdfeeder. Glenn Gould is humming along as he plays the French Suites *that emanate from my glorious new speakers.*

The laundry is in the works, and it's about time to tackle the wheels of the lawn mower. The images and message of the Bauby's book, The Diving Bell and the Butterfly, *resonate in my mind, especially the hysterical laughter and the difficulty of "repartee." Any witticism, quick as they come to mind, must be emitted into the waiting ears of friends. By the time they land, we've all forgotten what they were referencing. There is also the palpable manner in which some people, formerly little more than acquaintances, display deep empathy. On the other hand, some friends whom I believed were close are now distancing themselves from us.*

Marika and Helena's godfather has really let me down, and it hurts. He actually said, "You were determined that you had an incurable disease."

It is hard to listen to me; I'll admit that. Both he and his girlfriend have been remarkably silent for a couple of weekends. He gives me the feeling that I'm letting him down for not being tough, stoic, and recuperating so we can get on with it.

*   *   *

I didn't know where to turn for support. I went back to my former psychotherapist, but the sessions only intensified my feelings of helplessness and confusion. I left feeling worse. My therapist said I was trying to stifle my anger at Michael because he was not holding up his end of our marriage by earning a living. I was outraged by her interpretation. Money had nothing to do with the fear that gripped me. As much as I appreciated luxury, I did not need it. Money was only money. Loss of income was nothing compared to loss of communication and love.

Michael wrestled with his rage over being virtually ignored by his former employer. AFTRA's legal team, Laura Sigal and Stephen Burrow, could not make any headway whatsoever with the giant corporation. Although we had paid off our Connecticut mortgage in December and counted ourselves extremely fortunate, as days went by with not so much as a response from his former employers, our anxiety escalated.

On rare occasions, I turned to friends to vent my frustration. Why wasn't I strong enough to cope with Michael's moods? After all *it*, whatever *it* was, was happening to him and not to me. I couldn't separate myself from his anguish. Michael's pain infused me, dominating my life. Except for writing sessions with my partner, Melanie, or when I met with patients, the terror I fought to hold back seeped through. I felt like the boy with his finger in the dike, trying to hold back the inevitable flood.

I finally broke down during a telephone conversation with Beau. I told him I could no longer reach Michael and was beginning to think it was because he no longer loved me. Beau said he thought Michael loved me, but maybe I needed to jolt him out of his self-absorption by threatening to leave him.

I was speechless. I had called Beau to let off steam and possibly find some support or encouragement. Michael was bad-tempered and impossible, but would I ever actually leave him because of these traits? That was out of the question, and so was turning to Beau. I hung up feeling sick and more alone than ever.

I kept trying to challenge my growing depression with my Buddhist practice, chanting hours and hours each day. My prayer was always the same that Michael would be healed, that we would all be stronger and more compassionate towards ourselves and others as the result of our challenging experience. As long as I was chanting, I was charged with hope.

* * *

This morning, this sparkling morning, around 8 AM, I sit on the patio watching my old woodpecker pal trying to find the last seed morsel in the empty bird feeder. Meanwhile, not twenty yards away, a full feeder hangs in the magnolia tree. Yet another feeder is only ten yards away on the lattice near the sliding door. Maybe this bird is a shy guy.

I seem to have largely rid myself of the terrifying images and thoughts that startle me awake at night. I have symptoms consistent with ALS, although they may also be consistent with Lyme or some alternative with no such grim prognosis. The slow, pulsing tingling I have felt in the third fingertip of my right hand has now migrated to my thumb pad. (Our cardinal couple is at the feeder in the magnolia. I feel blessed.) The tingling seems to not be in my third finger any longer, so at least it's evidently migrating and not spreading unchecked.

My chief concern is still my right leg. The pain and difficulty persist and I must ask someone if that is one indication of ALS, or does it stem from the three straight days of tennis I played last weekend? I was already sore, but I played anyway, not wanting to screw up the foursome. The Korean lilac emits such a heartbreakingly sweet aroma, producing aching nostalgia. But, from what source?

*   *   *

Despite their best efforts, AFTRA had still received no response from Michael's employer. The only recourse was to consult an attorney to exert more pressure on the company. Michael turned to Michael Frankfurt of Frankfurt, Garbus, Klein & Selz, with whom he had served on the board of Creative Coalition. Michael Frankfurt's consequent letter stated:

"We and our client are surprised and dismayed that P&G would allow its twenty-five year relationship with Zaslow to deteriorate over this matter. There is no basis for canceling the Performance Contract, or reducing Zaslow's compensation. Zaslow does not want this dispute to result in arbitration. The parties have worked together successfully in the past, and Zaslow hopes to continue his relationship in the future. However, if negotiations cannot be completed within the next two weeks, our client will have no choice but to commence arbitration.

Lastly, there has been considerable concern among Zaslow's fans about his absence. Zaslow feels that he owes it to his fans of the past twenty-five years to allay these concerns and plans to issue a press release shortly."

How could they not respond? We waited. Distraction was the only thing that helped. I started reworking a script we had written together, anything to get his mind on something else. There were brief moments when love brought us back to our senses, and we remembered who we really were. These instances were increasingly rare.

One glorious summer afternoon, after a long lunch on our patio with our friend, jazz singer Susannah McCorkle we hatched a plan to finally go public. Susannah knew someone at *People* magazine, and offered to see if they would be interested in doing a story on Michael. They were. We geared up, as always, energized by the prospect of action.

While Michael continued to feel humiliated by the nasality in his voice, I observed, or thought I did, that this condition had not grown worse since he began the course of antibiotics. Was this only wishful thinking? I wanted so much to believe it was true.

* * *

It was becoming more difficult for me to communicate, especially on the telephone. I wished I could rise above the feeling of humiliation that emerged when I had to keep repeating myself, but often it was just too overwhelming. I called to order some chicken soup from our favorite Westside kosher establishment, and the person on the other end of the phone did an imitation of my nasal, slurred voice and called me a "yutz." My instinct to stand up for the underdog kicked in, but this time, the underdog was me! I was having a hard time.

Thank God for e-mails and my computer, for in that realm I felt more like myself. Had I known I'd be able to work again as an actor, it would have been bliss to have this much time in the country, playing tennis with my pal Pete Gurney, hanging out on my wooded hilltop. I'm still an actor, though, who loves to act and no matter how much I meditate and do Qui Gong, the uncertainty is a killer.

I busied myself communicating with colleagues such as Alec Baldwin, with whom I had worked at The Creative Coalition. My agenda was obvious—I needed support. I wrote him the following:

Dear Alec,

Exactly one year ago I opened in *My Fair Lady* at the Benedum Opera House in Pittsburgh, a tremendously fulfilling experience. As Henry Higgins, I played a speech pathologist, which is but the first in a continuing series of ironies. That was the latest (notice I didn't say last) play to date for me. In September, I had found a slight and strange difficulty in negotiating a phrase. This was the start of what has come to be, ten months later, a very severe speech impairment.

We still don't have a diagnosis, without which there can be no prognosis. Despite seeing three neurologists (and counting), medical doctors, ancient Chinese doctors, healers, chiropractors, acupuncturists, and, of course, speech pathologists, no clear diagnosis has emerged. I have had MRIs, MRAs, MRVs, EMGs (don't ask), and a CAT scan of the sinuses. I have had more tests than I took in high school and college combined.

Anyway, to the purpose of this correspondence: I was replaced at work. They asked me not to speak to the press, and released their own piece of disinformation that I had requested a thirteen-week hiatus because of an illness in the family. They continue to refuse to honor our contract, which runs through January of 1998, hence forcing AFTRA to file for arbitration. I have decided to tell my story to *People* magazine, and they are coming up to Roxbury on

Monday, July 14. I was wondering if you would be willing to speak with Cynthia Wang, who will also be interviewing cast mates. Thanks for your patience in wading through this fax that ran on."

Once again, I'm waiting for Dr. G up here at Montefiore in the Bronx. This prosthesis is reasonably comfortable as long as I don't talk. Which is not much use.

People with disabilities either like mine or more severe in nature are not disabled. That is the message we must keep sending to people. A very wise young woman who was also disabled once told me, "When a disability happens, one's life is changed, but it need not stop. Our dignity cannot be taken from us. It can only be given."

That philosophy sounds admirable, but sometimes the positive approach sucks. Here I am, stuck in this walk-in cubicle while Dr. G's gone to see what he can do to fix the offending portion of the device. The prosthesis renders me "denasal," which is quite a lot better than the hyper-nasality. Boy, have I mastered the lingo or what? It seems unbelievable that I will be stuck with this device, if I actually live out my life expectancy. Well, we humans are, so far, very adaptable.

Are the nerves responsible for this condition shot to hell, gone forever, or is there a possibility of regeneration? I've been on intravenous antibiotics for two weeks now. Dr. F is going to see me today at two-thirty. Susan is counting on him prescribing another two weeks. The information we have on Lyme disease suggests it may take months of antibiotics before symptoms are noticeably alleviated.

Dr. D, reprehensibly, has not responded to my queries about the swallowing test, the intravenous medication, and the leg and knee instability. What if it is neurological degeneration? Why didn't he put me on whatever drug is available to slow the process? Isn't there some institute or person somewhere who can diagnose and cure me?

Then there is this strange symptom of inappropriate smiling and laughing. It's almost as if I'm embarrassed by this condition. Like a child, like little Mickey, I sound slow of mind. This is so unbelievable.

13

HE DIDN'T HAVE ANY SYMPTOMS

"This is something I have thought about in hindsight. Michael wasn't sick yet, or didn't have any symptoms that I could see. I knew from Jill, my daughter who was in Marika's grade at Trinity, that he was having a problem. I had not seen him since his mother died, and went over to extend my sympathy. I could not get over the look of amazing pain and suffering on his face. I often think of that look and wonder if the emotions raging through his body could have triggered the ALS, which was probably lying dormant.

—Myke Schneiderman, friend

The chicken had been marinating all day. Marika had made and decorated a people birthday cake and another giant dog biscuit to celebrate Lily's first birthday. From inside our bedroom, we could hear our friends laughing on the patio. They were sipping wine as Helena fastened party hats on Lily and her dignified canine mentor, Brubeck, a golden retriever who belonged to Ric and Susan.

The anticipated birthday party buoyed Michael's spirits during the day, but now he was lagging. His anxiety centered around his coughing and I was trying to reassure him.

"Why wouldn't you be anxious?" I said. "Your father is in critical condition in the hospital."

"It's not that," he told me. "It's not anxiety. I feel like I can't breathe sometimes. If there were a plug, I'd pull it. I know it sounds awful."

"It isn't awful," I replied. "You don't want him to suffer. Stop being so hard on yourself."

"I keep adding his savings up in my mind and watching it dwindle without his benefiting from it. I guess I'm guilty of unfilial responses."

For once, Michael's speech was clear to me. "Unfilial responses" was a mouthful, and he had no trouble enunciating the words. I wanted to point out the good sign, but I knew he would protest. He did not believe, as I did, that the antibiotics helped his speech. At the very least they seemed to have stopped the downward spiral. He was definitely holding his own.

"We should go on out," he said as he stood up and headed for the door. He looked great. He was still playing tennis every day. I took comfort from his tanned muscular arms.

The telephone rang and he motioned for me to pick up. There was news both bad and good. Milton's heart had stopped, but the medics had revived him.

"What about the do not resuscitate orders?" Michael was becoming more agitated. I offered him the phone, but he pushed it away, so I spoke to the attending physician.

"There was a mix-up," I explained.

He sat down looking uncomprehendingly as I reported that, even with the mix-up, they expected his dad would die very soon.

"They assured me they would not take any more heroic measures," I said.

He shrugged. It wasn't getting through.

"We have to go to the hospital." He sat there, unable to come to terms with what was happening. Finally, he articulated that we couldn't go to the hospital because we had company and the children had camp tomorrow.

His response took me aback, as so many things did. His father was dying and he wasn't sure we should go to the hospital?

"You have to see him!"

He shook his head with the same indecisive, blank look. It was all too much for him. I put my arms around him. "We'll drive to New York first thing tomorrow."

He nodded. He looked crisp and handsome in the blue, flowered shirt we had bought three years ago when we all went to Maui to celebrate Milt and Edith's fiftieth wedding anniversary. I told him he looked handsome, but he shook his head as we went out onto the patio where Marika and Helena were passing snacks to our friends.

We didn't mention Milton's condition then, but brought it up later in the evening as we sat around the table sipping coffee. The most natural thing in the world was to turn to Beau, Marika and Helena's godfather. We were all only children and over the years we had come to rely on each other as family, in the truest sense of the word. We saw him through two divorces and numerous depressions. If he was alone, as he often was, we made sure he was included in our social activities. Michael had arranged photography jobs for him and I even played matchmaker, introducing him to a friend with whom he was now living. He had always been there for us and the children. Once, on our wedding anniversary, he arrived unexpectedly in the morning wearing a tuxedo with a bottle of champagne, flowers, and fixings for an elegant brunch. We knew we would always be there for him, and trusted he would be there for us and our children.

It seemed simple. We would drop Marika and Helena at camp on our way into the city. Since we didn't know exactly what we would find when we got to the hospital, we needed someone to pick them up at camp late in the afternoon. Either one or both of us would drive back out in the evening. Mostly, we wanted them to be with someone they loved and trusted, and that was what Beau was.

His negative response was a stinging surprise. He said flatly he couldn't do it. We didn't have the energy to dwell on it. We would cope. If Michael had to stay over in the city with his dad, I would drive back in time to pick up the children at camp.

The following day we spent in the Intensive Care Unit at Roosevelt Hospital with Kofi, the young man Michael hired to care for Milt. Joann Dorian, Michael's former wife, who had remained close to Milton, was also at his bedside.

*   *   *

I cried nonstop, as I tend to do lately. Dad had been so worried about me and I had not been able to be there for him because of my own health concerns. There was nothing I could have done and nothing I could do. When the doctor on duty came in, I signed the necessary forms that would allow Dad to be unhooked from the respirator. The doctor was sensitive, young, and caring. I counted his presence as a blessing, just as I counted Kofi's allegiance as a gift beyond words. He would not leave my dad's side and the hospital personnel commented on his devotion.

We had no way of knowing how long Dad would linger. Kofi and Joann urged us to drive back to Connecticut to be with Marika and Helena.

We left, driving up the West Side Highway along the Hudson River on a summer's day so stunning it made me weep. I dreaded telling them they would never see

Grampa again. Lately, I could not give the girls anything good and positive. I could no longer shelter and protect them. Wasn't that a father's duty?

The neon sign from our favorite market, Fairway, blinked up ahead, proclaiming: "Lobster: $4.99 per pound." Just last summer, we were all happily eating lobster on the Vineyard. We pulled off the highway and went into the store, where we purchased four two-pound lobsters in Dad's honor. At least I could give my darlings something they loved. I was happy to do it.

*   *

Cynthia Wang and her crew from *People* magazine arrived at our home in Roxbury on a sunny July morning. We worked non-stop until late afternoon. They photographed Marika, Helena, and Michael riding their bikes down a tree-lined dirt road as I drove our Jeep up ahead. We would prove to the world that he was strong and fit as ever. Everybody was laughing and kibitzing. It was more fun than we'd had in months. We rode up and down Upper County Road until the photographers were satisfied that they had their shots.

Michael was determined to squelch rumors that he was a "wizened old man," as he had been labeled by his former employer. Later, we went over to Pete Gurney's tennis courts for some action shots. I gained a new respect for the magazine. The sensitivity and commitment of the crew restored our optimism. We both felt the support we had longed to receive from the show.

*   *

Cynthia had the difficult task of interviewing me. Not only did she have to decipher my mangled speech, but, as I am more and more prone to tears, she had to bear with me as I dissolved regularly. I felt encouraged by her patience and empathy. Even though it was only a photo shoot, at the end of the day I felt a sense of accomplishment I hadn't felt in a long while. Being silent is not in my nature, especially in the face of injustice. By going along with my employer's terms, I had violated not only my own ethics but my very nature. It felt good to finally come out publicly against them.

*   *

We were flying high after the *People* shoot, but we were almost immediately confronted with another hurdle. Based on a report from another neurologist who said there was no improvement in Michael's speech, Dr. F said he could not ethically prescribe another round of antibiotics.

*   *   *

When I was no longer taking antibiotics, I became unbelievably depressed. The bandage covering the hepborn lock had symbolized hope. It had confirmed that I was a vital player in my own destiny, still capable of making things happen. At least I'd been DOING something. Now, I was back to zero. The low dose of Elavil I'd consented to take was not helping my depression. I felt drugged, enervated. When I looked in the mirror, I saw my father in his last days, thin, gaunt, with a blank and hopeless look.

*   *   *

Michael was not convinced that the antibiotics helped, but I thought otherwise. I wasn't sure his speech had improved, but at least it had not worsened and there were still no other symptoms. As soon as he stopped taking the antibiotics, his coughing increased. He moved to the couch in our bedroom so he wouldn't disturb me. He also began to complain about weakness in his right leg and admitted it was becoming more and more difficult to play tennis.

It made no sense to stop taking the antibiotics, especially in light of all the evidence suggesting that advanced Lyme disease may take years to reverse. I could not give up on it. During the day, I scoured the medical establishment for the name of someone who would put Michael back on antibiotics.

I called our internist Dr. A, who was coordinating Michael's medical portfolio. A chatty, hands-on physician who took temperatures and blood pressures himself, over the years Dr. A had become a friend as well as a doctor.

Dr. A was familiar with the whole saga of our Lyme quest. He too had been royally dismissed by the enfant terrible neurologist who stopped returning our phone calls. I was sure Dr. A would help us find someone to prescribe at least one more round.

"Listen, Susan," Dr. A's his tone was harsh from the onset. "Michael has to stop chasing around and face it. We don't know what this is. But it's bad. We could call it Zaslow's disease, but whatever we call it, it is a degenerative neurological disease and it is going to get worse. It is getting worse. Michael keeps trying to find a way out, but it ain't gonna happen!"

My knees buckled. Why was he angry with me?

"He has to accept it and you both have to forget it," Dr. A continued. "When my mother was diagnosed with terminal cancer, we talked about it *once* and then never spoke of it again."

I hung up, sat on the carpeted stairs next to the phone and cried. I wanted to kill the doctor who had been our trusted friend.

*   *   *

Heroic! That's how Dr. A described me on a recent visit. "You're heroic, aren't you?" At the time, I was sort of nonplussed by that. I mean, I have two young daughters and I am going to search the wide earth for help. Does that make one a hero?

"I love you, Michael, and we're going to get through this," Susan said. Well, I love you so much S, and I am so grateful that we are now on the same page with all of this. No denial, only determination.

*   *   *

Michael severed relations with Dr. D or perhaps it is more accurate to say he severed relations with us. Dr. D simply stopped returning our telephone calls. We also severed our decade-long relationship with Dr. A. Since we were getting nowhere, and, to my ears at least, Michael's speech was getting worse, I called Dr. F one more time, pleading for him to reconsider another round of Rocephin. He finally agreed that if we could get his colleague Dr. H to agree, he would prescribe more Rocephin.

Having been burned by one neurologist at this particular medical facility, we were wary. The waiting room and the receptionist were icy…literally. The temperature was frigid. Even the high gloss magazines were cold to the touch. There was no one else there, but when we took our coffee and bagel out of the brown bag, the receptionist showed us where we could throw them out.

Dr. H greeted us with an effusive manner, and asked Michael to strip to his underpants. He invited me into the examining room and was almost flirtatious as he performed the by-now familiar neurological test. This consisted of tapping Michael's knees and arm wrestling with him to test his strength. Michael bested him. Smiling, he declared everything, including the MRIs he had just reviewed, were normal!

Just as I was relaxing with the good news, Dr. H added that "something" degenerative was obviously going on, and it would get worse soon. He wasn't even sure there was such a thing as Lyme disease, and would definitely not support another round of antibiotics. He told us they wouldn't do any good. He cautioned us not to have false hope, and warned us not to bother with any drug trials. He himself had headed many drug trials and stopped doing them because they were costly and raised people's hopes. Michael might have ALS, he said, although it didn't appear as if he did. If it wasn't ALS, though, it was something else just as bad. It didn't matter what it was.

Dr. H looked at me closely and glanced at Michael, who was now fully clothed and standing in the doorway trying to deal with the verdict.

"It looks like you two have a good marriage," the doctor said. "My advice? Go home and have fun with each other."

We had a list of other top neurologists, but we held off visiting them until my writing partner offered to get us an appointment with someone at New York University Hospital. Dr. I was booked through September, but as a favor (my friend's father was on the hospital board) he would see us after he finished his office hours the following day. We were given an appointment time of 10 PM.

University Hospital was deserted on that sultry July night, and all the other medical suites in the building were closed. Dr. I was with another patient when we arrived, and it was 10:45 by the time we were shown into the examining room.

Dressed in an elegant, three-piece suit and a crisp, British-style stripped shirt, Dr. I looked as if he had just showered and shaved. He apologized for not having had a chance to study the stack of medical records I had sent over and asked that we remain in the room while he read them.

Michael and I watched as he read the reports and viewed the X-rays and MRIs, nodding and jotting notes as he went along. His concentration would have been impressive at any hour. We exchanged hopeful glances.

Occasionally, the doctor would ask me for clarification, but mostly he ingested the volume of information without comment. I felt as if I were witnessing an advanced species at work. Michael was smiling just watching him. This guy knew his stuff.

For more than a half an hour, we sat in silence. Finally, Dr. I looked up and politely asked Michael if he would mind putting himself through one more neurological examination. No one had ever asked us about our feelings before.

Michael grinned, happy to oblige this gentlemanly neurologist. Once again, there was the standard neurological examination with Michael, his legs dangling, sitting on the table in his underpants. Once again, Michael displayed the strength he was proud to still possess. Dr. I asked us questions we had not been asked before. He was particularly interested in hearing about Michael's emotional lability.

After Michael dressed, Dr. I said he was glad we had come to him, and Michael and I both agreed we were glad also. He was precise and clear in saying that Michael had Pseudo Bulbar Palsy, a condition characterized by difficulties with speech, chewing, and swallowing. He explained that these symptoms, all of which Michael had, closely resembled those of bulbar palsy, a far more severe, lower motor neuron disease. Although the hour was approaching midnight, Dr. I took his time educating us in the distinctions between upper motor neurons (nerve cells originating in the brain's motor cortex and running through the spinal cord) and lower motor neurons (nerves starting at the spinal cord or brain stem and ending at the muscle fibers). No one had bothered to explain any of this to us before.

*   *   *

I wept with gratitude as Dr. I continued and, for the first time, I did not feel ashamed of my tears. Ignorance had been supplanted by reason. The key distinction upon which he had rested this more favorable diagnosis was my emotional lability, the spontaneous or unmotivated crying and laughing which had begun to weigh heavily on my family.

Dr. I asked his secretary, who was finally closing down the computer in the outer office, to give me a prescription for Rilutek. He made a point of telling me that this was the one drug available for both bulbar palsy and ALS but that he was prescribing it to me for Pseudo Bulbar Palsy. He said to continue with the Elavil and increase it gradually so that I could derive full benefit for my depression. I was to continue my strenuous work out program and do whatever I could to reduce stress and I was to check in with him in two months.

*   *   *

As we were leaving Dr. I again emphasized that Michael was dealing with Pseudo Bulbar Palsy. I had been chanting for this type of specific diagnosis from a major neurologist. In retrospect I have often wondered and, I will never know for sure, if Dr. I offered this "tolerable" diagnosis out of a sense of compassion and hope. As we would later discover, Rilutek is the only FDA (Federal Drug Administration) approved drug for ALS. Michael began taking it immediately, albeit for Pseudo Bulbar Palsy.

It was going on one o'clock when we left University Hospital, and we were both smiling. Michael repeated the phrase "Pseudo Bulbar Palsy," as if he'd won it as a trophy. At last he had a name for the elusive something. We were both wired. Dr. I had restored our flagging faith in the medical establishment and that was cause for celebration.

"But the prescription he gave me is for ALS," Michael's doubts emerged even before we reached our car.

"He made a point to saying you had Pseudo Bulbar Palsy." I clung to the distinction.

He gave me a hug and we drove up Madison Avenue. Le Relais, one of our favorite cafes was just barely open. We sat outside, reveling in the thick, warm night air. Michael ordered steak tartar. A soft breeze began to rustle the trees along the deserted avenue and we drank wine and took in the beautiful night.

About a week later, Michael's former leading lady and friend, Robin Strasser, who played Dorian on *One Life to Live,* called us in Connecticut. She had a great idea to bring Michael back onto the show in his former role of David Rinaldi. She was outraged that he had been let go, and wanted to do whatever she could to bring him back.

Michael wept from both joy and fear. He was overjoyed at the prospect of returning to work, fearful that he would not be able to cut it. Robin and I said of course he could do it! Robin recommended he go into the woods where nobody was around, and recite *Macbeth* to the beech trees. Maybe he could put stones in his mouth like Demosthenes?

Every day, Michael practiced his speech with the tape recorder. It was agonizing to see how the very sound of his own voice hurt him. I told him his speech still did not seem to be getting worse, but since he was no longer taking antibiotics, I could not be absolutely sure. The bottom line was that as long as he didn't get worse, we could handle this. I reiterated my pep talk about going to law school, and I believed it. The sky was the limit as long as the symptoms did not worsen.

*   *   *

It was becoming more difficult for me to swallow and, whether by coincidence or not, dinner invitations from certain friends were fewer and farther between. Not that we'd kept a wild social pace in the past, but over our twenty-two years in Con-

necticut, the bulk of our socializing had taken place here. Suddenly, we found ourselves at liberty and when we were invited it was in isolation, that is, only our
family. I was almost certain this was because my drooling had become an embarrass-
ment.

I felt isolated much of the time. Someone I had considered one of my closest friends,
the godfather of our children, was chronically suspicious that my symptoms were
purely psychological. While other friends also had that same theory, most of them had
a way of gently teasing me when they pointed this out. I felt they were concerned,
rather than annoyed. I found myself less willing to return Beau's phone calls when he
did call.

With Robin busily working behind the scenes at One Life to Live, my agent
and dear friend Marilyn Szatmary received a phone call from producer Maxine
Levinson's office. Head writer Claire Labine was very excited about the prospect of
returning me to One Life to Live in my former role. They wanted to meet with me
as soon as possible.

I'm not sure who cried the most in that meeting, Claire Labine or me, but I left
with my doubts erased. I was still an actor. My work and talent were valued.
Although I was disabled, I was not perceived as useless.

A few days later, however, things began to fall to pieces. One Life to Live
wanted me, but they weren't sure for how many shows. In addition, my legal con-
sultants advised me that working for the show's parent station, ABC, could jeopar-
dize my case with my former employer. I was dying to return to work, but I could not
risk forfeiting the remainder of my contract for what might end up being no more
than several shows.

My euphoria over returning to work was replaced by an even greater depression
and hopelessness, interspersed with a deadly rage focused on my former employer. I
knew this anger could not help my health. Despite meditation, therapy, and the
countless inspirational and self-help books, I could not always control my anger.

Despite the calculated increase in calories, I was fighting hard not to lose weight.
I also noticed that my right eyelid tended to droop. Plus, when I was sleepy, I found
it hard to open my eye. I would periodically lose focus and just stare blankly. When
that happened, I would have to exert my will just to regain focus. It was as if I
would glaze over.

My right hand was still strong but the coordination was impaired. When I
played the piano, I was unable to execute trills. Since the ABC deal had died, I had
become more depressed and reluctantly decided to follow my psychiatrist's advice and
increase the dosage of the Elavil. So far I hated the stuff.

I also hated the damned obturator, that retainer-like device that fastens behind my teeth and is supposed to lift my soft palate to prevent air from coming out of my nose. I resented the hours I'd commuted to Montefiore Hospital for the fittings. I had believed the promises that this would solve my problem.

*   *   *

With each new day Michael became more depressed, even with the anti-depressants, which he claimed made him feel worse. He had always been a voracious reader but now, with time on his hands, he couldn't concentrate. I urged him to chant along with me and he tried many times, but always the sound of his voice plunged him into despair. Until the *People* article came out at the end of August, there was nothing we could do.

Neither Michael nor I were very good at waiting. I had to do something to jolt him out of his hopelessness, so I began lobbying for a trip to London. Our friend Vanessa had a house in Knightsbridge and we had stayed there previously. If we could use her house, we could have an affordable vacation with the children. Michael was ambivalent, but I booked flights, solidified plans with Vanessa, and hired someone to stay with our brood of animals.

I had not given up on getting someone to prescribe more antibiotics. By mentioning the name Roger to the receptionist in Dr. Patricia Coyle's office at Stony Brook University Hospital, I, or rather Roger, got an appointment for the next day. Whenever we were able to log another medical appointment, our hopes soared. Dr. Coyle was one of the preeminent Lyme disease specialists so this was quite a *coup*. Medical appointments had become our new *raison d'etre*. We couldn't help but hope that Dr. Coyle would diagnose Michael with Lyme disease. If this happened, Michael would be put on antibiotics for as long as was necessary. He would be cured and we could resume our lives, ever more thankful than before. While I was the one who spurred these hopes, I could usually lift Michael's spirits after awhile. With hope in the picture, things were much easier between us. A ferry ride across Long Island Sound from Connecticut sounded like fun. We were ready for a night alone. We would turn the trip to Stony Brook into a belated celebration of our last wedding anniversary!

We were having dinner down the road at Ric and Susan's, one of the few friends who still issued us invitations. Just as we were leaving Dr. Coyle's office telephoned to confirm our appointment for the next day. Even though it was short notice we were giddy with excitement. I knew Beau and Ann were driving into New York City the next day but didn't bother to call them since we would be seeing them at Ric and Susan's. It seemed natural to ask if the children and Lily could ride along so they wouldn't have to trek along to Stony Brook with us.

We gathered for cocktails around Ric and Susan's coffee table. My friendship with Ann predated my relationship with Michael by a good many years. We had been in an acting class together, and I had introduced her to Beau. Her family lived in Stony Brook, so I asked her to recommend a great place for Michael and me to stay.

I left the room to call for a reservation and when I returned, I asked Beau if he could drop off Marika, Helena, and Lily at our apartment. The cats would be okay for one night, and Marika and Helena would be well taken care of by our next-door neighbors, Diane and Richard, who were like family. Michael's appointment was at 8 AM, so we would be back in the city by early afternoon. It seemed like an easy plan. It never occurred to me that everybody wouldn't be as excited as we were about the appointment with Dr. Coyle.

There was a long silence. Michael struggled to chew a piece of the frittata that Beau had made. He was drooling profusely and pulled out his handkerchief, eyes affixed on Beau, waiting for a response.

Beau sat with the corners of his mouth turned down, silent.

I clarified that I was just asking him to give his goddaughters and Lily a lift into the city. It wasn't a question of staying with them or anything else. Again, there was a long silence.

Finally Ann answered for him, her voice louder than usual.

"Well, we don't want to drop Marika and Helena off!" she exclaimed.

Michael's jaw fell open, and he hastened to wipe his mouth.

"Why?" I was shocked. "You're going into the city, aren't you? We're not asking you to do anything but let them ride along so they won't have to go all the way to Stony Brook and wait around."

"Well we don't want them along. We don't want to deal with Helena's hyperactivity."

*   *   *

Feeling as if I had been punched in the gut, I sat, unable to articulate my feelings, my utter disbelief at their unbridled hostility. Susan wasted no time in expressing herself. The evening degenerated into open warfare and Helena worried the uproar was her fault. Luckily, she did not hear Ann's comment about the hyperactivity.

I reminded Helena about a talk we once had about kids always taking the blame for their parents' problems. I told her I had done it, we all had, but that it was really important for her not to shoulder the weight of this problem. If her mom and I were having trouble with Beau and Ann, it was our problem.

Susan's fierce rebuttal complicated matters, but Beau's attitude has been going down this judgmental road for a while now with his comment that I was determined to have a life threatening disease. After that ugly scene, we went home and I had an amazing dream about Dad. He was recovering and said he had a flat in England for $1,800 a month, overlooking the beautiful east coast, where he could walk his tootsies off. He was so healthy!

*   *   *

I had leveled totally inappropriate insults at Ann. Even at the time I knew they were way below the belt and I was embarrassed by my ferocious, un-Buddhist response. At the same time I really didn't care who I hurt or how much. I apologized before we left that night, but I was outraged by their lack of sensitivity, especially the comment about Helena, who once told me she considered Beau her best friend.

We scrambled to make other plans, dropped Lily at our veterinarian's office, and left with Marika and Helena early the next morning to take the ferry across Long Island Sound. We checked into a motel in Stony Brook, looking forward to a nice dinner. Surprise! Dinner was unspeakably wretched. The evening reminded all of us of our favorite British sitcom *Faulty Towers*. If only the maitre d' had resembled John Cleese instead of a mafia-mannered hit man. The only thing we could do was poke fun at my over-cooked, nickel-sized swordfish. We shared a damp musty room. A dog was barking incessantly in the next room and we wished we had brought along our well-mannered Lily. Marika and Helena were hyped up by the sleeping arrangements and, once the lights were out, we giggled and cut up until far too late. I felt like I was back in summer camp.

*   *   *

An unbelievably expensive rotten dinner with the smallest portions I have ever encountered sent us into gales of laughter. Afterwards, we cuddled in two queen-sized beds and reminisced about Helena's arrival from Korea at age two. The next morning I was nervous about the appointment with Dr. Coyle. I knew I had allowed myself to get too hopeful. Susan and I left the motel at 6:45 AM, with explicit instructions for Marika and Helena. We said we would call them on the cell phone from the hospital. I promised them we would have a really good time when we got back. I silently cursed our "friends" who had put us in the position of having to leave our children alone in a strange motel.

Dr. Coyle was even more impressive than her credentials. Her impression was:

"In brief, we have a gentleman who appears to have acquired motor neuron disease syndrome, principally affecting the bulbar muscles with mainly a progressive bulbar palsy picture, although he does have inappropriate laughing and crying features which would go along more with a Pseudo Bulbar Palsy. I am now beginning to see involvement outside the brain stem, with weakness bilaterally in the hands, and weakness proximally in his legs. I have told the patient that I agreed he has a bulbar palsy. Overall, the data to support any relationship to Lyme disease is weak. I have also told the patient that he does not have a picture of typical ALS."

*   *   *

I left Stony Brook hospital at my lowest so far. I was furious at Susan for whipping up my hopes. Also, the disclaimer that I did not have a "picture of typical ALS" did not reassure me. The promise to have fun with Marika and Helena loomed as yet another obligation I would be unable to fulfill.

*   *   *

I felt so guilty for firing up expectations about Dr. Coyle and Lyme disease. At the same time, I had come to understand the vagaries of Lyme and I could not stop thinking that somehow there was a connection with Michael's symptoms. I knew this was the wrong time to bring it up, but I couldn't give it up.

After checking out of the motel, we located a gourmet take-out shop and picnicked in the plaza outside. Michael was so sad. The news was not good and it was hard to avoid this fact. Understandably, the children wanted to have fun and all that they had to look forward to was another long, tedious drive. As we finished our picnic they spotted a pet store. We went inside and lost ourselves in deciding which of the squeak toys Lily would love the most. Michael tried to participate. I knew how miserable he was, I was battling the same sinking sensation myself. We left with two catnip mice and a bargain bag of colorful squeak balls, which Marika and Helena planned on doling out to Lily on future occasions.

14

YOU WILL ALWAYS BE THE ROGER

"It is really great that you are taking the time to talk to your fans."

*   *   *

"Please let us know what we can do to help you! A group of us are putting together a Web page. We miss you. Stay positive and remember that you totally ROCK and that you will always be THE Roger."

—*Anonymous, Fans*

*   *   *

My first official statement since being let go was released on the Internet:

"There has been a lot of conjecture and apparent misstatements about my condition. Thus far, I've been silent at my employer's request, but I've been feeling a growing need to let concerned and faithful viewers know my health and employment status.

I am feeling terrific. I am biking the Connecticut hills, playing tennis, swimming, and still doing 100 push-ups a day. These efforts are, in part, designed to put to rest my employer's assertion that I have a serious illness. In fact, there is still no definite diagnosis, other than the all-too-apparent symptom of impaired speech. Contrary to my employer's statement that I went on hiatus for three months (now extended indefinitely), which implies a voluntary act, they actually gave me no choice.

I had repeatedly requested that they find a way to incorporate what has happened to me into Roger's story. It seemed to me that the fans could accept Roger enduring a setback (i.e., accident, stroke, pharyngal cancer, the possibilities are endless), in the same way my own friends have accepted my problems and showered me with prayers, encouragement, and love. It may be that the writers would have welcomed the chance to explore how a character, who has survived more than a quarter of a century, would meet the greatest test of his life. Unquestionably, showing Roger's struggle with an unexpected, possibly unexplained problem, would encourage others who are challenged and troubled to keep fighting, to persevere, and not to give up. That would have been a very life-affirming and responsible message to send to viewers and to society in general. Indeed, One Life to Live made that choice, offering me an opportunity to return to my former role. Unfortunately my former employer placed a restriction on me, which would have affected my arbitration against them. My lawyers have forbidden me to discuss this in any detail, but I can say that Proctor & Gamble has not honored our contact, forcing us to seek legal redress, and placing even more stress on my family.

Speaking of my family, the girls have been so strong and resilient and my wife Susan has, through her humor and determination, been the life force that has held us together. All of us are working hard to view what has happened to me as an opportunity—even a gift—for us to grow and to open our sensibilities.

I just wanted to go on record because I feel such a strong bond with the all-important viewers, who have sent me such heart-felt, moving letters that have truly buoyed my family's spirits. I miss my coworkers and, of course, I miss Roger the Dodger. I assure you that I am still an actor and a fighter. Look for me. I am going to continue acting and, through speech therapy, I am determined to learn to speak all over again. As General MacArthur said: I shall return."

*   *   *

Michael was receiving a lot of publicity about his mystery illness, and well-meaning people would see my name in an article. My professional telephone number was listed, and I often received calls offering advice.

"I read an article about your husband and I know what he has," was a common greeting.

Usually I was eager for any lead, but on this occasion, I had an impulse to hang up. The woman's dull monotone touched some deep fear I struggled to keep buried. I was polite, though, and so inquired what she thought Michael might have.

"It's the same thing my husband had," she replied.

I leapt onto the word "had," figuring she meant her husband was now fine.

"It's ALS." I had picked up a pen so I could take notes and follow up.

I caught my breath as she added, "Don't worry, there's no physical pain with it. The only thing is…he died."

I hung up with the same nightmarish feeling of déjà vu I had felt on St. Barths. Her thick voice echoed like a curse in a Grimm Brothers' fairy-tale. There had to be something wrong with me if I gave credence to a stranger over the opinions of experts who said it was not ALS. I did not mention the call to Michael. I did not mention it to anyone.

*   *   *

I'm sitting on the wicker chair in our bedroom, waiting for our cat, Lucky, to finish eating. I don't want to disturb Susan, and if I leave Lucky in here, he'll raise hell until she gets up and lets him out. What a contrary cat!

I woke pretty much in despair. My chest is aching. What does that mean? My life is centered on trying to find clues. It seems that whatever this condition is, it's fairly dire. I've just got to fight it, do my speech drills, take Lily on bike rides, and pursue the possibility of working on One Life to Live.

I keep wondering about Beau and Ann. Her comment about Helena was so nasty, but what really distresses me is my relationship with Beau. I'm always revisiting his statement that, "You were determined you had a life-threatening disease." I rejoined that determined was a poor choice of words. Rather, I simply hadn't been able to find a neurologist who would pose a benign diagnosis. After that conversation, we didn't speak for three weeks. I finally called him and we mutually agreed not to rehash this nonsense. But now this awful scene at Ric and Susan's…do they not understand that we are stressed to the limit, trying not to alarm the children and determined to lick this by any means necessary?

I cannot call him this time, but in the absence of his ability to make contact with me, I may write to him. He has been so good to me, coming to San Diego to get Dad. Susan has reminded me of his generosity many times. He has been there for Susan, taking her to dinner on one wedding anniversary when I was away working and, of course, he has lavished many generosities on my sweeties. Does he not comprehend that I am locked in a fight for my life?

I am determined to live, because I have so much to lose. I want to live to watch my girls grow and to enjoy my life with Susan. I am confronted with a challenge. I will develop my strength of character to breathe trough the coughs, to meditate, to chant, to educate myself on holistic remedies while simultaneously pursuing a traditional medical course.

Last night was nice. We all watched a tape of my movie, You Light Up My Life. *I was awfully cute back then.*

*   *   *

The Sunday morning before we were due to leave for London, my friend Nancy called from Chicago. She was out of her mind with excitement.

"I know what's wrong with Michael!" Nancy cried.

Nancy had talked with her friend, Sandy, a voice teacher in Pittsburgh, who knew a woman, like Michael, who had mysteriously lost her voice. The woman was totally cured. Nancy gave me the telephone number and said the woman was expecting to hear from me.

"Call me back and let me know what happened!" she said positively.

I let out a whoop, ran downstairs and out onto the patio. Michael was in the process of washing down thirty-some vitamins and sipping his latest Chinese herbal mixture from the Qui Gong Center.

"She had exactly the same symptoms as you," I told him. He looked dubious as he picked up the *New York Times.*

I raced back upstairs and called the woman, who sounded perfectly normal as she described how slurring had rendered her speech completely incomprehensible. She had also experienced severe depression and even mentioned being "overly emotional." I was delirious. This was the answer we had been searching for!

Returning to our patio, I filled Michael in on the details.

"She gave me the name of her specialist in Philadelphia, Dr Sataloff," I said. "Singers come from all over the world consult with him. He treated her with Botox shots and fully restored her voice. They still haven't established what caused the slurring, and she has to return periodically for Botox shots, but so what?"

We yelped and danced around the patio. Marika and Helena came out to see what was going on and we shared our good news. Although it was Sunday and I knew there wouldn't be anyone in Dr. Sataloff's office, I called anyway and left a message.

The next morning, I was up early, trying to secure an appointment before we left for London. Once again, Roger came to our rescue, and I didn't even have to mention his name. Dr. Sataloff's assistant was such a major fan she recognized Michael's name and volunteered to fit him in the schedule two days later.

*   *   *

I did all my exercises—100 push-ups in sets of 25, 200 sit-ups, dumbbell work, and legwork with weights. Nancy called again, and it seems this Botox treatment is actually promising.

*   *   *

The train to Philadelphia reminded us how much we love to travel, particularly on trains. We savored Crispy Creme donuts, sipped coffee, read the *Times*, and arrived at the 32nd Street Station, where a cab bumped us over cobble-stoned streets.

We entered Dr. Sataloff's office, which was in an elegant eighteenth-century building. The ambiance was warm, the antithesis of the opulent, modern facilities we were used to. Michael smiled and said he felt like he was coming home.

We were greeted by Dr. Sataloff's assistant, a serious fan who was as excited about our visit as we were. Dr. Sataloff was about Michael's age. He introduced himself, acknowledging how hard it must be for Michael, as both a man and an artist, to lose control of his voice. Such a personal approach was definitely a new twist. Together with Sataloff, several nurses, and some interns in training, Michael and I entered a small examining room filled with the latest equipment.

*   *   *

Dr. Sataloff addressed me as a colleague rather than a patient. I recognized his drive and his ambition. He was good because he worked his ass off, probably a perfectionist, like me.

I dreaded the test because it involved swallowing some noxious stuff, which allows the doctors to view my swallowing on the monitor. Sataloff encouraged me to watch, another new twist, and delivered a coach-like monologue as the test progressed. The monitor revealed the liquid gurgling down, the pulsating of the pink uvula, and the mechanical process of swallowing. I, as have most of us, took this process for granted all my life. I felt the suspense in the room and heard the word "normal" uttered more than once. My swallowing was still normal!

I was weeping, admittedly not that unusual for me. I was still aware that everyone in the room was rooting for me. They were all as overcome with emotion as I was.

*   *   *

Michael passed the dreaded swallowing test with flying colors! I was hopping up and down in the little room. Once again, though, the sweet bubble of hope soon burst. Dr. Sataloff was very concerned about the progressive nature of Michael's dysarthria, and immediately picked up the telephone and made an appointment with a neurologist colleague for later that day. Michael, it seemed, was not a candidate for the miracle Botox shots. Once again the dreaded initials "ALS" entered the picture.

Earlier, we had selected a cute outside cafe where we planned to have lunch, but neither of us felt much like eating. We walked slowly down Pine Street, discussing whether or not Michael should stay in Philly and see yet another neurologist. He liked and trusted Dr. Sataloff, so he decided to stay for the appointment late that afternoon. Since I had a dinner meeting in New York about a possible writing job, I would have to take the earlier train. This job would be a strong step towards firming up our financial uncertainty.

I did not want to leave Michael to face any more bad news alone, but he insisted he would be fine. If I got the writing job, there would finally be something to celebrate.

He helped me into a cab, and I turned to look out the window as we headed back to Union Station. The sight of him walking tentatively down the street almost prompted me to jump out of the cab. I tried to stifle my tears. I could not hold them back. I felt cornered, trapped. No matter which way we turned, the path to freedom was blocked. Something good HAD to happen! I had to get this job! Several days later, we received Dr. Sataloff's report, which basically stated that the doctor found no structural or functional abnormalities with Michael's vocal cords. The physician, however, was concerned that Michael's condition was worsening, and that Michael might, in fact, have ALS or some other motor neuron disease.

The two back-to-back disappointments were shattering. I had acquired a constant queasiness in my stomach, but I was glad I had persisted and made arrangements to get away for a week. We hired a local Connecticut fan and friend to stay at our house and care for Willy, Lily, Lucky, and Fred the Frog.

After the usual packing chaos and false starts, we finally jumped in the Jeep to head for Kennedy International Airport.

As was his habit, Michael put on a tape as soon as he got in the car. When it turned out not to be music, but a recording of his father's memorial service in California, I exploded. Was this any way to start a vacation? He bristled. His dad's friends had taped the memorial since he was unable to fly out. He was oblivious to the possibility that Marika and Helena and I might not want to listen to a painful reminder of our loss. Not that man anymore.

At the airport everything was more of a hassle than usual. Every time Michael tried to hoist a bulging suitcase we were terrified he would fall. The rest of the world was moving at its normal fast pace but we could no longer keep up. We boarded the plane, a frazzled bickering family but as as soon as we took off, almost magically, our spirits lifted. Michael relaxed immediately and I knew we had made a good choice. We settled into Vanessa's lovely Knightsbridge townhouse located in the quaint, cobble-stoned Pont Mews. Jet lag and all Michael was his old buoyant, enterprising self. For weeks he had avoided making telephone calls, now he confidently spoke with various contacts, making reservations to see all the shows on our list.

London was warm, sunny, and filled with tourists. We tramped around everywhere from Buckingham Palace to Westminster, Piccadilly to Bloomsbury. Michael and I had spent a lot of time in London, and it was fun to revisit our favorite spots. Marika had been to London before, but this was Helena's first trip and Michael delighted in sharing it with her.

Although we had previously spent hours at the Tate and other museums, we had somehow managed to miss the British Museum. Marika's unbridled enthusiasm for the "Elgin marbles" finally got us there.

*   *   *

Steps were growing more problematic, and the day at the British Museum was frightening. I was aware with every step that there was something wrong. I still managed to lose myself in London's theater scene. Our first night, my dear friend and former costar, Brynn Thayer, and her husband, David Steinberg, had arranged seats for the hit comedy ART. I had not laughed so hard in months, and the sound of Helena laughing next to me sent the evening over the top. We were having fun! It was still possible.

*   *   *

We indulgead our theatrical appetite, taking in performances of *The Ideal Husband, The Inspector Calls,* and, to satisfy Marika's appetite for scary plays, *The Woman in Black.* We dined after the theater, often outside at the Café Rogue around the corner from Vanessa's house.

We initially made plans to take the train to Stratford-upon-Avon to see two Royal Shakespeare Company productions. As the days went on, however, Michael's anxiety surfaced. The evening we attended the Irish Theatre production of *The Weir* at a tiny theater, he began to worry about his breathing.

The minute the first actor lit a cigarette, I stiffened. We were practically on top of the actors and five minutes into the play, everyone was puffing away. Michael was on the aisle trying not to cough. Every time he shifted in his seat, we all tensed, knowing that he was sensitive to smoke.

The play was brilliant but agonizing, and it was a relief to leave the smoky theater. We all loved Indian curry and, blessed with yet another warm summer night decided to dine at an outside Indian restaurant. From the moment we were seated, Michael was jittery, harping on the smoky theater, complaining about the service, and criticizing the exotic aromas he used to love. As soon as we returned to Pont Mews and climbed the steep stairs to Vanessa's flat, he announced he had to go back to New York right away.

After Marika and Helena went upstairs to bed, he told me he was having trouble with the stairs. It was true there were a lot of stairs at Vanessa's. There was one steep flight from the courtyard entrance, then another steep flight to the bedrooms. He went into the kitchen and demonstrated what he said was his lack of coordination in descending the stairs.

"You were on your feet all day," I said. "You're tired." I honestly could not see what he was talking about.

"I don't want to go to Stratford," he said.

I thought of the hours he had spent on the telephone making the arrangements for the tickets.

"Maybe you'll feel differently tomorrow when you're rested," I encouraged him.

He moved around the room, agitated. I urged him to sit next to me, but he said he could not sit down, that he felt like he was going to choke.

"I feel like there's smoke in my throat, like I can't get my breath. I need to go home."

"Please sit with me." I led him over to the sofa and eased him down next to me. His restlessness was palpable. He sat for a moment, then he was up again.

"You're working yourself up," I told him. "Try to breathe. Let's do yoga breathing exercises."

I him drew back down beside me. Suddenly his body stiffened, his head fell back, mouth open. I thought he was hyperventilating and held his head and tried to rouse him. He did not respond. I shouted for Marika and Helena who were upstairs getting ready for bed. I was supporting his body so he would not topple off the sofa and told Marika to take over while I dialed 911. 911 got me nowhere, no buzzing, no ringing. Nothing. Michael was still not moving. I fought against being paralyzed by my own hysteria and ransacked Vanessa's drawers trying to find a telephone book so I could find the British equivalent of 911. Helena was crying. I dialed "0" for operator, but there was no response. I didn't know the system.

Finally, I tried calling Vanessa's daughter but an answering machine picked up. Marika was still holding Michael, who showed no sign of life.

"Go knock on doors," I screamed at Helena. "We need help!"

I tried to make sense of the London phone book, trying to find at least the name of a hospital. Helena was shouting for help in the courtyard below us, as Michael's eyelids fluttered. He was still limp, unable to sit without support. Seconds later, Helena returned with two young men, one of whom was a doctor. While the doctor checked Michael's vital signs, his friend called an ambulance.

Michael was adamant and struggling to articulate that he would not go to a hospital. Almost immediately, though, the ambulance arrived and, over his objections, he was put on a gurney and hoisted down those narrow stairs. I sat in the front seat with the driver and Marika and Helena, who refused to be left behind, sat beside their dad as we sped through the wet, deserted London streets.

The emergency room at Chelsea Hospital was small and homey. Nobody asked us for insurance, and we were all invited to join Michael in a little cubby that was sectioned off with what reminded me of floral curtains from a British sitcom. Michael laughed when I said if John Cleaves had walked in with a stethoscope around his neck, I would not have been surprised.

We spent the rest of the night waiting for the doctor on call to come in. Marika and Helena kept busy making trips across the street to the all-night market, returning with British goodies, unlimited Smarties for their daddy and themselves.

It was a gray and drizzly dawn when the doctor finished all the tests and reported that he saw no indication of a stroke. Everything, he said, appeared to be normal. We took a cab back to Pont Mews and fell into bed around 6:30 AM.

When I woke, I heard Michael negotiating with the airlines to leave as soon as possible. I was amazed by his resilience. As hard as it was, he made himself understood and, with his usual magic touch, managed to get us booked on a flight the next day.

15

THE MELODRAMA THAT
JUST HAPPENS TO BE YOUR
LIFE

Your letter arrived as a wonderful surprise and welcome relief. It meant so much to hear from you, to be certain that your mail has been forwarded, and especially to know that, in some very small way, I made you feel a little better.

Quite honestly, on the day I received your card, I'd reached my lowest ebb in the months-long melodrama that just happens to be your life. It was so hard to know absolutely nothing about you for months, and then, just as we're eagerly expecting your story in People, *we get blindsided by an online report that it'd take a miracle for you to recover, much less ever return to GL. Four months of silence was just plain scary—especially from you! I've just never pegged you as a "keep your mouth shut" kind of guy!*

Your card assured me that your passionate spirit is alive and well. The main thing I want to say right now is this: If you need us, we are here. We have your best interests at heart, and would never do anything to hurt you. When we decided to create a Web page in your honor, we did it because we wanted a place where people could go and learn more about you. We've received lots of online notes wanting to know, "What can we do to help Michael?" So that's the big question—if there is anything we can do to help in any way, please let me know, because we'll do it for you.

—*Teresa Brown, assistant attorney general of West Virginia, fan*

I returned from our abbreviated vacation to the usual piles of letters and e-mails. In addition to these items, there was a petition to my former employer from two fans, Kristi Miller and Teresa Brown. They were protesting my dismissal and consequent treatment. Feeling the groundswell of support, I dug in with a new sense of purpose. I spent most of my time sitting in Marika's room at her Macintosh, which was where I felt most like myself. This was the one place I could still communicate (slow fingers aside) with my usual confidence. As long as I could write and reach out, I felt a sense of hope. The voice inside my head was still my own, and with the computer, I could access my message and send it forth.

I was ecstatic! I struck up a letter and e-mail relationship with quite a few people, among them Teresa Brown who, as we later discovered, was to become a top flight angel in our lives.

*   *   *

Whoever Kristie Miller and Teresa Brown were, I loved them. Michael did an about face as he saw the ranks of fans forming behind him. He was fighting mad, determined to right the wrongs, which, in this case, had been done to him. Immediately upon our return from London, he made an appointment with Russ Warren, the orthopedist who had performed his most recent knee surgery. On August 21, Michael went to the Hospital for Special Surgery, which was where Dr. Warren had performed the successful six-hour operation on his right knee in May 1991. Warren saw arthritic deterioration in the X-rays and found the right knee to be looser than the left. He said that looseness could unquestionably be contributing to the weakness in Michael's right leg. Cutting straight to the point Warren declared it was time for Michael to have a knee replacement.

This was amazingly good news, as far as I was concerned. This diagnosis suggested that Michael's new symptoms were related to his old knee injury and not to whatever degenerative neurological disease we were doing everything to dodge.

*   *   *

Once again, I was hopeful and hope mobilized my outrage over the way I had been treated. My former producer was quoted in the People *article as saying, "Thorpe has great strength and power. It didn't seem characteristic for us to stop, then begin telling a story about whatever Zaslow's problem was." His obvious implication was that if one has an impairment, it necessarily follows that one cannot have strength or power.*

On August 31, I posted the following response to my caring fans:

"My family and I are very much moved by your support and prayers. Your response has strengthened our resolve and furthered our hopes that there is indeed

light at the end of the tunnel. Maybe I've been given a new mission…a new purpose in life. Surely, I've been given a new instrument and I am determined to put it to use in the service of compassion and love. We are all responsible for each other. I have never been more certain of that eternal truth."

*   *   *

There was still no certain diagnosis for Michael, but it was obvious that whatever it was, it was getting worse. For my part, I continued to follow leads associated with Lyme disease. At dinner one night with our friends the Prioleaus, Phillip, who had originally supported us in that area, suggested that we might give the "guessing" Dr. C another chance. Phillip knew Dr. C, and thought he might be open to looking further into the possibility of a Lyme disease connection.

I was not enthusiastic. I would have preferred to wait until the gentlemanly Dr. I returned from vacation, but Michael thought he might have misjudged Dr. C. He made an appointment, and wrote a letter bringing him up to date.

Dear Dr. C,

Susan and I are ready (we think) for more information on my diagnosis, which I believe is Pseudo Bulbar Palsy. Is this a diagnosis or a syndrome? Does the continued normalcy of my EMG test call this into question? Is there literature you could show us? I have contacted the New York chapter of the ALS Association, and they have established a full-service ALS Center at Beth Israel Medical Center. Do you recommend that I visit them? My speech pathologist at Montefiore recommended that I investigate (with your help) the NIH Neurological diseases Center in Bethesda, Maryland. I wonder if you could call Dr. L to see if I would benefit from making the trip. I know of the Sanofi trials now taking place and have enclosed the information I have along with the 800 number. I don't know where the trials are being held, and would appreciate this information.

I have noticed reduced function in my right foot, ankle, and knee lately. My foot tends to drag and it catches on rugs. I can't rotate my ankle swiftly or tap my foot quickly, and the foot feels uncoordinated. I visited Russ Warren at the Hospital for Special Surgery and he asks that you communicate with him. I am uncertain if my right leg problems are related to this motor-neuron disease, or simply attrition stemming from my 1971 basketball injury. Well, I guess we'll talk when you get this rather lengthy letter. I am so uncertain about so many issues. Susan and I wish to face our prospects head on, and help our daughters to understand what their daddy and family are facing.

*   *   *

Once again, the ritual neurological examination saw Michael stripped to his shorts, legs dangling from the narrow black table. I observed from a corner of the small room. I was biased against Dr. C, but in person he was pleasant and charming, if not a bit too cavalier. He put Michael through the strength paces, and I applauded as Michael bested him.

When Michael remarked on his continuing upper body strength, Dr. C smiled knowingly.

"Have you experienced any fibrillations, involuntary muscle twitching?" Dr. C inquired.

Michael shook his head, and I concurred.

Dr. C looked strangely pleased.

"You will," he said cryptically.

"What does that mean?" Michael asked, defensive. I didn't blame him. After all, he had bested Dr. C even with his right hand.

"It means I'd still put my nickel on ALS," Dr. C told us.

Why was this doctor smiling? I had to control myself, and I could see Michael was also angry. He certainly didn't need me to add fuel to the fire.

"I'm still wondering about Lyme," Michael controlled himself and struggled to form the words. "You have Dr. Coyle's report."

I jumped in. "She said if Michael were to have another spinal tap, he should send it to her because she does some new tests that aren't done elsewhere."

"How about we do the routine Lyme test and see what happens?" Dr. C asked. "If those results come back positive, we'll go from there."

I stopped myself from interjecting what he had to already know, that the test was notoriously unreliable.

As Dr. C left the examining room I gave Michael a high five, and we focused on the positive, pinning our hopes on the slimmest possibility that the test would come back positive. While Michael dressed, I followed Dr. C into his office and we exchanged a few words about mutual friends. I wanted our relationship to be positive so that he would want to help us.

As we walked back into the hall, Michael was coming out of the examining room. He wobbled as if he was walking on ice, lost his balance, and fell. I ran towards him as he struggled. As I helped him up, I glanced up and saw Dr. C still standing outside his office door, watching us. He made no move to help, and did not ask Michael if he was all right.

Michael gave me a look. I knew he was thinking precisely the same thing I was. Still holding his position, Dr. C asked Michael to walk in front of him. I stood to one side. Michael did what he was told but he said later he felt sick inside as he was doing it.

*   *   *

I was having trouble walking. I had said as much, and the doctor had seen me trip. Shouldn't he have done something, even something as simple as asking if I was okay? It occurred to me that I should call an orthopedist and see if something could be done to help my walking. But why, I wondered, hadn't that occurred to Dr. C? The answer was obvious. He was a neurologist, and tripping had nothing to do with his specialty. I called and made an appointment with Leon Root, one of many fine orthopedists at the Hospital for Special Surgery, and a tennis-playing friend from Roxbury.

*   *   *

We were impatient to get the results of the Lyme test. Four days later, just as Dr. C had dictated, I called his office to see if the results were back from the lab. When his secretary hesitated, I made a point of saying not to disturb Dr. C. She put me on hold for some time. I assumed she was checking the day's mail for the report but then Dr. C picked up.

"I told you the lab report would take four or five days," he said, admonishingly. "You are to call on Tuesday and not one minute before! Now is that clear?" I felt like a child being spanked for my bad manners. Why was I surprised at his harsh tone? Here was another lesson in patient subservience to the Almighty.

It was a relief to see Leon Root, who fit us into his busy schedule the following week. An examination revealed Michael had a mild weakness in his right foot and leg, which accounted for the tripping. Dr. Root ordered a posterior leaf orthosis. He scratched his head and asked Michael if he had investigated the possibility of Lyme disease.

When we explained that the most recent Lyme test, done by Dr. C, had returned negative, he shook his head. He reiterated what everyone pretty much accepted. The standard blood test was unreliable. A negative result was not conclusive. He did not understand why the spinal tap had not been repeated.

We had been asking the same thing for months. Even on the remote chance that Michael's condition was Lyme disease, why not explore every avenue? If it were a question of health coverage, we would have happily done anything to establish a diagnosis for which there was a treatment!

*   *   *

I have to face the fact that my toes and the tripping are definitely due to the disease, and not my old knee injury. I know this is a blow to Susan. She lost it today when she spilled a smoothie. It is very difficult for her. She is always making smoothies, phone calls, and plans. She keeps trying and chanting for things to be better. I know how she feels. It feels difficult because it is. It's mind-bendingly hard. This is the greatest challenge of my life, but I am determined to meet it head-on. I will exercise my body, my mouth, my speech, and get my libido back! I am going to buy a journal for Susan, Helena, and Marika, and we will try to get back to communicating with each other.

Nobody but Helena can understand me when I talk. Mostly, I try not to talk. It's too humiliating to hear my voice. Therefore, I spend as much time as I can in Connecticut. When I'm alone up there, puttering, chopping wood, I feel like myself. I bought everyone in our family a blank book, so we can begin communicating again...if only in writing.

9/1/97 7:17 PM

My darling Helena,

I am so excited to express myself to you and you to me.

I can't believe that you and Marika and Mom got your desk up and working in your new room! It's going to be wonderful for you to be so independent and in charge of your very own private space. This is a very special time for you and all of us. Also, I'm glad you are back in school and not in my presence as much. You were always worried about me this summer—especially in London—always asking, "Daddy, are you all right?"

No child should have those worries, and now you're back with your friends and homework and baby-sitting Rachel and just hanging out.

I like seeing you carefree and relaxed and yourself again. Anyway, I love you so much! You're such a unique, special person. We often don't see our own attributes as clearly as we discern the qualities of others. That's the trick of life—to learn to appreciate one's self and be our own best friend.

Your ever lovin' Daddy

PHOTOGRAPHS

Michael & His Dad
Los Angeles 1952

Michael
Los Angeles, 1970

Michael
Age 7

Michael as Perchik,
FIDDLER ON THE ROOF, 1971

Michael
ROGER THORPE, 1975

Michael, Susan & Fred Lipson
FIDDLER ON THE ROOF, 1971

Michael as Henry Ward Beecher
ONWARD VICTORIA, 1980

Michael & Susan
Wedding Dance, 1975

Michael & Deli Gan
YOU LIGHT UP MY LIFE, 1977

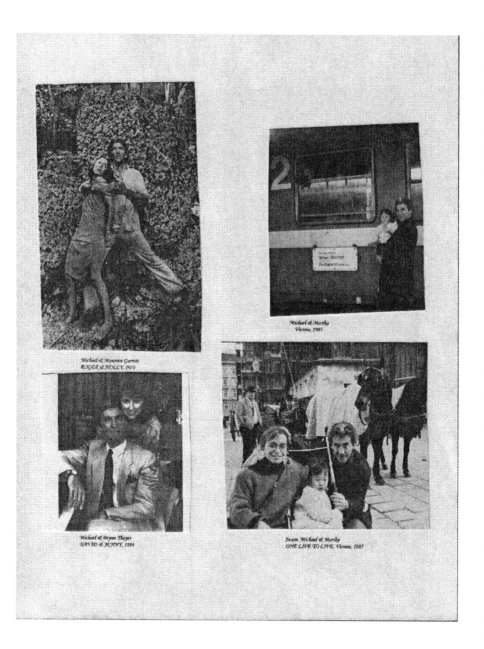

Michael et Maureen Garrett
ROGER et MOLLY, 1979

Michael et Marily
Vienna, 1985

Michael et Bryan Thayer
DAVID et JENNY, 1984

Susan, Michael et Marily
ONE LIFE TO LIVE, Vienna, 1985

Michael & Martha
Roxbury, 1983

Martha, Helena & Michael
Maine, 1989

Michael & Susan
Roxbury Thanksgiving, 1984

Martha, Michael, Helena & Susan
Roxbury Thanksgiving, 1990

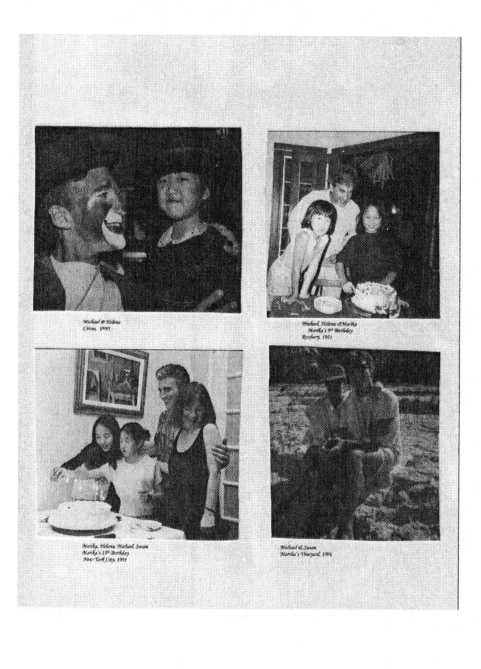

Michael & Helena
China, 1990

Michael, Helena & Marika
Marika's 9th Birthday
Roxbury, 1991

Marika, Helena, Michael, Susan
Marika's 13th Birthday
New York City, 1995

Michael & Susan
Martha's Vineyard, 1994

Michael & Lily
Lily's 1st Birthday Party
Roxbury, July, 1997

Michael & PAL, Chris Prendergast
New York City, June, 1998

Helena, Michael & Bryan
SOS for ALS
New York City, September 1998

Marika, Susan, Helena & Michael
SOS for ALS
New York City, September 1998

Michael at The New York Yankee

Tony Hearns, Michael, Dorino Gordon
ALS Sports Benefit, October, 1998

Michael, Helene and Dave Winfield
ALS Sports Benefit, October, 1998

16

UNITELLIGIBLE

Most of my knowledge of Michael came from writing scripts for him. He was a joy to write for because he always made the scene sound better than it had looked on the page. Nearly two decades later, Mimi Turque, with whom I was collaborating on a musical project, asked if I would present our material in her friends Michael and Susan's living room. This was shortly before they had received a definitive diagnosis, and Michael was plagued by frequent coughing spasms. His speech was virtually unintelligible, but he was still able to walk and to communicate his thoughts to us by looks and gestures. His immediate concern was for my comfort at the piano. After moving the piano himself so I wouldn't have to twist my neck to be seen by our little audience, he addressed the lighting situation. Was there enough light for me to see the music? Although I thought I could manage, Michael wasn't satisfied. He went out and came back with a somewhat rickety stepladder, insisted on climbing it himself, and adjusting some overhead lights so they would illuminate the music. I held my breath, fearing he would fall, but he didn't. He fixed the lights and came down from the ladder. Then and only then, when the stage was right, could we begin. I never saw Michael again, but I will always remember and admire his consideration for my comfort when he must have been in such distress himself.

—Nancy Ford, writer, composer

I slept from eight something last night to around eight-thirty. Twelve hours! I am really down! I can't help observing that I am slipping. My strength is in a downward spiral and I've got to fight!

I lifted my dumbbells this morning and it is getting harder. Maybe that's because I missed all week since the dumbbells were in Connecticut. I've embarked on the ozone therapy and supplements at Gary Nulls, which is just down the street.

I am such a sorry guy. Where is my spunk and spirit? I've got to fight these blues. I'll raise my hands up in the air in exultation while proclaiming my depression. Then, I'll curl up in a ball and whimper: "I am depressed." I imagine myself, five years from now, appearing on The Gary Null Show, *having reclaimed my strength and voice and recounting how I beat this rap with the help of so many wonderful facilitators.*

I'm writing this in the plant-filled room at Gary Null's, waiting for my ozone treatment. As usual, they're running late, so I may have to do the ozone after I meet with my new therapist/healer, Michael Ellner. He suggested Susan join me, and she should be here soon. I take my notebook everywhere because writing has become my only means of communication. I also use it to record my passage through this dark and thorny jungle. I'm hacking my way through with my machete, never knowing when I'll be attacked by a snake or a lion or swallowed up by some other disaster.

This drug, Elavil, is wiping me out. I'm up to seventy-milligram doses, and it really makes me feel blotto. At least I had the sense not to drive the car over to have the MRI done. Susan drove me, the sweet darling! This MRI is for the thoracic area. Dr. C wants to rule out compression of the spine.

Imagine what he would say if he knew I was flying off to the Shealy Healing Institute in Missouri to see a holistic shaman?

I can hardly imagine it myself, even though Dr. Shealy is a bona fide physician. Oh, I am so weary of feeling this way. It is truly not me and neither is this miserable disease, and I must focus on that reality.

*   *   *

Suzy Duella, the wife of one of Michael's oldest friends, Keir, was fighting ovarian cancer. Suzy rejected conventional treatment and nutritionist Gary Null was treating her with alternative vitamin and ozone therapies. She and Keir were wildly enthusiastic about Gary, who told them he had never lost a patient. Since the Gary Null Center was only two blocks from us, Michael added intravenous vitamin C and ozone treatments to his regime.

Michael felt stronger on the days he had treatments. I could actually see a difference. I noticed a healthy glow to his face, which had grown increasingly gaunt. The treatments were expensive and time-consuming. Sometimes I would bring him thick power shakes from the health food store across the street and sit with him during the treatment. Gary himself was lean, fit, and perennially tan. He wore crisp, colorful shirts and snazzy loafers like someone fresh off a Caribbean cruise.

Michael was wary of Gary's cocky manner. While we were dubious about his guarantee of a cure for Suzy, we held fast to the belief that anything was possible. If Dr. C characterized medical pessimism, Gary stood for hope.

I never doubted that Gary believed in his methodology but his office, though well meaning, was hopelessly chaotic. Michael would arrive on time either to wait or to find out that someone had made a scheduling error. If we tried to phone ahead, sometimes the phone was answered and sometimes not. From my first visit, I found it ludicrous that in order to reach the healing center, one had to climb two flights of dauntingly steep stairs. The message seemed to be: "Gary Null Health Center—Everyone Welcome Except the Disabled!"

Through our friend Teresa Hargrave in Connecticut, Michael learned of Dr. Norman Shealy, a founder of the American Holistic Medical Association and head of the Shealy Institute in Missouri. Always the student, Michael loaded up on Shealy's books, some of which were written in collaboration with medical intuitive Caroline Myss.

Shealy's innovative research intrigued him, and we contacted the Institute and arranged for Michael to be admitted for treatment. I very much wanted to go along. It would have been a vacation of sorts, but in addition to being away from the children I was in the process of trying to get a writing job and would be writing a sample script during that period. Michael was upbeat about the trip and I had a positive impression from speaking almost daily with someone at the Institute. I would relay Michael's inquiries that he would write on one of the ubiquitous yellow legal pads. I was anxious about him making the trip alone, and felt torn and guilty even though I knew it was best for me to stay behind.

Out of the blue, three days before he was to leave, we got a phone call from Dean Compton, one of Michael's favorite friends from UCLA. Dean was the sort of person who could drop out of your life for decades, and then reemerge as if he had never left.

The timing of Dean's call felt like a positive sign. And, he was in Missouri, twenty minutes from the Shealy Institute! We could not think of a more ideal companion for an offbeat, alternative healing experience. At the time, we didn't realize exactly how offbeat it would turn out to be.

*　　　　*　　　　*

Dr. Shealy wants me to increase the dosage of Elavil before I leave. Maybe that's what is slowing and stopping my speech? That's wishful thinking. Maybe if stress brought this on, I can reverse it by focusing on the positive.

I am scribbling this in the brace shop of the Hospital for Special Surgery. I'm awaiting the device that will lift my toes and stop me from dragging my right foot and stumbling. I've got to start having fun! I am such a drag. We're having dinner with Steve and Carrie and Madison tonight as a celebration of Marika's fifteenth birthday. Maybe if I am in a relaxed state, they can help me heal myself at the Shealy Institute. I am leaving on Saturday. My breathing difficulty and cough have subsided and that's a positive sign!

*   *   *

Michael was to fly to Missouri on Parent's Day at Trinity School, so for the first time, I went by myself. On the way home, I stopped at Whole Foods and bought an array of gourmet organic foods for the plane. I picked up our car at the garage and drove Michael to the airport. On the drive back to Manhattan, when I wasn't crying, I was chanting with all my heart for Dr. Shealy to heal him.

17

THE EXORCISM

I never thought I'd see my rational buddy Mike at an exorcism. Lordy, lordy was it ever something!

—*Dean Compton, friend*

It is now 6:50 PM, and we've crossed the dateline, so it's 5:50 PM Missouri time. I made short work of that organic chicken Susan picked up at Whole Foods. The breast was a little dry, so I didn't eat all of it but the dark meat was yummy. I'm now plowing my way through the green juice, which isn't as good as mine—no carrots to sweeten and enliven. The strawberry smoothie and peanut butter cookie have also vanished into the confines of my stomach.

The air has always been a good place to gain perspective. This well may be the dreaded initials, but who's to say the progression can't be halted? I've got to have faith and believe. Susan believes, the girls believe, our friends believe it can happen. Susan has been so nurturing and accepting about my withdrawal from familial responsibilities. And Lily? I haven't walked her in ages. I am sad that this is happening. I don't deserve this, but no one does. I had this realization during therapy with Edy. I have always expressed my stress and anxiety and I have been able to laugh and cry and grunt, unlike a lot of men. Did I ask for this?

I don't think I did. I couldn't contain myself when Mom was dying. I just wept openly and loudly, and when Dad died, same thing. I don't restrain my emotions. As Helena says, I am the first to cry in movies, whether for joy or pain.

*   *   *

Michael and I spoke nightly with Dean as an interpreter. The Shealy Institute, founded in 1971 as the nation's first comprehensive pain and stress management clinic, was nurturing and positive. The staff of experienced medical professionals was dedicated to alternative therapeutic options. Dr. Shealy traveled all over the world in search of new techniques and technology geared toward treating neurological disorders.

Dr. Shealy was particularly interested in some of the vibratory technology coming out of Russia. According to Dr. Shealy's report, Michael was introduced to the GigaTENS usage for the Ring of Crystals. Several days later, the Ring of Earth was added. These treatments would be continued at home, together with the Liss transcranial stimulator, tiny electrodes applied to specific areas of the head.

Prior to coming to the institute, Michael had been instructed to record his temperatures, which were found to be low, averaging significantly below ninety-eight degrees. A treatment protocol was begun to raise Michael's core temperature.

Brain mapping was performed and evaluated by Dr. Shealy, who observed a significant abnormal pattern, in which extremely high levels of delta waves were made in the frontal lobes and a very small amount of beta waves were provided. Michael was outfitted with RelaxMate glasses that looked like large protective glasses worn by welders, only with dark lens. The glasses emitted blinking pulses of light at various intervals, according to the setting. They could be set to stimulate Theta waves and could markedly decrease delta wave activity.

It was Dr. Shealy's impression that theta wave reduction might be therapeutically helpful, but that Michael would need to continue this form of therapy once or twice daily for a minimum of three-to-six months. The glasses became a fixture in our lives and Michael, who found them quite beneficial referred to them fondly as "my Shealys."

In addition to the electrical devices, Dr. Shealy prescribed various supplements, including the Gary Null Antioxidant, twice daily. He also suggested taking Amantadine for several months in case the etiology was viral. Michael was introduced to specific meditations and given literature to support a variety of forms of spiritual healing. The institute acknowledged "while some of these approaches are admittedly experimental, they would be safe and it would be anticipated that potential benefit could occur with very little in the way of side effects or problems. Michael or his wife, Susan, is encouraged to call us should any questions or problems arise."

*   *   *

Here at the Shealy Institute, I'm beginning to see that maybe I've been protesting too much with regards to holding in stress. In addition to Mom's unexpected death and Dad's degeneration, I've always held myself to higher standards than those to which I've held my friends. I never gave myself any slack, except in my hippie days.

I realize I'm not unlike other type As, ambitious people, but perhaps my constitution was just not able to handle it. Lucy, the healer/nurse/psychic, worked with me today to draw out this ambitious streak. Diane, the nurse, did much the same type of catalytic work the day before. Susan, you have been right all along. The added stress of that June in 1996 and my unrelentingly high standards have no doubt landed me here. Diane, in a tragic run of events, lost her mother in 1995 and both of her sons two months later. She says we are all put here to learn. We are not masters when we start out, and it is asking for trouble to demand that of ourselves. She said she took herself apart when her sons died, and she felt as if she had failed them.

Most people here have this religious streak. When I allow myself to be open it's all right. Shealy has a mystical bent. He asked me if I believe the soul reincarnates and if I believe that evil forces can come back, unbidden, to possess a living person. Heavy stuff. It's not exactly the political ideology I was weaned on! Dean and I had the best red snapper steamed with veggies in a Thai restaurant. I wanted to take home every dish that came out of the kitchen.

*   *   *

With Dean at his side and buoyed by the adventurous spirit of the institute, Michael asked if he could extend his stay by two days. This was completely his idea. The Shealy Institute did not play on his vulnerability nor did they ever suggest that he return for periodic treatments. Without any promises of cure or improvement, the experience restored Michael's dignity and hope.

The night before he was to leave, Dean called as usual. I could hear Michael's gurgling laughing sounds in the background. Dean told me that Dr. Shealy had scheduled Michael's final treatment—an exorcism.

Michael came on the line and garbled "the son of Trotskyites at an exorcism?" He and Dean were whooping it up. Michael was game, but riddled with trepidations. He requested that Dean be present. I wished I could hop on a plane and join them.

The following day, they called with the details of the exorcism. Dean did most of the talking, but I could hear Michael's muddled speech in the background.

Dean described a solemn and ritualistic ceremony witnessed by several staff members. The shades were drawn, the candles were lit. Michael lay on his back in the center of the room, unable to believe what was happening. Dean stood apart from the participants as the exorcism conductor intoned a request for guidance from the powers of light. He summoned the powers to enter the room and dispel the evil spirits that possessed Michael's body. Despite his skepticism and resistance Michael was convinced of a change in energy as the powers of light and love came into the room. Their presence was palpable to everyone present. Michael felt shivery warm sensations and, against all the logic of his mind, believed his mother, Edith, was present. Dean, who had known Edith, felt her distinctive energy. Suddenly the positive sense of light and benevolence shifted and an eerie heaviness swept over everyone present. Moments later, the conductor let out a cry of alarm. With difficulty he articulated that he was wrestling with an adversary of unearthly dimensions. An alien.

I was prepared to hear a weird occult account but when Dean mentioned alien spirits from the other side I was caught me off guard. Alien body snatchers belonged in the science fiction category rather than the spiritual realm. The notion of an alien inhabiting Michael's body was terribly unsettling and made me doubt the authenticity of the entire experience.

Michael flew back to New York reeling and questioning, but hopeful. That hope was hard to hang on to in the face of his continuing loss of speech and other blatant reminders that he was not that man anymore.

*   *   *

What an intense week in Missouri! Dr. Neil, Norm's associate, is terrific and I believe Norm is authentic. The exorcism actually became a sharing of emotions, after the strange business was through. The love and compassion of all of the staff was awesome. It was a very healing experience.

I think what I've learned is that nobody knows the path my illness will take. Going to the Mayo Clinic would be an exercise in futility. They are very traditional, and we'll get the same answer we've heard from the slew of other traditional neurol-

ogists. *They don't understand bulbar palsy, or for that matter ALS. So it's up to us to fight tooth and nail to live. Since I (Hallelujah!) got upgraded, the food on the flight home was reasonably good. I ate chicken and bowtie pasta with olives and anchovies. I also managed to down a glass of good white chardonnay without once choking, coughing, or sputtering. My mouth feels smaller and slower. I take dainty bites, deliberately and consciously. I prepare my mind in a Zen-like fashion.*

*   *   *

Most lives have a roller-coaster quality to some degree, but our life consistently went from highs to lows in an instant. Michael was positive and determined when he returned from Missouri. Two days later, he plunged to the depths. The muscle twitches, which Dr. C blithely foresaw, sent him into major gloom. He was back to blaming the Elavil for his lethargy, and stopped taking it. I was certain he needed something to counteract the depression. We bickered about taking Elavil or some other anti-depressant. One afternoon, he scribbled a seething condemnation about my nagging, and accused me of taking advantage of his muteness. I countered by promising never to speak to him again. From that moment on I too would communicate by writing on a yellow legal pad.

Like idiotic adolescents we scribbled insults back and forth until we were both in tears. I hated that I could speak and he couldn't. I had to accept it. Couldn't he understand how I struggled with guilt every time I opened my mouth?

*   *   *

I had a dream involving Arthur Miller, our neighbor in Roxbury. He embraces Susan and I and proudly shows us his new digs. He is living in a commune-like, hippie bunker layout, which is very nice. There are lots of friends around, and then suddenly Susan and I are in the hallway outside of our New York apartment. Our neighbor, Rachel, a delightful four year old, her father, Richard, and mother, Diane, are there. Diane offers me a cookie from a tin she is holding. I accept and clown with Rachel. Then, Susan and I enter our apartment. The radio is playing It Had To Be You, *and I start to sing along.*

I am really singing! Not great, as yet, but actually singing with articulation and range! Susan and I can't freaking believe it. We are going wild, dancing around our kitchen, whooping it up.

Suddenly, I stop. Susan sees my worried expression. I tell her that this has happened before in my dreams. I am afraid, aware now that this too is a dream.

"I thought so, this is REAL," Susan says. At that point, we are delirious, dancing around our kitchen. I hit a high note, and we're both ecstatic, breathless with euphoria.

Then, cruelly, I wake. I feel lower than I have ever felt, and I think, "Cruel, cruel." The next day I am struck by the thought that if I can live like that, even in my dreams, there is hope. Such joy and liberation in dreams is better than nothing.

I long to revisit that oh so joyous feeling!

*   *   *

In lighter moments, we joked about whether Michael would rather have the use of his voice or of his legs. Communication won, hands down. Now that his speech was totally indecipherable on the telephone and to me as well, he took matters into his own hands. Since his efforts to communicate his various requests to me were becoming too time-consuming, he started spending hours relaying his requests through writings, faxes, and the Internet.

After six months, Michael's employer still had not responded to Laura Sigal and AFTRA's efforts to negotiate a settlement for his lost salary. At Laura's suggestion he contacted Ann O'Shea to determine if we could take legal action by viewing the dismissal as a disability case.

*   *   *

I am determined to get some justice here, and, one way or another, I will. It is very difficult not to be bitter.

Between doctors, I finally found time to fax Brynn Thayer the following update:

I am virtually unintelligible now, especially on the phone and except to Marika and Helena who are truly amazing at understanding me. I am increasingly thankful for my trusty fax, and, as you can imagine, e-mail, which we finally installed is a godsend!

We finally found a neurologist we can relate to! I was shopping at a health food store and came upon The Brain Wellness Plan, *written by the nutritionist and neurologist Jay Lombard. The book details various neurological diseases and recommends what supplements might be helpful. The notion that nutrition and supplements could be beneficial was brand new to us. We had been used to neurologists who approached motor neuron diseases with a passive attitude. Finally, here was a guy who was willing to join with patients and their families to wage war against these scary dragons!*

I tracked the author, Jay Lombard, down and Susan and I drove to his office in the Bronx. We felt like we'd journeyed to another city. There were small buildings, lots of sky, kind of old world, and there was no Manhattan glitz whatsoever. What a relief to walk into a waiting room that did not feel like a page out of Architectural Digest! *I'm afraid a lot of our medical institutions think they can soothe or distract patients with extravagant, marble lobbies and fountains. Here there was definitely no marble, no thick carpeting, only the reassuring hum of conversation emanating from the secretaries.*

We met with Dr. Lombard and we were not disappointed. He has been interested in neurological diseases since he was in high school. After the same old neurological exam I asked him point-blank: "So, do I have ALS?"

"It doesn't matter so much what you call it," he replied. "What matters is what you do about it." We were both weeping. Imagine, somebody was saying we could do something!

Susan and the girls are my lifelines, and are doing great! Susan remains a fountain of wit and compassion, and the girls are looking after their daddy. I am still in quite good spirits, though my right leg and foot have degenerated to the point that I can no longer bike or play tennis.

We are trying to take the positive outlook that we are going to slow, stop, and reverse this lousy turn of affairs, which is the only outlook that has a chance of success. Negativity can be more toxic than all the pollutants in the world. I know that you and David comprehend this simple truth because you guys are the real McCoys.

Hey, have you seen The Full Monty? *We loved it! How about* Shall We Dance? *Anyway, that's about it. My former employer is still stonewalling, despite the tons of mail they get in support of me. My next step is to file suit with the EEOC on the grounds of discrimination against people with disabilities.*

*   *   *

We sat across the desk from Jay, as he insisted we call him. He gave us a crash course in the current thinking about ALS and made a list of the top researchers in the field. There was still no definitive diagnosis, but Jay said that is not uncommon with ALS. Both Michael and I read everything we could get our hands on, and it seemed to me that ALS may not be a single, discernable disorder. What is labeled ALS seems to affect people differently and runs its course in various ways. The physicist Stephen Hawking has lived with ALS for over twenty years, yet the literature states unequivocally that patients survive only two to five years.

Dr. Lombard's point was that scientists still do not know precisely what we are dealing with. Is ALS one disease or many? Why does Stephen Hawking live for more than twenty years, while others survive only the briefest of years? The mystery has eluded researchers, but Jay said the good news was ALS research has made enormous progress in the past five years. Most significant is the discovery that the gene for one form of familial ALS is linked to the gene for superoxide dismutase (SOD). This discovery led to the development of animal models such as transgenic mice with mutant SOD that Jay opined marked a giant leap forward in ALS research. He was optimistic that a breakthrough was maybe not exactly around the corner but finally on the horizon.

Hope. Michael folded up Jay's hastily drawn diagrams and tucked them into his pocket. Jay seemed almost embarrassed by our gratitude. He gave us what he referred to as a "short list" of the five top ALS researchers. His manner suggested he felt reverence for their work. He emphasized that they, not he, were the real experts, but that he would be happy to implement any protocols they might suggest.

We drove home and I telephoned all five neurologists on Jay's short list. The first appointment to come through was with Dr. J at a major research center in a nearby city. Once again, "Roger" paved the way and we were squeezed into the schedule, instead of having to wait the usual two months.

Meanwhile, wedged in between Michael's schedule I saw clients in my office located across the street from our New York apartment. I was long overdue for a visit to my dad in Ohio. I had put the trip off, not only because I dreaded it, but because there was never a free moment. Once I finished writing the sample script I booked a flight to Dayton and spent the next three days with my dad at the nursing home. I told him everything was fine with Michael.

My dad was not an easy patient. He had managed to live alone for the past six years, mostly through a combination of grit and gumption. A former sheriff, he was famous in our small town for being a John Wayne sort of guy who shot from the hip and was to be trusted, not crossed. I encouraged him to participate in physical therapy so he could regain his strength, but he was dubious.

We had a couple of good afternoons together where he allowed me to help him do a few exercises. The best times were singing old tunes together and reminiscing over the past. As my departure time approached, however, Daddy grew testy and irritable with the nurses. As I left to head to the airport, I heard him railing at someone for doing something "stupid."

I returned to New York and, three days later, Michael and I were driving to our appointment with Dr. J who assumed we had come because of a new Sanofi drug trial. We had no prior knowledge of the trial, but of course we were interested when he said they were in the process of selecting candidates. The timing of our visit felt auspicious.

*　　　*　　　*

Getting into the Sanofi drug trial required more qualifications and determination than auditioning for a Broadway show. Although I fit the required medical profile I needed to pass a breathing test to qualify. Because of the lack of strength in my lips I could not grasp the testing instrument in order to get an accurate reading. I was blowing with all my heart but the air kept escaping. Susan and two nurses cheered me on. I don't know how many times I tried, but I just couldn't do it. I knew I had the lung capacity, but I just couldn't get the necessary score to make the cutoff.

*　　　*　　　*

I felt like Michael's acceptance into the drug trial was a matter of life or death. The test involved a little monitor, like a scaled down version of a carnival strength-testing machine with a little ball that went up and down. We urged Michael on as he took in the biggest gulp of air he could manage. I held my own breath each time he released the air, but he just couldn't make that little ball go up high enough. The nurses were determined to get him into the trial. Finally they sent us down to the cafeteria so Michael could eat and gather his strength. When he returned, rested and fed if not relaxed, Michael rose to the occasion. He blew hard enough to send the meter over the top, like a macho powerhouse slamming the hammer down. Like the crowd at the local carnival we all cheered. Such are the victories we treasure.

Michael officially became a participant in the Sanofi drug trial being conducted by a French pharmaceutical company. The trial was designed to see if Sanofi could regenerate nerve cells. Of course, there was no guarantee that Michael would even be taking the drug. Only one-third of the participants would actually receive a full dose while the other two groups would receive a placebo or a half-dose of the drug. Since this was a double-blind study, even the doctors would not know who was getting the drug.

As we drove back to New York I told Michael that based on his amazing record as a lucky gamblin' man, he was sure to get the drug. Just in case, though, as soon as we got home, I began making inquiries into the illicit drug market. I knew there were Sanofi trials in Europe. I telephoned friends with contacts in those countries to see if we could buy the drug over there.

*   *   *

While surfing the Internet, I found a heart-stopping interview with Dr. Lewis Rowland of Columbia. Although he was known as the preeminent ALS expert, Susan and I had avoided him because he was rumored to be mired in the negative, old-fashioned views of ALS. Toward the end of the interview, Rowland mentioned "spontaneous remission" that can occur in ALS, and claimed to have seen a dozen or so such cases. Immediately, I faxed Jay Lombard the piece. I had several burning questions in my mind regarding these cases, and feverishly desired more information. Were these spontaneous remission patients studied? What if anything did they have in common? Did they DO anything? Alternative medicine? How can we get more information?

*   *   *

There was so much to do and so many leads to follow, but the news of spontaneous remissions from one of the most highly respected and conservative neurologists was astounding. It seemed unusual and quite disturbing that there had been no follow-throughs. Why hadn't the ALS Association gathered every shred of information possible about these survivors? I pledged to inquire about this and added Rowland's name to my growing list of things to do.

My daily routine included follow up to the Shealy Institute on replacement for Michael's Shealy glasses, and finding an update on the Russian Giga-TENS, which had reportedly been approved by the U.S. Food and Drug Administration. I ordered Noni Juice and various other nutritional supplements. Twice a week, I drove Michael downtown to see a physical therapist/nutritionist. Again I was stupefied at the challenge he faced in entering this person's office. Each visit required that he negotiate a steep swirling staircase that appeared like something out of an old MGM musical. I was terrified, but the friendly practitioner cheered him on, as if he were cresting an unexplored peak. Why did she think he needed one more challenge?

Like the detective I had imagined myself to be as a pre-adolescent I was always on the lookout for a new clue. My sleuthing led me to a well-known Manhattan pharmacy, which shall remain nameless. The pharmacy was known for obtaining drugs not yet approved by the Federal Drug Administration from foreign countries. Their practice was illicit, but in my estimation, ethical. The owner was clearly not out to make a killing because he volunteered the name and phone number of his British sources so that I could contact them directly. Thus I was able to acquire Idebenone and several other drugs. I tried to return every call concerning Michael's treatment. I spoke with many amazing people, some compassionate and eager to help, others trying to sell their wares to make a living.

18

LAUGHTER AND TEARS

We are here for each other, learning to live one day at a time. There is so much laughter and tears in our home. We are living very full lives now. We are closer than ever before, learning valuable lessons from each other. And that goes triple for our daughters, Marika and Helena.

—Michael Zaslow

The next neurological appointments to materialize were with Dr. K and Dr. M. Dr. M was affilliated with a nearby institution while Dr. K was a five-hour flight from New York. However, Dr. K's office asked me a question that intrigued us: Had Michael ever visited the island of Guam in the South Pacific?

The answer was "Yes." Michael, while still in college, had visited Guam during a USO tour. If we were dealing with ALS, a very high percentage of cases existed on the island. That did it! Although the logistics of the long trip were overwhelming I made the appointment immediately. Maybe Dr. K was working on a treatment related to some virus that people who had been to Guam might have been exposed to?

As I continued my daily routine I clung to the thought that Dr. K would not have asked such an esoteric question if it did not have potential signifi-cance. I was on the phone constantly with my dad's fleet of health care work-ers in Ohio. He was so miserable, begging to leave the nursing home, pleading with me to come and get him out, threatening to walk home, even though he could no longer walk since his last fall.

With each day seeming to bring a new crisis with my dad in Ohio and with Marika and Helena in school we knew there was no way I could accompany

Michael. When Brynn learned he was going on his own, she generously insisted upon flying from Los Angeles and meeting him there. It was an amazingly generous offer. I was thankful she would not take no for an answer.

*   *   *

I am to be given the Silver Circle Award at the National Association Television Artist's Society award dinner on November 17. This honor, though welcome, seems to confirm my status as an endangered species. Since I have managed to get an appointment with another esteemed neurologist, Dr. K, the same day, Susan will accept on my behalf. She will offer the following speech as my acceptance:

Dear Members of the Academy,

First I want to tell you how sorry I am not to be here with you tonight to accept this honor personally. I am otherwise engaged seeing my fourteenth neurologist (that's a conservative figure) in the hope of getting some useful answers to my speech puzzlement.

I miss work so much and the company of my cast mates and crew. I thank my coworkers for their support tonight, as well as throughout the black hole of this experience. I also want to take this opportunity to thank my wife, Susan, and my darling daughters for their humor and wealth of understanding in putting up with my more than occasional bleak moments.

Now I want to address this honor, before someone gets the can and hooks my wife's beautiful neck. I would be ecstatic to belong to any club that had Betty Rae as a member. It is to this singularly classy lady that I owe my career in daytime television. The mold was indeed shattered when our lady of the casting was created. When I tested for the part of Roger Thorpe in 1971, I was a swarthy young man with a helmet of black hair and a beard. This was a period in which there were few, if any, Mediterranean-looking fellows on TV or in films. Troy Donahue was still the paradigm of the day. I was playing Perchik in the original run of Fiddler on the Roof *at the Broadway Theater at the time, and Susan was playing Hodel. I was asked to shave off the beard for the second test for* Guiding Light. *I agonized over the decision before deciding that it would make it too important—I would have had to wear a fake beard and apply spirit gum to my face for every performance of Fiddler. I imagined the perspiration ungluing the moustache and me inhaling it as I drew a breath for my dreaded high note in my big number,* Now I Have Everything. *Anyway, I said if they offered me the part on* Guiding Light, *I'd shave my beard. And I showed them a picture of me sans beard to assure them that the beard wasn't hiding some monstrosity. Betty Rae convinced the powers that were to hire me for what was then conceived as a short-term plot device for the character of Roger Thorpe. Thanks Betty, and thanks to the folks at NATAS for this tremendous honor. It comes at a perfect time and really lifts my spirits, which need all the elevation they can get. I will treasure this moment forever. My spirit is with you right now. Love you, Zaz*

Brynn Thayer met me at Intercontinental Airport Sunday evening, having over-ridden my protests that she would have a far better time sticking with her plan to go to New York with her husband, David Steinberg. Together with Clyde, the skycap from American Special Services, and the first of many special people we were to meet, she escorted me to the black Rodeo she had rented. The trip to one of the largest medical complexes in the United States, if not the world, was uneventful. We checked in, stowed our bags in our rooms, and went down to have a beer. We succeeded in closing the bar.

The next day, Brynn called me at 6 AM. I wasn't allowed to eat breakfast because I was scheduled to have blood drawn later that morning. We walked directly over to the outpatient unit, where we were assigned a large room with two beds and three comfy chairs. We set up shop and studied the Internet material on ALS in preparation for meeting with the great man, Dr. K. Meanwhile, Dr. N put me through the same strength test I had performed easily seventy-five times since my first visit to a neurologist. Once again, I passed with flying colors.

Dr. O came in and did a simple pulmonary test. Brynn was insistent that the blood work be done so I could have breakfast. I was ravenous, my appetite blissfully unaffected by whatever else was going on. She returned from the hospital cafeteria with a bagel, a banana, cinnamon bread and some orange juice just as the "vampire" (which was how the staff referred to her) came to draw blood. Forty vials! We laughed in disbelief.

Twenty minutes later, the vampire left with her booty, leaving me spent and sprawled on the bed. Finally I could eat, but I didn't have the strength to rise up to a sitting position for a good ten minutes. By that time, Dr. P had arrived to repeat the strength test she performed earlier. Strangely, she seemed determined to best me in arm wrestling. I thought it was a draw, and she thought she won—at least on the right side. She insisted she saw fasciculation in my muscles, even on the left side. I was very protective of my left side, which I wholeheartedly believed was unaffected.

Dr. P said there was a fellow in the adjoining room who was anxious to meet me. Apparently, he had carried the People magazine article around with him, and had even considered traveling to New York to meet me. At that moment, Dr. K came in, accompanied by the two doctors who had been in earlier, plus another eight young residents.

Dr. K asked me why I had traveled all this way when there were certainly plenty of excellent neurologists in New York.

"I'm in search of a diagnosis that isn't ALS," I answered, half joking.

He then lowered the boom on me—smack, right between the eyes.

"I see you've been to all the top guys," he said. "Dr. D, Dr. J, Dr. C, to mention a few. You've done your legwork. I'm wondering if they have been direct with you."

I didn't like how this was going. "What? What do you mean?"

"You're a classic ALS patient," Dr. K said, "You have to accept that. Now. You have to accept that you have ALS, so you can get down to the task of defiance and battle the disease. I'm sorry to be so blunt."

"You can't keep going all over the world looking for someone to tell you it's not true," he said. "It is."

19

HONESTY

Everybody says you must be honest. That honesty is the best policy, but I don't know, particularly with this unfortunate diagnosis. There is nowhere to go with it, unless you believe in counterculture stuff, which I, myself, don't. If you found out six months later, well, you've had those six months without knowing. This is not a piece of information that I would want to know myself."

—Ivan Strausz, MD, friend

I wept uncontrollably, emitting humiliating sounds that I normally only emitted privately. I hated this doctor, this man who had sealed my fate. He was a sadist beyond anyone I'd met. I could not stop the awful blubbering until well after the room had cleared and the group continued on their rounds. Still weeping, I repeated my litany that he who takes away one's hope is the devil.

"Eat," Brynn said, and handed me the bagel. "You're hungry. Eat." I shook my head.

"I hate him," I said. The pencil cut through the yellow pad as I scrawled my communication in huge, angry letters.

I tore into the bagel as Brynn seized the moment.

"I think he did what he had to," she said. "He didn't take away your hope…only your denial. You've been going nuts trying to figure out what this is, and now you know. He's right. Now that you know, you can focus on other things."

I listened to her because she clearly was totally in the moment, an icon of wisdom, love, and compassion. We weathered a very tough moment, gaining tremendous power as a result.

Dr. O came to repeat the simple pulmonary test with a larger mouthpiece. By that time Brynn was back with a BLT and fries. I held the good doctor at bay while I *stuffed my face. He was very gentle and understanding, and much happier with these results.*

Brynn's cellphone rang, and it was Susan—hooray! We'd been trying to reach her, and since it was too difficult for me to be understood, especially over the phone, Brynn related what had occurred so far.

*   *   *

For more than a year, we had done everything possible to avoid this moment but here it was. I could hear Michael's indecipherable utterances in the background as Brynn conveyed his message: He was relieved and hopeful. I was definitely not relieved, but that only made me fight harder to remain hopeful.

The scene, which was recounted to me where Dr. K hurled his diagnosis at Michael in the presence of a dozen or more interns made me sick. What did the doctor's public declaration have to do with compassion? If such forthright candor was his style, would it have made more sense to make this diagnosis in private? Although I did not say so at the time, Dr. K's performance struck me as medical melodrama having nothing to do with the Hippocratic Oath. I guess it was a good thing I was not there. I know I would not have stood by without jumping in to protect Michael.

*   *   *

I took the phone to hear Susan tell me how much she loves me and how hard we are going to fight and how we are going to win. I returned a garbled second of that emotion and listened as she instructed me to make sure I ate heartily.

"Let me talk to Brynn again," Susan said. She then repeated the eating instructions, creating a diligent monster out of the already vigilant Brynn. This added emphasis on calorie intake ensured that I was not to be without some nourishment or other in front of me for the next three days.

An EMG followed, despite my protest that I was unsure if the insurance company would pay for it, having had my most recent EMG only five days ago. Brynn phoned my insurance representative, Cheryl Fredy, at the AFTRA (American Federation of Radio and Television Artists) Plan. Cheryl and I had developed a close relationship by fax, as I had required increasingly more attention. I don't know what I would have done without her, for she never failed to write me little notes of encouragement and drawn little smiling faces.

Cheryl assured Brynn there wouldn't be a problem because my health fund wasn't an HMO. This was not exactly what I wanted to hear in this case, because I actually wanted to avoid having to take the painful test. No such luck.

Brynn held my left hand while they applied the shocks and needles to various sites on the right side of my body. The needles under the chin into the tongue were, as always, the worst, but in the hands of the able Dr. Q, it was a piece of cake. When I wrote on my pad to him that his was the best of eight EMGs (something of a record, I was told) he blushed a deep red. He was, like everyone we'd met, brimming with compassion and confidence—a combination of attributes I had come to discover was sadly rare in the medical field.

Finally, the testing was over. Brynn wheeled me back to my room, and I managed to get myself to the hotel gym for a workout. We ate delicious takeout at a movie theater. It was nice to eat in the dark. I had become increasingly self-conscious about my inability to eat with my mouth closed. Chewing was getting harder and harder, and I had to sneak my finger inside my mouth to help my tongue guide the food to my teeth.

Later, we again closed the hotel bar and said "goodnight."

Back in my room, I was greeted with the most moving voice mail from Susan describing how she and Helena had accepted the Silver Circle Award on my behalf. Three full tables of cast members from Guiding Light—*including Jerry VerDorn, Kim Zimmer, Tina Sloane, and Maureen Garrett, had shown up in my honor. Susan was so happy that I had worked out at the gym after such a brutal day. I cried again, and listened to the message three times before going to bed. I saved it and listened again the next morning, playing it for Brynn later in the day.*

First thing the next day, I was wheeled up to the pulmonary facility. It was dazzling. Dr. O, again a paragon of gentleness and encouragement, guided me through the elaborate tests. One of the tests involved sitting in a booth very similar to the one used on that game show The Sixty-Four Thousand Dollar Question. *The test was designed to evaluate my breathing capacity. I scored poorly because of leakage. My lips were just too weak to provide the necessary compression. There was really no way of measuring my true breathing capacity.*

Down in the hospital room, we visited our neighbor, David Goodbar, his wife, and his daughter. The People *article had deeply affected David, who had also been in search of any alternative diagnosis to ALS. He and Vicki didn't want to believe he had the dreaded initials any more than Susan and I had.*

Just as David was revving up, Dr. K showed up with his medical entourage trailing in his wake. I scribbled for Brynn to ask him about pitching the idea of an ALS story to the ABC network.

"Michael and I are thinking his character, David Renaldi, could return to the show with ALS," Brynn said. *"Think of the exposure that could be gained, and the increased awareness of the disease."*

"It would be incredible," said Dr. K. *He immediately saw the impact this kind of exposure could have on a disease that had been previously shoved aside, ignored, and basically hidden. Since Lou Gehrig had the disease over fifty years ago, there had been no progress in finding either a treatment or a cure. In the collective mind of the medical community, ALS was a metaphor for hopelessness. It seemed to me that ALS was as frightening for those in the medical community as it was for those of us who had it. I scribbled furiously on my yellow pad and shoved it in the good doctor's face.* *"Maybe we could get you to come on the show."*

Dr. K's face lit up.

"I'd do it," he said, willingly. *"I'd do whatever I could to take ALS out of the shadows."*

I fought back my tears, which was no easy job in my mental state. I explained how I was going to be a man living with ALS. Rather, David, the character I play, will be a man living with ALS instead of dying from the condition. We can show the public what it's like to lose your speech, to not be able to trust your own legs, but that the mind still isn't affected. We can prove that people with disabilities aren't their disabilities, but are still their former selves. I'm still me, Michael Zaslow. David Renaldi is still David, even though he can no longer play the piano or conduct. We can let the audience see how David struggles to communicate. We can raise awareness and money for research!

Suddenly, we had all moved to a new level. Dr. K was not the devil. He revealed the recent loss of his beloved wife from colon cancer only three weeks before. This explained why my earlier appointment had to be pushed back. He spoke passionately about his commitment to ALS and to his patients. He saw the potential in my status as a daytime celebrity and was as eager as we were to exploit this status. I now had a mission, and we all felt a new sense of hope.

I was wheeled up to the muscle biopsy center into an adjoining operating room. There, Dr. R, a cheery woman, filled us in on what I might expect in terms of discomfort. She then shocked me by saying that the biopsy would be on my left leg, the good one.

I had assumed it would be on the right leg, which was noticeably weak and atrophied in the thigh. I feared I would not be able to walk at all if the biopsy was done on the left leg.

When Dr. K returned, I voiced my concerns.

"If the diagnosis is definite, why do the muscle biopsy at all?"

"I want to make sure there is lower motor neuron involvement," Dr. K replied. "We need to know this. I don't mind if it's done on the right."

"Would it be as beneficial to you if it's done on the right?"

He leapt on my question. "The point is—is it good for you? I can see you're a nice guy. ALS is the nice guy's disease. In my experience only nice guys get ALS. If a guy is a son of a bitch, I'd have to reconsider the diagnosis."

To everyone's amusement, I scribbled on my pad, "I can be that guy!"

I agreed to the biopsy, only if it was performed on my weak right leg. When that was over, Drs. N and P entered and asked us if we would consider appearing in front of all the medical residents. I would have my strength tested again and be questioned. I would have Brynn's assistance of course, since I could only scribble replies on my yellow talk pad.

My only reservation was my extreme emotional lability. I was afraid I would lose control in front of thirty young, healthy strangers. Dr. N reminded me that my emotional lability was a symptom of ALS and it would be educational for the residents to see it firsthand.

Brynn, as always protective of me, suggested I might like to sleep on it, but I scribbled: "What the hell, I'll do it!"

Back in my hotel room, we called Susan and happily filled her in on what had taken place. After Brynn returned to her room I struggled to get the local e-mail address so I could send direct greetings to my girls. It was close to 2 AM when I packed, did my electrodes, and fell asleep with my Shealy glasses blinking away.

The next day, Brynn wheeled me over to meet with various therapists. We lined up in our wheelchairs like planes awaiting a control tower's signal to land. I was armed with all sorts of pamphlets on communication devices and other medical equipment I might need.

At 1:15, Dr. N escorted us to the residents' demonstration. I wrote jokingly: "Do I need makeup?" We entered a large room where more than thirty residents awaited us. A young Indian doctor was chosen to conduct my strength test, and I triumphed over her. She was all of ninety-nine pounds, but the victory was still sweet!

One of this doctor's tests, unfortunately, confirmed weakness in my eyelids. I was unable to keep my eyes open against even modest pressure. I was so excited to be keeping my cool and not dissolving into bathos that I was actually able to clown and tease. What a difference from our first day in Houston!

Our performance was a smashing success! We were due to meet Dr. K, who came with a list of questions about new drugs and treatment. He said straight out that if Myotrophin was approved by the U.S. Food and Drug Administration, he would have me wave bye-bye to the eighteen month Sanofi trial I had just begun.

"*I want you settle in with the diagnosis awhile before we make any moves on the question of drugs,*" *Dr. K said.*

I scribbled, "I trust you," and he pulled out a picture of a dollar bill with bears on it. He explained that what he looks for in his resident interns are not simply high test scores, but something called the huggable factor. He explained that if a patient doesn't want to hug the residents when they leave, there is something sorely lacking, and Methodist Hospital doesn't want them.

Brynn had allowed two hours to get to the airport. Ordinarily, it is a half-hour jaunt, but we kept getting lost and had to double back several times. When we finally reached the car rental, Phil, the man on duty, clearly smitten with Brynn, drove us directly to the check-in. Phil was another in a cavalcade of angels. Brynn was positive our earthly realm was chock full of angels.

"*I wish I could believe that,*" *I said. "Especially now, I wish I was one of those fortunate people who could believe. But I've been raised an atheist.*"

"*I know you've said your parents didn't believe in God,*" *Brynn said.*

"*They were revolutionaries,*" *I scribbled. Trotskyites, then socialists. Religion was suspect in our home. They believed in humanity, in helping people. Nobody could have given more time, money, and energy to causes than my folks. They put their money where their mouths were, but it wasn't in the name of religion. If there actually is an omnipotent God, he or she would have to be very mean-spirited, not to mention a poor administrator. Look at all the injustice and misery in the world. "So talk to me, tell me, convince me of his presence,*" *I said.*

Brynn laughed. "You're a tough sell."

"*I wish I could be sold,*" *I wrote.*

"*Well,*" *Brynn thought for a moment, "I see evidence every day. For example, your marriage. How many years is it? Would you call it a match made in heaven? And Marika and Helena. Is it not pretty miraculous how they came into your lives?*"

I could not refute the logic of that. In so many ways, I have found that since my illness, many people whom I've come in contact with are brimming over with good will.

Brynnie and I sat together on the flight. When we landed, she commandeered a wheelchair and secured a wagon driver to take me to the gate for the flight to LaGuardia. She then instructed the check-in woman to make sure a wheelchair and attendant would meet me at the gate in New York and take me to the driver of the car service that Susan had ordered. It was about this time that Brynn realized she had lost her own ticket to Los Angeles.

Typically, she was unflappable. She knew they would have a record, and simply issue her a new ticket. Susan and I learned the following day, fortunately, that someone had turned the ticket in to the appropriate gate. Was this another of Brynn's angels at work?

Brynn and I boarded the plane where she alerted the flight attendant that I was speech impaired. The attendant asked Brynn to buckle my seat belt, assuming I was also helpless. Brynn assured her I was up to that task, and left me with a hug, a kiss, and one more sandwich. I find it difficult to pucker and give a smooch because of my weak lip muscles, but I can definitely manage on the receiving end!

The final sandwich on the flight was divine. I downed most of it before we were airborne, and then I took out my computer and began recording the account of our seminal journey. If I was going to describe my odyssey to Susan, I would have to do it by laptop. I assumed my encounters with angels had ended, but I was wrong. Arriving in New York, a young fellow with a wheelchair met me at the gate, and wheeled me to the baggage carousel. He instructed my driver to get his car and meet us at the "F" sign by the curb. My bag was the second one on the belt and he started to wheel me with one hand and the baggage wagon with the other. Suddenly he began whistling a tune that had been my introduction to music when I was two years old. My parents told me that I played that record till the grooves were worn out.

I wrested my yellow pad out of my pocket and scrawled for his benefit: Eine kleine Nachtmusik. *He nodded with excitement, and began extolling the virtues of the timeless composers—Mozart, Bach, Beethoven. What were the odds meeting such a kindred spiritt?!*

Angel? As this lovely man pushed me to the car I wrote: "One year ago I could whistle, sing, and speak."

"Did you have a stroke?" he asked.

"Neurological disease," I wrote.

"Have you tried alternative medicine?" he asked.

"Indeed I have," came my answer. "Acupuncture, IV drips loaded with anti-oxidants, yoga, meditation. I try everything I can."

He nodded approvingly. He was elegant, calm and so in the moment even though at 12:30 AM he must have been exhausted. For the first time in our magical encounter, I tried to speak.

"Could you write your name for me on my pad?"

He understood and wrote: "Gaudens Yapo." He included his home and work telephone numbers. American Airlines baggage handler, Sky cap...angel.

20

PARADISE LOST

"The mind is its own place, and in itself, can make a heaven of hell, a hell of heaven."

—*John Milton*, Paradise Lost

I slammed an umbrella against a framed poster. Slivers of glass flew everywhere. I swore. I sobbed. I screamed. I chanted. My Buddhist practice and studies taught that under the principle of *ichinen sanzen*, every human being has the potential to become a Buddha. It tells us that true happiness exists within ourselves. The greater the obstacle, the greater the opportunity to evolve. It seemed there was no greater obstacle than ALS. I was not ready to meet the challenge.

I knew that as long I thought my suffering was caused by Michael's ALS, by a force outside myself, I would waste away from anger and bitterness. Although I had received profound proof and benefits from my Buddhist practice, I was terrified. We are told to chant for total victory, and I did. But who knows precisely what "total victory" looks like? I thought I knew, but I learned otherwise.

*   *   *

Mr. Yapo settled me in the car, my driver back to the city was flawless and as we pulled up in front of our apartment building, Leon, the night elevator man, to whom I'd given the mountain bike I could no longer ride, was waiting for me. Susan had alerted Leon to be on the lookout, and he hurried out to take my luggage the second the cab stopped. Upstairs he helped me to our front door, which was covered with little post-it notes welcoming me home. There were even "meows," "woof-woofs," and "glurgs" from the cats, Lily, our dog, and Fred, the frog. Once inside I also discovered an elaborately colorful sign over the bathroom sink from Helena. The sign proclaimed: "I LOVE YOU SOOOOO MUCH DADDY, YOU ROCK! YOU ARE DA BOMB!"

*　　*　　*

I steeled myself every week when I called my father. He was more miserable, more depressed and more emphatic with his demands to go home. The cost of hiring a full-time nurse was out of the question. Had I known about long-term care? Of course not. I thought I was being responsible by going behind his back and putting him on the waiting list at the "best" retirement home in the area.

I made countless phone calls trying to line up someone to stay with Daddy at home. I tried to get him placed at a facility where his best friend, Crop, lived. Finally, I asked his neighbor and friend, Joanna, if she would work for us. Together we hatched a plan and created a schedule in which Joanna would take care of Dad in the evening and a visiting aide, Rhonda, would be there during the day. I made arrangements for a hospital bed and other necessary medical equipment to be moved in so that the house was ready whenever the nursing home thought he was strong enough to return home. My life felt like nothing but medical miasma.

*　　*　　*

Since my only means of communication now is writing, going for psychotherapy is more difficult even than before. However, I have been seeing Edy Nathan, a colleague of Susan's. Edy is smart, compassionate, and seems to be a good choice. She is urging me to be in touch with ALL of my feelings.

Dear Susan,

I think I am in touch with all my feelings—hope, optimism, sadness, and the feeling that I've had a better life than 90% or more on the planet. If the worst happens, I know I'm not being cheated. I'm a realist. I know that the odds are against me, but I'm a fighter, and so are you. Edy still says we have to share our sadness with each other. I asked her: Why state the obvious? She said she wants us to exhume the sad feelings, or the toxicity will poison us as we live and breathe. I've been thinking of my mom and dad lately, and about how happy they were down in Del Mar by the

Pacific. How Mom would laugh full out. I miss her laugh. It's been a hell of a two-and-a-half years.

I'm not afraid of death. There have been times when I would have welcomed that macabre reaper, but not anymore. I am, however, afraid of spiraling into helplessness and dependency.

A few more words about last night: Edy said I should not put on my "brave face" when I saw you but to share my sadness with you and allow you to share yours with me. I'm not very good at that and maybe my timing was off. (I'm not very good at timing either.) I did smile and hug you when you first arrived. I know you had a hard road with your dad in Ohio and I want to hear about it. (I've become a very good listener lately.)

Do you know I can't blow my nose any more? Or chew food with my mouth closed? My tongue is just too weak. to push the food to my teeth and I've been wondering how much longer until I need a feeding tube. Edy suggests I should find out all about that.

*   *   *

My husband felt a new sense of urgency, different from his old compulsion to try and prove he was a good guy, worthy of being his parent's son. There was much to accomplish. We made plans to create a non-profit, ALS awareness organization that could also raise money to find a cure. It was unconscionable that in the fifty years since Lou Gehrig died, there had not been one single effective treatment found, let alone a cure. The ball was already set in motion for a possible return to the ABC network. Michael's former employer had finally responded to the legal requests regarding his financial compensation, and Michael's contract-dispute negotiations had finally begun. Our lawyer at AFTRA, Laura Sigal, predicted we would have a settlement by the first of the year.

Walking was becoming more difficult for Michael. Although he believed we would find a cure he remained a staunch pragmatist and was determined to take full advantage of every moment. We were veteran travelers and, for years, since reading Thomas Flannigan's *The Year of the French,* he had yearned to go to Ireland. He was adamant about taking the trip immediately while he could still walk.

The timing could not have been worse, but I submitted.

I booked a low fare on Aer Lingus and we made reservations at Keir and Suzy Duella's favorite inn, The Ballymaloe House, in County Cork. I was nervous about Michael's tendency to choke and I took a CPR course, just in case. Our Connecticut friend Susan Monseurd offered to stay with Marika and Helena. Meanwhile, things got more complicated as I was receiving daily phone calls from the social worker at my dad's nursing home. Evidently, his hip had healed, but he remained uncooperative, obstreperous and steadfastly against any physical therapy. Three days before our scheduled departure to Ireland, I was informed by the social worker that he no longer qualified to stay in their medical facility. His insurance covered only a specific number of days. Plus, he could only stay there if he agreed to physical therapy, which he was refusing.

The timing was excruciating. I pointed out that they should have given me more notice. I tried, without success, to get Dad's deadline extended by a few days so I could be there when he was moved back to his own home. I offered to pay out of pocket so he could stay where he was until I was back from Ireland. The social worker accused me of irresponsibly capering off on vacation and shirking my parental care responsibilities.

Meanwhile, Joanna and Rhonda were standing by, and the house was equipped with all of the medical equipment he would need. The date of my dad's discharge fell smack in the middle of our trip. I had to either stick with our plan and go to Ireland, or cancel and go to Ohio to be with my father.

Overriding my guilt and fear that I would never again see my father alive I chose to go with Michael. My Buddhist practice gave me courage. I truly believed that one advances toward true happiness and enlightenment by overcoming obstacles. The Ohio social worker was devilishly relentless. She left phone message after message about my irresponsibility. How could I desert my own father? As if to test my faith one more time, the evening we left I got a call that one of my patients who I had helped check into a hospital after a near fatal suicide attempt had checked herself out of the hospital and disappeared. At the airport with Michael in a wheelchair waiting to board, I was on the phone with my patient's sister and the psychiatrist on the case. Minutes before boarding I found out she had been found and was alive.

The ALS Association of Greater New York had secured a voice computer for Michael to use on our trip and when I told him the good news about my patient he pecked out: "Let's get out of here before something else happens!" We laughed. I knew I was doing what I had to do.

*   *   *

As far as I can tell, the only advantage to being disabled is the treatment one gets during air travel. No waiting in lines, no laborious dragging of luggage at New York Kennedy Airport, and when we landed at Shannon Airport the following morning, I was wheeled hither and yon, smoothly bypassing the usual snags. Susan and I emerged into a singing wind and a gray drizzly dawn. The car rental was conveniently located, and I managed to follow the signs out of the airport and onto the highway. Against all odds, we had made it. THIS WAS IRELAND! It was love at first sight, just as I had known it would be.

*   *   *

Although I didn't share Michael's soul connection to the land of Celts and fabled wee people, I felt a strong literary connection, due to my love of W.B. Yeats, Synge, and Joyce. The rain had soaked the moss on the trees. The patchwork of green leapt out at us as we drove south on thin curvy roads toward Cork. We rolled down the car windows and, even though it was December, the air was fragrant and spring-like. It was heaven to be together on the road again.

After that first burst of euphoria, I noticed that Michael was having trouble steering the car. The roads were single, narrow lanes bordered on either side by lichen covered stone walls. I held my breath fearing that any moment we would careen into the piles of ancient rock. I controlled my nervousness for as long as I could but after one too many swerves I suggested maybe I should take over.

We both chalked Michael's shakiness up to his exhaustion because, as far as I knew, he had not been having trouble with his hands. I felt rested because I, as usual, had slept on the plane. Michael had always been the assigned driver on trips to England, mostly because I am dyslexic and the thought of driving on the left was too terrifying. Even in the States, I have mixed up my right and left and found myself barreling headlong into oncoming traffic.

So it was with trepidation that I took over the wheel. Michael tied a red ribbon around my left wrist and programmed "stay on the left" into The Light Writer, his newly-acquired voice computer. At every roundabout the digitalized voice alerted me: Stay on the left. For the past two months, Michael had literally been unable to make himself understood. The Light Writer was like a welcome addition to our family.

By the time we reached Cork the sun began to break through the blustery Irish gray, and two hours later, we arrived at the Irish Manor house. Michael tapped into the computer, "I feel like I have come home."

The Ballymaloe House was everything Keir Duella had promised. Elegant, but homey with children and dogs running in and out, the old manor house pulsed with the lilt of the Irish brogue.

*   *   *

Everywhere we went, people were fascinated by my voice computer, and, if I do say so myself, impressed with my appetite. I dined like a king, relishing fresh vegetables from the organic garden, the fish caught just miles away, and the luscious deserts oozing with butter and cream. Keir and Suzy hadn't told us that a famous cooking school was connected to the Ballymaloe House and as "Francophile Foodies," we were overjoyed. Over long dinners, we drank wine and laughed that we had found the perfect spot. I would return robust and quite a few pounds heavier. We felt lucky then and, even with the Light Writer lying between us on the table like a technological middleman, we were able to come together.

*   *   *

As grateful as I was that we were in Ireland laughing and even conversing thanks to the blessed Light Writer, a bittersweet loneliness permeated most of our activities. Not only was I the designated driver for the first time, but there were days when Michael was just too exhausted to enjoy tooling about in our usual manner. Michael was with me, but at the same time, he wasn't. I missed his boundless energy. His loquacious friendliness had inevitably elevated previous trips into the realm of high adventure.

Still, we managed occasionally to carry on in our old impulsive spirit of adventure. After hours of driving to find a nunnery that we had been told made the most exquisite Irish lace, we finally arrived. We'd been circling around for so long that we both had to go to the bathroom. The lace had become secondary to the more essential necessities. We tapped on the door of the solid somber edifice and when no one answered, we tried the knob. We peered into a bare and chilly stone foyer with a stairway off to the right. A large oil painting of Jesus was the only indication that we had reached our destination.

We called out and listened for a response, but heard only the hollow stillness of a building long deserted. We went outside and double-checked the address, which corresponded to the information the hotel had given us. We then went back inside cautiously, almost surreptitiously, like kids sneaking into a deserted, supposedly haunted house.

"Wonder where the nuns are?" Michael tapped on the Light Writer. "Wonder if there is a toilet?"

He and his cane went off in one direction, and I ran off in the other. After only a few minutes, we reunited, laughing, under the oil painting of Jesus. We had not found the lace we were searching for, but we were both a lot more comfortable as we climbed back into the car.

We headed back north after five days. We had made reservations at the Adaire Manor, which was only an hour's drive from Shannon Airport where we had an afternoon departure the following day. On the advice of friends we chose a route that took us to Blarney Castle. Legend has it that whoever kisses the Blarney stone will have his or her wish granted. As much as Michael was a man of reason, he was determined to leave no stone unturned. Although it was out of our way, no matter what he was going to make a pilgrimage to the Blarney stone.

He was tense during the drive. He complained of stiffness and was afraid he was catching a cold. It seemed our light-hearted respite was coming to a premature end. At the same time, he became testy when I suggested we pass up the Blarney stone and head for our hotel so he could rest. He would kiss the stone or else!

We arrived and went to get our admission tickets, but found the employees would not accept payment from Michael, who was limping noticeably and communicating with the Light Writer. We both noted that the man at the gate treated him with an almost reverent attitude.

It was immediately obvious that Michael could not continue walking up the steep uneven stone stairs that led to the fabled stone. He wanted me to go ahead and kiss the stone for him. He, who had always forged ahead, sat on a bench looking after me as I began the ascent. I recalled how he had once scaled the sheer cliffs in Mexico like a mountain goat. I, on the other hand, had suffered a vertigo attack and had to crawl back on my hands and knees to perceived safety. I kept my eyes straight ahead and ignored my queasy stomach, finally arriving within sight of the magical stone. In order to kiss it, I would have to lean far out over a sheer drop. The few tourists who managed to kiss the Blarney stone were being protectively held by their companions. Even without my vertigo, I would have been unable to position my rather small self in order to kiss the stone. I considered asking someone to hold onto my arm but was overcome with dizziness and images of my body falling through space.

On the way back down, I felt unbearable grief and hopelessness, not because I believed in the magic of the Blarney stone, but because I could not fulfill my mission for Michael. I wish I could have lied and said I kissed the stone, but I could not.

In the car Michael began to shiver, and by the time we reached our destination, he was pale and feverish. I left him in the car and went inside the Adaire Manor to register. The massive stone lobby had fifty-foot ceilings and at one end stood a towering Christmas tree, more grand even than the fabled Nutcracker tree.

The concierge handed me the key to our room, but when I saw it was on the third floor, I knew there was no way Michael could make the climb. I explained that my husband had motor neuron disease, as ALS is called in Ireland, and explained that he had great difficulty walking. Without hesitation the concierge smiled and said she was happy to accommodate us on the ground floor.

Hugely relieved at overcoming this obstacle, I helped Michael out of the car and we followed the bellhop to our room. Our jaws dropped, probably in unison, when he opened the door to what we later discovered was the "Premiere" suite in this extremely lavish hotel. The regal chamber overlooked a rushing stream upon which the wee people might surely have frolicked. At one end, there was an enormous four-poster bed with angels carved atop every post. There were four larger angels carved in bas-relief above the headboard, and angels carved into the heavy molding. There were angels above the closets and above the windows. There were angels everywhere.

Amazingly, the shivers and fever that kept Michael in bed during our stay in the "angel" room at the Adair Manor were gone by the time we arrived back in New York. We were rejuvenated and laden with Christmas presents purchased at the Ballymaloe House.

Michael tapped out that we should go back to Ireland next Christmas to do our shopping. As always, when we returned from a vacation, he was already planning his return.

According to my agreement with Joanna, who was caring for my dad, I would not call from Ireland and she would not call me unless there was an emergency. I had not heard from her, so I assumed he had been successfully transported back to his home. I called the moment we got in and learned that the nursing home had discharged him with a high temperature. After four hours at home, Joanna called an ambulance to take him back.

My heart was breaking for my father, but it was almost Christmas and I did not feel I could leave Michael, let alone Marika and Helena. I did what I could to negotiate on his behalf with the staff at the nursing home. I was and am grateful for the love and care that Rhonda, Joanna, my Aunt Jo, and my Uncle Bob showered on him.

Another Christmas in Connecticut, and although we did not cut our own tree, Helena and Marika hauled in a ten-footer and we decorated it, topping it as always with the feathered cat angel. On Christmas morning, we opened our gifts, saving the huge box that had come from Brynn until last.

The box had been the subject of much anticipation and conjecture. Various stickers on the outside alerted us to "Handle with care," "Keep upright," and "Keep in cool place." Was it animal, vegetable, or mineral? A Pandora's box, out of which might spring…anything! We were all revved up, and, as I gingerly ran a knife along the packing tape, I realized I was as hyped-up as Marika and Helena about Brynn's mysterious present.

I stuck my hand inside the box and let out a little squeal, for it seemed I had touched a live thing, a bird, something fragile with feathers. I withdrew a great, feathered angel bird, a splendid symbol for our newly conceived ZazAngels organization that would lead us to a cure for ALS.

But that wasn't all. Brynn's package was loaded with celestial beings. Helena and Marika rooted around in the bubble packing material, squealing with delight as they unwrapped dozens of small rabbits, dogs, birds, Cupids, and cats, each one an angel.

21

KEEP CHARGING THE ENEMY

It was one of those all-time, best days of your life days. We'd just come from our first ZazAngels meeting. ABC had embraced our idea of returning Michael to One Life to Live. *We had pushed several tables together at the neighborhood Chinese restaurant around the corner from Michael and Susan's apartment. It was our "hang-out." We had a mission. Michael was our inspiration and our leader. Always had been, always would be. Susan was the force. We laughed and plotted and planned and laughed some more. Why did it always feel so good to make Michael laugh? From the first day I met him in 1981, hearing Michael's laughter was always a priority for me. It came from such a deep place in his being. Not like anyone else. Michael was using his computer to speak, but he didn't need his computer to laugh. ALS never took his laugh. I remember thinking I never wanted the night to end. When the time came for the traditional opening of the fortune cookies, they were the usual: "Money is the root of all evil," "Take the next job you are offered." Then came Michael's fortune. The small piece of paper rolled up inside his cookie said, "Keep on charging the enemy so long as there is Life."*

We all cheered. That was Michael. If you couldn't fight for yourself, Michael was there. If Michael believed in a cause, he was your front man. If the underdog was right, Michael pled the case. Michael fought all his battles with courage and dignity and laughter. This latest battle would be no exception.

—*Brynn Thayer, actor, friend*

The meeting with Randi Subarsky and Harriet Abrams at ABC could not have gone better. Michael looked gorgeous in a black turtleneck, his angular face still glowing from Irish cuisine and Christmas cookies. Randi and Harriet looked relieved. He was his usual handsome, charismatic self. Brynn and I exchanged hopeful looks as they discussed various scenarios for the return of

140

David Renaldi to *One Life To Live*. They were as excited as we were. This time Michael wasn't the only one who was laughing and crying. We all were.

*   *   *

I had my life back again, and I was more determined than ever to win. The negativity and hopelessness that surrounded ALS offended my sense of logic. Of course there would be a cure. Nothing was impossible. People had to know that. It was revelatory that current National Institute of Neurological disease (NINDS) spending for ALS research amounted to only $333 per patient each year. That compared unfavorably with AIDS and Parkinson's, which receive many more times, and in the case of AIDS, ten times more, financial attention per patient. Believe me, I am not suggesting that we should be in competition. In a just and reasoned world, there would be enough to share.

*   *   *

Thanks to The Creative Coalition, the advocacy group which Michael had devoted time to before ALS took over, we held our first ZazAngels meeting on January 27, 1998. The meeting took place in a conference room at the HBO Building on Sixth Avenue. We both agreed that Brynn should be the president of our new organization. As always, she was totally prepared with a newly-purchased copy of Robert's Rules of Order, sharpened pencils, pads, platters of fruit, and bottles of Pellagrino.

We had notified a number of people about our first meeting, but we weren't at all sure who would show up. When two unfamiliar young women walked in, we knew they could only be Kristie Miller and Teresa Brown, the two fans responsible for organizing the opposition in the form of a petition to Michael's former employer. Although we had never met we yelped and hugged and hollered and kissed like long lost kin.

Michael sat at the head of a long conference table with his hand resting on the Link, the new augmented speaking device with which we had replaced the Light Writer. The Link was larger and capable of more than a few sentences. It also offered several digitalized voices. Michael selected a voice that sounded just like the voice on the pocket-sized Weather Watch machine we kept in the junk drawer in Connecticut. Initially, we found this coincidence hilarious. We had been listening to that dopey "guy" for years, and now here was Michael with the same robotic intonation that had been the butt of our jokes. Eventually, however, the Link would prove so frustrating and unreliable that Michael threatened on several occasions to throw it out the car window.

*   *   *

I was overwhelmed with gratitude and a growing sense of confidence as friends and colleagues came in. Among those present were Pete and Molly Gurney, Mimi Turque, Ellen Levine, Ivan Strausz, Billy Baldwin, Meir Ribalow, and Michael Collyer. All the seats were filled, and my buddy Steve went out for more chairs. The energy that night was palpable. I knew it would make me well. Together we would raise awareness about ALS and raise the funds for a cure!

*   *   *

Urgency was our guiding principle. A Cure by 2000 was our slogan. By aligning with an existing entity, we could begin raising awareness and money immediately. The ALS Association of Greater New York and BAA, another organization focused on neurological diseases, both sent representatives. Both organizations were eager for Michael, with his celebrity status and fund-raising potential, to join under their auspices. Almost everyone present agreed that our cause could best be served if ZazAngels affiliated with an existing non-profit organization that had "ALS" as an identifying logo. If we went with the BAA, which raised money for numerous neurological diseases, that organization's initials would dominate. Most people didn't even know what ALS stood for. With Michael returning to the ABC airwaves, there was an unprecedented opportunity to educate the public about Amyotrophic Lateral Sclerosis.

The day after the meeting, I received an urgent message from one of the neurologists with whom we had consulted. There could be only one reason for the doctor's upbeat manner. He had information, either about a treatment or perhaps (still the lingering hope persisted) an erroneous diagnosis.

I could hardly contain my excitement as I dialed. The doctor greeted me by my first name like we were old friends. Never had a neurologist been so chummy. This was it! Finally an end to this nightmare!

He said he'd received a report about last night's meeting. I thought that was a bit odd, considering his demanding schedule and the location of his medical facility, which was thousands of miles from New York. Why would he be so interested in what went on at our first ZazAngels meeting?

"Did you find something for Michael?" I blurted out.

He chuckled. "Don't I wish. But you can be sure Michael will know the minute I get my hands on something."

Then why the excited urgency in his voice? Once again, I felt duped. I grew resentful as he explained he had heard that ZazAngels was going to affiliate with the ALS Association. He was worried that we would be disappointed if we partnered with such an inept organization.

I could not fathom what he was saying. Why was this so important to him?

He suggested we reconsider and work with BAA.

I still didn't get it. Why did it matter? We were all fighting to cure ALS. Naïvely, I explained we chose the ALS Association for the very simple reason that we wanted the initials "ALS" in our message. How could we raise awareness about ALS with the initials BAA?

Ignoring my logic, he reiterated how ineffectual the ALS Association was. Would we at least consider affiliating with a medical institution, not even his own, he hastened to say, but for instance maybe a facility in New York City? I assured him Michael would gladly appear for any organization that was working to find a cure. I couldn't see a problem, but he hammered away even when I said Michael would volunteer to appear on the BAA telethon.

"Give it some serious thought. Talk to Michael."

Michael groaned as he tapped out: "HIS INSTITUTE IS COMPLETELY FUNDED BY BAA!"

The next day, I got phone call from a gentleman at BAA who was also concerned that we would be disappointed if we worked with the ALS Association. He stated he had our best interest in mind. Did we know what we were getting in to?

I suggested that ZazAngels also include the BAA initials in our publicity, adding how great it would be for everyone to join forces and work together.

My offer appeared to rattle him and he said he'd have to get back to me. When he called the next day, I could tell by his tone that we were no longer buddies. We could not use the BAA initials if we were also using the ALS name. He was cordial but cool, and before we hung up, he too warned me that we would regret our decision.

Brynn, Michael, and I were unprepared for such intrigue. Still naïve about the scope of ethical implications regarding such competition, we laughed that it rivaled a daytime soap opera story line. The only thing we cared about was finding a cure for ALS.

Brynn had relocated her life from the beautiful Pacific Palisades home she shared with her husband, David Steinberg, and had found temporary quarters in a variety of far less comfy New York apartments. Her devotion and skill were awesome. We both worked non-stop. We arranged for the creation of a Michael Zaslow's ZazAngels Web site. We wrote and printed up flyers and information with which to begin soliciting funds for research. We designed logos for T-shirts and baseball caps. We fed off of each other's sense of urgency, and often joked that it was pretty amazing that two such strong-willed, opinionated women could work so well together. Often, we felt like we were on some drug that infused us with energies and ideas we could not rationally explain. Non-stop was what we were.

My dad's eighty-ninth birthday was coming up, and I made plans to fly out to visit him. I had to cancel the trip, however, because Michael came down with a terrible cold. Daddy was not only more miserable since he had been transferred into a ward with Alzheimer's patients, he was frightened by the bizarre behavior of the patients who wandered into his room at any hour of the day or night.

My father was a very difficult patient but he did not have Alzheimer's disease nor had such a diagnosis ever been mentioned. Obstinate as he was he was also a respected businessman, former sheriff, president of the election board, and a pillar of our community who had lived a productive and worthy life. Considering that this was the most highly-touted and costly facility in the area, I had expected a great deal more. I called other retirement homes, including those near us in Connecticut. My father said he wanted to die, anything to get out of this very upscale establishment.

Michael's cold was almost gone, and with Brynn nearby, I made a reservation to go to Ohio. Two days before I was to leave, however, the nursing home telephoned me to fly out immediately. Michael offered to come along, and as much as I wanted his support and the presence of another person, I could not imagine trying to care for both him and my father.

Before I got into a cab to go to La Guardia, I bought a bouquet of daisies, Daddy's favorite flower. I was calm until I boarded the plane and buckled into my seat. Suddenly I was seized with a stifling and profound sense of grief. I turned to the window, unable to stop crying. I looked at my watch. It was two o'clock, and the flight to Cincinnati Airport was an hour and a half. I tried, but could not stop the flow of tears. They persisted even as I stood outside the airport, waiting for Joanna to pick me up.

Finally, she arrived and I sat with the daisies in my lap. Joanna told me she had stayed with him at the nursing home until the ambulance came. She had sung to him and held his hand. She said he smiled and was happy when he heard I was on my way.

When we arrived at the hospital, they could not find his name on the register. I was still holding the bouquet when a staff member ushered us into a windowless cubicle to tell us that he had died at two PM on the way to the hospital.

I went back to his house. I had not been able to be there for him. I forced my mind through the thick swamp of guilt and attended to the details. I took Joanna to dinner at the Golden Lamb Inn, and we told Bill stories and drank martinis. How lucky he was to have had a friend like Joanna Klontz. How lucky I was that she was there for him, holding his hand, and singing to him. The next morning, I met with the funeral director and my father's lawyer, and held a small reception for his neighbors in the afternoon. When everyone left, I locked my father's house and my friend, Ginny, drove me to the airport.

I was back in New York by 7 PM, in time to join Michael for our first official meeting with Dorine Gordon, President of the ALS Association of Greater New York. There were also several other representatives from the National ALS Association present. Once again, we met at our ZazAngels "office," the Chinese restaurant around the corner from our apartment.

22

THE FIGHT IN THE DOG

We were winding down a meeting with the head of ALS research at Susan and Michael's favorite neighborhood Chinese restaurant when the inebriated table across from us became even louder and uglier. One of the men was imitating Michael's slurred speech and mimicking his voice computer. The other two egged him on, laughing. I told myself, "Ernst, you better do something!" In the seconds it took me to get up, Susan was in the middle of them like a dart. The diminutive Ms. Hufford had, in those few seconds, turned into a mack truck! I am telling you, she had those guys frightened! It reminded me of a story my father told me when I was a child…it's not the dog in the fight, it's the fight in the dog.

—*John Ernst, Chairman Emeritus, ALS Association of Greater New York*

The process of eating was taking longer and longer because of swallowing difficulty. Also, I was downing some eighty vitamins, receiving electrode treatments, IVs, acupuncture, and qui gong. Still, I continued to read everything I could get my hands on about Amyotrophic Lateral Sclerosis. I spent hours on the Internet learning about the latest alternative treatments. I scanned countless testimonials from people with the disease.

Many people were living long and productive lives with ALS. One man claimed to have been cured by a vitamin regime and religious experience, after having been diagnosed in 1982 by sixty different neurologists! I felt the odds were in my favor. I would hang on until we found the cure. We were flooded with well-meaning advice, some of which we took. Susan was always on the phone with people who were promoting micro-clusters, magnetic mattresses, Noni juice, red crystals or tablets containing seventy-two trace elements, miracle waters, or purple algae.

How to explain the eleven spontaneous remissions alluded to by Dr. John Rowland of Columbia Presbyterian? And how to explain the theoretical astrophysicist

Stephen Hawking who was in his third decade with a disease that purportedly kills people in three to five years? Although he can move only a few facial muscles and a single finger on his left hand, Hawking managed to write the best seller A Brief History of Time, *and lives a full life with his wife and family.*

Of course, I wanted to believe there was a cure, a solution to the problem. More and more, in light of my reading, it did not make sense to believe otherwise.

*   *   *

We strained our minds to digest the scientific vernacular relevant to ALS. Our new friend Teresa Brown scoured the Internet from her home in West Virginia, and compiled a thick volume of ALS-related treatments.

The work of Dr. Stephen B. Edelson, who practiced chemical molecular medicine in Atlanta, caught Michael's attention. According to Edelson, "every ALS patient I have seen was loaded with toxic materials, either mercury or toxic chemicals." Edelson's view was that ALS was at least partly an environmental disease, and that we would be seeing more of it. We both found Edelson's hypothesis intriguing. It was difficult to understand why the ALS Association and other groups devoted to finding a treatment or cure were not pursuing this theory. Money, of course, was always the excuse, but we were beginning to wonder if there wasn't another reason as well.

When he wasn't studying ALS, he was downing vitamins, eating, or exercising to stave off degeneration and weakness. He continued to go to Asphalt Green, where he worked out with a trainer. If the workout was good, he was in high spirits. If not, his mood plummeted.

Sometimes, I would go along because it was more and more difficult for him to get around. I was constantly afraid that he would fall, which he had begun to do with some regularity. Half-teasing, I suggested he wear his bike helmet everywhere he went so he wouldn't damage his wonderful brain before we found the cure.

We were aware that people, and not just medical people, thought we were living in a fantasy world to consider it even a remote possibility to discover a cure by the year 2000. We were unfazed. I reminded Michael that throughout the horrors people endured under the regimes of both Stalin and Khruschev, I refused to refer to Leningrad as St. Petersburg. Then, lo and behold…without warning, without bloodshed, the beloved city of all those Russian novels I thrived on in my youth was officially, was again, St. Petersburg. The impossible was as possible as anything else. I had to believe that ALS was no exception.

I would fall into bed at night with my brain scrambling to evaluate information on ALS-related items such as allopurinol, Alpha Lipoc Acid, neurontin, and wet cells. I continued to plot how to get Michael onto Myotrophin, which was due to come up for review by the USFDA in a month. Molecules of the so-called "Buckyballs" delayed the onset of symptoms and death in mice genetically altered to carry an inherited form of ALS. What could we do with this knowledge, though? My mind was deluged with scientific developments. Each one was like a narcotic, compelling me to keep searching.

Michael devoured each new shred of scientific data. I believe the flow of information nourished him far more than the vitamin-laced smoothies I made. Later I came to realize that this scientific obsession was characteristic of most people with ALS. Since everyone knew that the one USFDA-approved drug did next to nothing, information was the only treatment that had a favorable impact. I could quite literally see a difference in Michael's gait and face after he digested a helping of provocative scientific speculation. He received the following correspondence:

"Dear Mr. Zaslow,

I felt compelled to write to you after hearing about your story. I suffer from multiple sclerosis, another neurological disorder. Through all my research, I am convinced that most internal maladies are caused by delayed food allergies, such as the yeast organism Candida Albicans.

Most traditional doctors will not agree with this. There are only two labs in the U.S. that do the testing, and I urge you to call them. Though this is not a cure for multiple sclerosis, changing my diet has made a huge difference in the quality of my life."

We received many such letters targeting food allergies as a relevant factor in ALS. Dr. S, a gentle, bike-riding internist whose office was on the ground floor of our apartment building, had briefly treated Michael's dad. Always friendly, he stopped to see Michael one day and told us he was investigating ALS on his own.

Michael was moved by Dr. S's concern. Dr. S urged him to make an appointment with Dr. T, a young doctor who had joined Dr. S's practice and who specialized in identifying and treating food allergies. Michael immediately made an appointment. They drew blood, took hair samples and other specimens drawn at the times designated by Dr. T. These were sent to an out-of-state laboratory.

On first impression, Michael was not impressed with Dr. T, whom he described to me on the Link as "very young, very arrogant, and very sure that he can cure me."

Dr. T's protocol required no drugs, only a complete dietary makeover, which we implemented immediately. We were told that people normally have to adhere to the anti-Candidiasis diet for two to six months to show progress. Those patients with cancer, AIDS, chronic viral illnesses, or auto-immune diseases such as ALS, however, may require a longer commitment, we were told. A sugar-free, yeast-free, mold-free diet, as the program recommends, is not easy to follow. There were restrictions on practically everything that Michael loved to eat. We were essentially already very healthy eaters, and consumed lots of salads and raw vegetables, fruit, fish, chicken, and hardly any meat. Only recently, since Michael had begun to drop weight, had we resorted to increasing calorie intake with unlimited helpings of ice cream and cookies. Now he could not eat any wheat products, meat, dairy, salads, or fruit. Almond butter, almonds, and avocadoes became our staples.

After one week, the pounds literally fell from his already wasted body, and he was constantly ravenous and irritable. He loved to eat, and since being diagnosed with ALS, food had remained his one source of pleasure, even with his drooling and difficulty swallowing. I was against continuing the diet, but he held on.

By the second week of the diet, Michael had dropped another unbelievable twelve pounds. If he continued at this rate, ABC might take one look at him and rescind their offer. More importantly, I seriously questioned if the diet might damage his already precarious health. Meanwhile, Dr. T found it impossible to communicate with Michael through the Link, and suggested that I come to an appointment with him so that we could communicate more effectively.

When I arrived at his office, Michael was tucked away in a little waiting area, inhaling a BLT and a milkshake, both forbidden foods.

He was not only starving but angry. He had weighed himself and found he had lost several more pounds. Dr. T had reassured him that he would not continue to lose weight and that an initial loss was positive and consistent with the treatment. For weeks Dr. T had been insisting that Michael would soon be healthily gaining weight. Once again, he felt betrayed.

When Dr. T saw my husband gobbling away, his face flushed and he accused Michael of trying to kill himself. Here he was going all out to save Michael's life, and this was how Michael was repaying him? He lectured

Michael about how harmful junk food was, as if we were fries-and-burgers people. He spouted forth some obtuse data on Candidiasis, claiming he was on the brink of a scientific breakthrough that would revolutionize medicine.

Michael, of course, could not reply. Even with the Link, it was impossible to adequately defend himself. I interrupted on his behalf. Dr. T was speaking to my husband as if he were a child, or worse, an imbecile, as if Michael's animal-like moans, his only means of objecting, were symptomatic of a slow mind. Had Dr. T known the real Michael, he would never have dared to speak so abusively.

At one point, Dr. T turned to me, with a conspiratorial smile. "I can't understand him!" he whined, as if Michael not only could not speak, but couldn't hear either.

It was obvious Dr. T knew little about ALS and the dangers of weight loss. He knew even less about compassion. We left the office together, and I redoubled my commitment to put back those lost pounds. We drove downtown to the premier vitamin and supplement establishment. Michael waited in the Jeep while I went in to load up on supplements and vitamins, including Creatine Fuel Powder, Coenzyme Q 10, Lipoic Acid, Carotenoids, NAC, Polyphenols such as grape seed, pine bark, Astragulas, Ginko, Omego 3 Flax Oil, DHEA. That night, for the first night in weeks, he went to bed happy, with a full stomach.

We both continued to read and evaluate the steady stream of information sent to Michael by the many people who wanted to help. The following letter was particularly intriguing.

Dear Mr. Zaslow,
I need to share with you what we feel is wonderful news, and you may feel free to do with it what you will. There is a scientific paper currently being reviewed by a peer review committee for publication in the *Lancent*, which I believe is a British medical journal. This paper cites scientific research proving that ALS is a virus.
The study was done on seventeen ALS patients, and only two did not have the genome sequencing of the virus. The studies do not lend an explanation for how the virus arrives at the anterior horn cells. The researcher made it clear that the new anti-viral drug to treat herpes will also do the trick for the ALS mutant virus. Until the new drug arrives, he has a couple of suggestions…

I faxed Jay Lombard the lengthy document, and with his approval, we began to implement an altered regime. It was dizzying to sift through the plethora of data for the possible treatments and cures that were being proposed by so many well-meaning people. I was afraid to ignore any new idea that came in. What if I passed over something significant? Although we were becoming educated in the ways of the disease, we did not fancy ourselves experts.

On the other hand, we sometimes feared that those researchers who received funding year after year had developed a kind of tunnel vision. Most of the medical community had been thoroughly indoctrinated with a negative view that precluded the possibility of finding a cure any time in the near future. Did anyone know what, if anything, Stephen Hawking and other long-term ALS survivors, had in common? In addition to all of the studies on ALS mice, had data been collected on existing ALS patients? Could any commonality be documented? Were there reliable demographics on the number of new cases in the United States? How about in other countries? Were there any countries where, like the island of Guam, there was a particularly high incidence of ALS? Did we know for certain that ALS, long considered a disease of people in late middle age, was not striking men and women at younger ages? We knew of several other ALS cases in our tiny community in Connecticut. Since that was an area particularly infested by deer ticks, was Lyme disease in some way triggering ALS? Or were environmental factors at play, similar to those factors responsible for the high incidence of ALS in Gulf War veterans?

Questions such as these gnawed at us. We understood that such inquiries were not considered "pure science." Still, our questions seemed relevant to unlocking Pandora's box. The answers to all of those questions, we discovered, was "No."

Now that Michael was scheduled to go back to work, we were inundated with requests for interviews. The daytime magazines were among the first to jump on the bandwagon. Since the first piece had been so successful, *People* scheduled another interview, which took place in our New York apartment. The subsequent article included a shot of Michael surrounded by the fifty-some bottles of vitamins he was taking. In another photo, he was grinning as he flipped an omelet in our kitchen while I looked on. We did not seek publicity, but when it came Michael welcomed it for the chance to put a face on ALS and to stir the public into action.

Preparation for interviews consumed much of our time. What time was left was devoted to medical appointments, psychotherapy, IV drips, physical therapy, and, of course, the ongoing and relentless quest for new treatments and a cure. There were still the monthly trips to Johns Hopkins to monitor his health as part of the Sanofi drug trial. On more than one occasion, duties with the children prevented me from going with him to Johns Hopkins. I was fortunately able to hire sometime to drive him down in our car, but there was one time when I had to put him on a train alone. Although he was still able to walk, he was unsteady and often fell. I was in terror every time he left the house.

Brynn was a resilient and resourceful fund-raiser, and the ZazAngels research fund began to swell. Beau designed a logo for hats and T-shirts. We were working against the clock to get our A Cure by 2000 campaign underway. Brynn, a perfectionist to the end, haunted the "ribbon" district and came up with a classy blue-and-white ribbon reminiscent of the New York Yankees' uniforms. We still needed someone to coordinate ZazAngels' rapidly expanding projects, and hired Kristie Miller, who along with Teresa Brown, had organized the petition protesting Michael's dismissal. Kristie was an amazing bundle of energy and ideas. Her passionate spirit reminded both Michael and me of his mother's zealous and vocal commitment to justice. Kristie hopped back and forth between her home in Baltimore and temporary abodes here.

Kristie was on top of every detail connected to ZazAngels and ALS. On March 8, she e-mailed Michael about the USFDA's Peripheral and Central Nervous System (PCNS) Advisory Committee meeting to be held on April 9, 1998, in Bethesda, Maryland.

The meeting was critical. Once again, the drug, Myotrophin (which I had been trying to get from European sources) would be presented for review. ALS patients all over the country had been waiting for approval of this drug. Those who had managed to get into the first trial and who were actually on the drug attributed their improved conditions to Myotrophin. Dr. K unofficially believed in its efficacy, and told Michael if he could get him on Myotrophin he would do so immediately.

We made plans to go to Bethesda, and contacted our media sources to cover the public testimony, another first. PALS (people with ALS) everywhere were encouraged because now that Michael was a PAL too the disease was finally getting media attention. We were all certain the long-awaited approval of Myotrophin would finally come to pass. Three days before the public hearing we received word that the FDA meeting was canceled because the most recent Myotrophin trial had proved inconclusive. Had the FDA not known of these results before? The abrupt decision was not convincing to us or to the other desperate PALS whose only treatment was one FDA-approved drug that everyone knew was next to useless.

We continued working non-stop, and when we weren't making copies, telephone calls, or ALS ribbons, our minds buzzed with future fund-raising plans. Brynn, always able to accomplish the impossible, secured a meeting with Casey Steinbrenner. This meeting resulted in plans for the first ALS fund-raiser at Yankee Stadium since the time of Lou Gehrig. It was happening, and Michael had made it happen! The critical mass he believed would create the cure was gaining momentum. The date was set for September 12, 1998. There would be a pre-game softball competition with teams composed of daytime stars. Everyone who came to the Yankees game on that day would get to see the face of ALS.

Meanwhile, we decided our main ZazAngels fund-raiser should be a theater event. Our friend Pete Gurney offered his wonderful play, *Love Letters*. Michael and I knew Gerald Shoenfeld, president of the Shuburt Organization from Roxbury, and I wrote to inquire if the organization would donate one of their Broadway theaters. Alec Baldwin had phoned me several months earlier, after running into Michael and me at our neighborhood Indian restaurant. He made it clear that he would be there for us over the long haul, and offered to help in any way he could. Michael e-mailed Alec to see if and when he might be available to star in *Love Letters*. Alec responded with an immediate yes and the date was set for December!

A performance of Pete's *Love Letters* was already scheduled for August 15 in Washington, Connecticut. Pete generously designated ZazAngels to be the recipient organization of all the funds raised.

It was impossible to fit everything in. We were both lucky if we got in bed before midnight, and many nights it was much later. I would get up early, make breakfast, and drive the children to school. They certainly were old enough to have gone on their own, but I loved the morning ritual of driving them, even with the chronic squabbles over who got to sit in the front seat. I knew how much Michael missed chauffeuring his darlings, and could not always assuage the twinges of guilt I felt over being able to move about freely.

The constant frenzy of activity, while exhausting, stabilized our lives and fed our hope. A cure was not the only reason for excitement. Marika was making her theatrical debut in her school's Gershwin Revue. ZazAngels baseball caps arrived the day of opening night, and as I pulled the Jeep up in front of the school, Brynn leapt wildly off the curb, waving her chic ZazAngels cap.

Michael wept throughout the show, and we all cheered when Marika tapped her heart out to *I Got Rhythm*. She looked happier than she had in months, and after the show, we went back to our apartment to celebrate with her friends and ours.

Suddenly, there was a crash. Everyone froze. Michael lay on the floor. There never was any warning. Just a sudden, heart-stopping crash. This time, there was no blood and we helped him to his feet. He defused the situation by making light of the fall on the Link, and the party continued. The following week, I came home to find that he had purchased a shiny blue walker with a little basket.

Michael had worked with Donna Hanover, the first Lady of New York City, when she appeared on the *Guiding Light*. Donna had been impressed by Michael's professional generosity and commitment to his family, and he was won over by her independent sprit, her warmth, and her devotion to her children. When she heard that he had been diagnosed with ALS, she offered to do whatever she could. Coincidentally, Donna had written a piece for *Good Housekeeping* on another ALS patient, Pat Pepper. This intrepid, gorgeous, brilliant, outspoken spirit was as determined as we were to find a cure. Pat was our kind of person—health conscious, athletic, and very political. Like Michael, Pat was furious over the cruelty and rudeness of this disease. ALS had reared its head just as she had found happiness with a wonderful man to whom she was now engaged.

Pat introduced us to the physical fitness trainer she had brought with her from England to do proprioceptive neuromuscular facilitation (PNF), a form of physical therapy used in England with stroke victims. She was convinced it was helping her, and she arranged for Michael to have a complimentary session in the workout room of her Fifth Avenue apartment. Michael felt immediate benefits and this treatment became part of his regime three times a week.

*   *   *

After Pat's trainer returned to England, I began doing PNF at home, with the young Irishman he had trained, Tony Hearn. My left side was still as strong as before I had contracted the disease, and we were already seeing improvement in my right side.

In addition, I took IV drips twice a week with powerful antioxidants. I challenged my insurance company to reverse its position and cover the drips. They had finally agreed to reimburse Susan and I for the voice-activated computers. This rep-

resented a major breakthrough for those of us who could not otherwise communicate. I do feel good that I had a hand in setting that precedence. I still find it disgraceful that so many PALS have had to suffer in silence until a "celebrity" managed to grab the attention of the powers that be.

This is not only an ugly disease but frightfully expensive. Between PNF, various therapies, and IVs, I see our savings dwindling. Ah, but I am once again going to be a working actor!

*   *   *

We were scheduled to tape our first major television interview with ABC's *20/20* at our home in Connecticut on Good Friday. Since the children had school on Thursday, we decided to drive up early on Friday, rather than battle the Easter traffic. I arranged for Joe Pffering and his crew to arrive ahead of us, so they could set up their equipment. Susan Monseurd, who lives down the road, let them in and by the time we got there, our furniture was rearranged. Huge lights were set up and focused on the couch where Michael and I were to sit. I joked that as a person who loves to move furniture around, I had never thought of that particular configuration, but really loved it.

Michael had prerecorded responses to the questions the interviewer would be asking. Recording them was a time consuming process, since the Link was notoriously finicky. I had begun to detest the thing. So far, we had returned three of the devices because they had stopped working properly after a few outings. Because of the Link, we had again been up until 2 AM the previous night, and because it was Easter weekend and we were having guests and our annual egg hunt, the Jeep was more loaded down that usual.

The resultant chaos probably explained why, when we began recording, we had to stop immediately. I had a big hole in my black tights. I knew it was there, but had lacked the time to go out and buy a new pair, or even focus on what I should wear. As usual, I just threw something on and went. I don't even think I put on makeup. I kept crossing my legs so no one would see the hole, or draped my hand over it when the camera was on me. The camera picked it up anyway.

One of the cameramen gave me a piece of black electrical tape. I patched up the hole, and we all had a good laugh.

On May 6, 1998, two days after a trip to Johns Hopkins to monitor the Sanofi drug trial, we attended a press conference. This conference, thanks to Donna Hanover, was held at Gracie Mansion. Michael and Brynn would speak on behalf of ZazAngels and a thirty-six-year-old woman recently diagnosed with ALS, Jenifer Estess, would announce the formation of her own fund-raising organization, Project ALS.

Brynn spoke eloquently about ZazAngels' mission to raise awareness and find a cure for ALS. Several times, she was overwhelmed with emotion and had to pause. After a statement by ABC President Pat Fili-Krushel, it was time for Michael to present the speech we had prerecorded on the Link.

"Thank you, Pat. You and the people at ABC and One Life to Live *have demonstrated that working for a giant corporation doesn't necessitate relinquishing one's humanity. ABC is exhibiting tremendous social responsibility in writing David Renaldi's return with ALS, something that has never been done before. I, and the 300,000 PALS living with ALS in the United States alone, thank you. You are giving us, and indeed the entire neurological community, an opportunity to vanquish this disease and save our collective lives."*

I was sitting with Jay, who had come in for the occasion. After the first few lines, the Link sputtered and stopped. Michael laughed. He did not need words to communicate the implications of the moment. His expression said it all. With great poise, he pressed the rewind button. Everyone applauded, laughed, and cried as he started the prerecorded speech from the beginning. This time, the Link made it to the end, and there was more applause as people rose to their feet.

Three days later, on a balmy, sunny, spring morning, Michael went back to work. For once, we were ahead of schedule. I got the car out of the garage, and pulled around in front of our building as Michael was helped out by our friend and elevator man, Martin. It would be a long day. In addition to taping the show, the entertainment program *Access Hollywood* was coming to the Sixty-sixth Street studio to do an interview.

Michael, who was always professionally prepared, was more than prepared. What neither of us was prepared for was the gigantic banner outside the studio: WELCOME HOME, MICHAEL!

Brynn was grinning and bobbing up and down as I pulled up in our Jeep. Michael was greeted by Bob Krimmer, Robin Strasser, Laura Kaufman, Bob Woods, directors, technicians, David the wonderful doorman, and ABC executives from across the street. They were all as excited as we were.

Later, Donna Hanover stopped by to watch part of the taping. Marika and Helena came down as soon as they got out of school. Michael, silent as he was, was radiant and articulate. As pianist and composer David Renaldi, he was as debonair and elegant as ever, sitting in "David's" wheelchair. A hush fell over the studio when he and Robin did their first scene. I think, on this occasion, Michael was the only one who was not crying.

Two days after taping his first show, we were off to Washington, D.C. for the first ALS Advocacy Day. ALS patients, their families, and caregivers had traveled from across the United States. They were there to lobby their representatives for ALS research funds, and to support House Bill 2009 so that ALS patients without health insurance could get Medicare.

As usual, we were up until the small hours of the morning programming a speech Michael was to give during our scheduled meeting with House Speaker Newt Gingrich. Getting anywhere on time had become a major battle, because it took Michael much longer to perform normal, everyday habits, such as brushing his teeth or putting on his socks. By the time Steve Yates arrived to drive us to the airport, we were frazzled and more than a little testy with each other.

It was a sunny day, the cherry blossoms had already bloomed, and D.C. was August hot. We were met at Reagan Airport by David Hogan, who had lost his father to ALS. David drove us to the "war room" where, for the first time we were faced with a room full of PALS. Even though we had known what to expect, the sight of so many people with ALS was sobering. There were PALS in wheelchairs, newly diagnosed PALS—some of them in their early twenties, PALS with walkers and PALS completely immobilized, on ventilators with family members or caregivers in attendance.

The constant hum from battery-run ventilators was chilling. The PALS on ventilators were strapped into huge wheelchairs that reminded me of an electric chair I had once seen at the Warren County Fair in Ohio. Their necks were supported and their faces were frozen into blank expressions with gaping, drooling mouths. Their hands were stretched lifelessly on the arms of the chair and their legs were still as sticks. I had never seen a person on a ventilator. I'm not even sure I even knew such a mechanism existed. There was something scary about such helplessness. I averted my eyes, frightened of the future that lay before us, and I felt ashamed for not being stronger.

Michael was amazing and, I may add, in his element. The ALS patients were greeting him, those who could shaking his hand, others emitting the same primitive sounds that now came from my husband. We had already appeared on several network television interviews, and his first show would be airing soon. Already, the public service announcements were playing on ABC, showing Michael as a man living with ALS. Never before had this disease been made visible to so many people.

Just as I had turned away from some of the patients on ventilators, so had the world had turned its back on this ugly disease. When we entered the room that day, Michael's presence electrified the ALS community. Faces lit up. PALS who still could speak called out their encouragement and gratitude. Everyone was smiling. Even those with the vacant expressionless masks that characterize PALS in the later stages of ALS conveyed a sense of joy. They had a spokesperson. Feelings of hope were palpable, and love was all around.

Chris Prendergast, founder of the Ride for Life, together with several PALS had ridden in their electric wheelchairs all the way from Yankee Stadium to D.C. ALS patient Kyle Hahn and his partner, Terry, had carted their block long Banner of Faces from Ohio. The angry, irreverent Fernando, whom we had met at Yankee Stadium at the Ride for Life send-off, greeted me like an old friend. As I connected with PALS that day, I felt like I had been lifted from this earth into another realm. Elevated. The energy of hope and determination from so many ALS patients brought out the best in us and also, I would later discover, in many people.

At one point in the reception, Sarah and Jim Brady stopped by to show their support. Little more than a year before, Michael had appeared robust as he walked to the microphone to emcee the Brady's Handgun Control Benefit. Although Michael was still able to walk, the physical demands of the day were such that he finally agreed to use a wheelchair. As I spoke to several ALS patients about the formation of ZazAngels and Michael's appearance on *One Life to Live,* I looked over at him. He was signing autographs, clasping hands, giving without reserve, as he had always done. In moments like these, I knew that, despite the more frequent bickering, the anger and frustration, I had never loved him more.

We traveled between government buildings on "the underground railroad." We met with our New York congressman, who kept saying he already was an AIDS supporter. Michael, on the Link, gave this man a lesson in ALS that I think he will never forget. Gratefully, he has been an ALS supporter ever since.

Our sense of urgency accelerated as I wheeled Michael down the wide halls of the House of Representatives for our meeting with the Speaker of the House, Newt Gingrich. Considered left of liberal by our friends, we were amused that Michael had been chosen to meet with the force behind the new conservatism. I teased him that it was a good thing he couldn't speak, or we might be booted out.

Michael insisted on leaving the wheelchair outside the Speaker's sumptuous chambers. Michael walked in with only the aid of his cane, and we, Dorine Gordon, and several other representatives from the New York delegation trailed after him. In one corner of the chamber sat a television set. Michael noticed it first. His eyes grew wide, and he gestured wildly. *One Life to Live* was playing. Maybe the Speaker himself was a fan? We all laughed, and Michael pecked into the Link: "It bodes well."

And it did bode well. The Speaker entered, and he and Michael shook hands. There was an immediate spark of recognition between the two men. Michael, who had come to rely on his expressive brown eyes, conveyed both a sense of dignity and urgency. The Speaker met his gaze, unflinching. Michael pressed the button on the Link and, as the programmed speech played, the two men did not break eye contact.

"The fifty-nine years between Lou Gehrig's diagnosis and mine have seen woefully little progress in ALS research to find even an effective treatment, let alone a cure. The one FDA-approved drug costs $12,000 per year, and prolongs life by three to four months. The Banner of Faces implores you and challenges you to see yourself or a beloved family member through our eyes. The NIH (National Institute of Health) and NINDS (National Institute for Neurological diseases) spend a total of $333 per patient per year, yet the incidence of ALS is about the same as multiple sclerosis, and five times greater than Huntington's disease. MS and other diseases have effective, life-prolonging treatments that enable patients to advocate for themselves while we, with our projected lifespan of two to five years following diagnosis, have had fewer numbers, our voices not loud enough to be heard.

Until now. As of this month, we are no longer an "orphan" disease. We are going to be heard.

We challenge you to walk a yard in our shoes and those of our families. House Bill 2009 will begin to help. It will allow people with ALS to get Medicare if they don't have adequate insurance. And it will pry loose needed money for promising research. Once a cure is found for this granddaddy of neurological diseases, it will unlock the answers to a host of related diseases, such as Alzheimer's.

I fell twice yesterday, once in our bedroom and once in the living room. After Helena, our twelve year old had gone to bed, she heard me fall, a sound to which my family has, sadly, become accustomed. Helena sprang out of bed and saw me, helpless as a baby trying to get up by holding on to some furniture. I could see the anger and sadness in her eyes, and heard them in her voice as she helped me.

What we need from you is a sense of compassionate and empathetic URGENCY. Once you have developed such a sense, the money for research will follow and the

FDA will allow open studies to replace the double-blind, placebo-infested, eighteen-month studies presently taking place.

This decade has been designated 'The Decade of the Brain' by the medical community. It is fast drawing to a close. The challenge is apparent. Let's pull together to meet it. A Cure by 2000 can be a reality.

Thank you for your time and attentiveness."

*   *   *

The two men embraced, and the Speaker shared a personal story with us. He assured us of his support for House Bill 2009 and ALS research funding.

Despite our exhaustion, our spirits were infinitely better on the plane ride back to New York. There really was no need to speak. We held hands, knowing we were united as never before. In some way, after my initial reaction to seeing so many helpless ALS sufferers, I had fallen in love with the ALS community. I knew that even if Michael was cured tomorrow, I would never be able to turn away again. And I knew that whatever happened, Michael would always be there for his fellow PALS.

23

ONE OF THE EASIEST DECISIONS

The decision to hire Michael to return to ABC on One Life To Live *was one of the easiest decisions I've ever made. I never hesitated or asked for approval because I knew it was right for Michael, right for the viewer, and the right thing to do. When I first received Michael's letter describing his journey with ALS, I was moved by how suddenly his life had come to a screeching halt. Here was a talented, powerful man, a man with a family, and a whole life ahead of him, who lost control of his life, almost overnight. I couldn't help thinking that it could happen to any of us.*

As time went on, I saw how ALS tested Michael's strength and watched him rise to the challenge. Everyone he touched was given a rare opportunity to make a difference. We were brought together in a way we never had been before. Working with Michael put our lives in perspective and made us feel better about ourselves. It cost us nothing to give him back his dignity and give him a chance to feel like a man again. Even without words, Michael's talent and strength were powerful presences. It is something I will never forget."

—Pat Fili-Krushel, former President ABC Television

Interspersed with the bliss of going back to work was the ongoing pain from the fallout with our friend and godfather of our children, Beau. For years, it had been assumed that as "family," we would spend holidays together. Since the clash the previous summer, though, we saw them less and less frequently. Memorial Day was coming up, and, since we hadn't heard from them, I called to see what was up. I offered, as always, for everyone to come to our house so we could watch the local fireworks from the cornfield across the road.

Beau was uncharacteristically cagey and ignored my invitation. Finally, he said they already had a "gang" coming over to his house. I was hurt, but I persisted. Nothing lifted Michael's spirits more than a night with good friends. I said we would help out and like always bring whatever he assigned us. He glossed over my offer, but I pushed him until it came out that the "gang" was all of our friends, including people we had introduced to Beau.

Michael had been unable to spring to my defense at the dinner table the previous summer. On this occasion, though, he fired off an incendiary e-mail. There ensued a barrage of recriminations that proved only one thing: e-mails are a dangerous form of communication when one is hurt or angry.

Over the course of the next weeks, I tried to reconcile with Beau. Neither Michael nor I could believe that our friendship could disintegrate without making every effort to rebuild our relationship. After numerous attempts to meet and sort through our feelings, Michael wrote Beau another e-mail. He labeled the subject "Love and Death."

*   *   *

Dear Beau,

I have loved my Susie for twenty-seven years, lived with her for twenty-six, been married to her for twenty-three. When you hurt her, I leapt to her defense and wrote a lashing letter to you, expressing honest rage. I do not hold that evening last summer, before we went to Stony Brook, against you. You were both very clear in your apologies and we forgave you completely. My apology comes with love for you both, from my heart.

We have been hurt by you. When you excluded us from the reception for your son, whom we have known and loved for so long, we were pained. M and B, in separate phone calls, said "We'll see you at Beau's," and we didn't have a clue. I'm not going to pursue the reason why you didn't invite us, or at least give us a choice, except to offer a guess. You possibly feared the reception would be about me and my disease, rather than, as it should have been, about your son. Beau, you're very organized and meticulous, and the spectacle of a pal with bulbar onset ALS is unappetizing, to say the least. Here I am, wetting down your napkins and drooling because my tongue muscles have atrophied.

Shame on you for ignoring Susie's plea to meet with you and to attempt to heal this wound. Now we get to the love and death part. We so love you guys that we both had a rotten night's sleep after Susie received your letter. It seems clear to us that you take no responsibility for lapses in real communication. I wept at Marika's school musical saluting George Gershwin. It was so good, and there was our darling, tapping away, blissfully smiling. I was weeping because they ended the show with just the seniors doing a number, and I have less than a fifty-fifty chance of seeing my darling graduate. I feel positive most of the time, but the medical community, with very few exceptions, views me as a dead man walking. There are no guarantees but hope, as I have said in speech after speech. When I am faced with bodily facilities being slowly chipped away, suffice to say, I have my moments.

All I really want to say is, "How about the big picture?" I'm the one with a deadly disease, and you slam down the cards and figuratively stride away. You did not even pick up the phone to talk to the girls, and they were hurt. It's hard having a sick dad who can't talk. They need all the healthy adult males they can find.

As I am, for now, a one-handed typist, I will close, but not before beseeching you to do the right thing. I am attempting to be mature, and I expect the same from you. Let's get past this bump in life's road and deeply learn from our wrong turns. I so adore my vida, my Susie, and I can't even kiss her. I can still receive kisses though, and caress her with my left hand and arm, as I did this morning. A tear is making its way down my cheek. She is so determined to save my life, as am I. That's what we are about for now. But we need moments with our long-standing (and sitting and lying down) friends. I keep thinking of you while reading The Tortilla Curtain *by T.C. Boyle. Have you read it? If not, have I got a read for you!*

*   *   *

There was no response. I met Beau's partner, Ann, and we sat in the woods talking about the rift. I begged her to get Beau to meet with Michael face to face. When we parted, I was hopeful that she would intervene. As the days went by, Michael's largesse turned into a cold fury. The mention of Beau or Ann set him off. If Ann called to speak to me, he would type angrily on the Link, "I don't want her calling here."

The last time Ann telephoned, she wanted to know what she could to help me now that Michael was no longer able to share the physical load. Could she weed the garden? Maybe water the plants when we were in the city? I should tell her what I needed and she would do anything.

I took the cordless phone outside so that Michael would not know I was talking to her. "Michael is dying," I told her. I heard myself say something I had never even allowed myself to think let alone speak out loud.

"I know," she responded. Suddenly, I was as angry at her as I was at Beau. "I've already told you what I need you to do. Screw the garden! If you really want to help, get Beau over here, so he and Michael can make up. If you can't do that, what I need is for you never to call here again!"

Inside, Michael knew instinctively who I had been talking to, and he scribbled wildly on one of the yellow legal pads: "If the worst happens to me, I do not want them to come to my memorial. I do not want them to wallow in a grief that is as shallow as their love."

My husband was a man of extreme tolerance, generosity, and undying loyalty. If he gave his heart to you, he gave it all and forever. To see him so wounded by a friend, in addition to everything else, was unbearable.

As painful as this loss was for us, it was more painful for Marika and Helena. I was conflicted about whether or not to deprive them of their godfather's company. On the other hand, I was not going to inflict any more pain on Michael by arranging for them to see him secretly, as one friend had suggested. Perhaps I should have been more relentless in my determination to get the two of them to meet face-to-face. Maybe I didn't try hard enough. Beau had been the best of friends for many years, and I know that he must have been as grieved as we were.

We had to let go of our regrets and anger. While no new friend replaces an old one, vital, interesting, crazy new people entered our lives. Many of Michael's scenes at the studio were with Bob Krimmer, and during the months to come, Krim, as we called him, was a ray of wit and unflagging loyalty. His wife and two adored children remained in their home in California when Krim came to New York to work. Fortunately for us, he was on the show often, and as he and Michael grew closer, he spent much of his time in our home. Krim had an uncanny ability to understand Michael, and they would sit and communicate for hours. Krim was definitely an angel, a rollerblading angel who brought laughter to our entire family.

Another angel was Tony Hearn, Michael's physical therapist. Like Michael, Tony was a gregarious raconteur. Michael was always uplifted by Tony's spirit, as well as by his politics, which were as liberal and passionate as Michael's. Tony's lilting Irish accent was an added bonus. Both Krim and Tony had not known the old, talkative Michael, "not that man anymore," but both had the capacity to see through the disability into Michael's spirit. Both Tony and Krim were able to bring out the best during the worst of times. I will always be indebted to them for the generosity and humor they brought into our lives.

I, on the other hand, did not always bring out the best. I was exhausted and tense. I was exasperated by our dealings with the National ALS Association.

Michael and I agreed that they lacked creativity and a sense of urgency. Tucked away in the suburbs of Los Angeles, they seemed almost blasé about the vast media opportunities made possible by Michael's celebrity and his willingness to do just about anything for the cause. Michael, together with ALS patients Pat Pepper and Chris Prendergast, drafted a letter to the board of the National Association addressing the absence of PALS on the National Board. In return, these three brilliant people were sent a placating letter thanking them for their interest and assuring them their suggestion would be considered. Where, we wondered, was the sense of urgency?

I knew anger was counterproductive, but despite my intentions, I caved in to my feelings of resentment. I loved Tony and valued the physical therapy sessions that always left Michael invigorated. I was coming home day after day to a living room filled with people and dominated by a massage table. The furniture's askew placement was making me more irritable. I had never thought of myself as a control freak, but as time went on, I lived in dread of what new front would be invaded by forces beyond my control. I could no longer recognize my life. I had loved my old life. I wanted it back!

Before Michael became ill, we had been looking for a larger apartment. Much of the tension in our family was because there was simply no longer enough space to contain us and ALS. If we had needed more space before, we definitely needed more space now. What I did not know at the time was that most PALS are forced to change their living situation to accommodate the disease. Doorways need to be widened for the inevitable wheelchairs. Ramps need to be built, bathrooms need to be reconfigured, all of which contributes to a family's staggering expenditures for dealing with ALS. These costs can be upwards to $200,000 a year.

Michael, as always, was game for change and we plunged into the real estate adventure. A steep flight of steps from the street to the lobby made access into our building increasingly hazardous. I notified our real estate agent that we were only interested in buildings with flat, easy access. The major concern was money. Upgrading would increase our expenses considerably and, even though he was working again, the future was fraught with financial imponderables.

When I realized Michael was cutting back on physical therapy treatments to save money, I decided to see if Marika and Helena could get financial aid from their school. I am fairly certain there was an angel, in the form of an anonymous Trinity School parent, who helped facilitate an immediate and unbelievably generous response. When I told Michael that Trinity was giving both of our children full financial support, he wept with relief and gratitude. With our children's education secured, we continued our search for more space with our usual gusto.

Around this time, several people called to tell me about a healer who had appeared on *The View,* a show on which Michael and I were scheduled to appear on June 19. This healer had actually performed treatments on the air. In addition, the show played a clip of a woman with ALS who was as lifeless as a rag doll during her first treatment with this healer. Over the course of several months, she progressed to the point where she was presently walking and leading a normal life. Several doctors confirmed the woman's diagnosis of ALS, and the woman gave a moving testimonial to this healer's powers.

When I watched a tape of *The View,* and witnessed this amazing cure with my own eyes, I knew I would do anything to get Michael an appointment.

This healer kept a very low profile. Through various sources, I learned that he was booked well into the fall. Except for Penney Leyshorn, Michael had soured on healers, but watching this healer, he was excited. Seeing was believing. The rag-doll woman who had been carried to her first treatment was walking and talking like a normal person!

Meanwhile, our twenty-third wedding anniversary was approaching. Even with the progression of the disease, we decided we would celebrate both this year's anniversary and last year's, which had passed in a fog of depression and resentment. I was still hot on the trail of this healer, and came up with a phone number that, under no circumstances, was I to give out to anyone. I had been told that this healer's wife handled all of the business. I knew the cost of a single session was $1,000, but I was only later informed that payment was accepted in cash only.

I did not hesitate. I made an appointment for Sunday, June 7, our wedding anniversary. I didn't tell Michael what was happening, only that I had a really big surprise. I confided in Brynn, who shared my excitement. She was spending the weekend with us in Roxbury, and we had fun tantalizing Michael with hints about the big surprise.

On Sunday, I drove the Jeep into the city, battling summer traffic, and running late as usual. I was wired and afraid we would arrive late. Brynn kept calling ahead on her cell phone as we inched our way to the healer's office on the East Side. Michael was grumpy, the whole surprise game had worn thin. The children were restless, the cats were meowing, and only Brynn and our dog, Lily, remained calm and pleasant.

Finally, we pulled up in front of the healer's brownstone. We had dinner reservations at the Park Avenue Café afterwards, and Michael was adamant that he did not want to use his walker. He insisted he could manage with a cane. We would take a taxi to the restaurant and he could definitely walk the few steps to get inside. Brynn and I exchanged glances, knowing it was not worth trying to convince him otherwise.

"Where are we?" Michael asked. It was uncanny how the Link's digitalized voice could convey irritation.

"You have an appointment with this healer," I finally told him. His grumpiness metamorphized into that unique blend of ALS crying and laughter. Brynn said she would drive Marika and Helena home, and come back to chauffeur us to our anniversary dinner. We protested, saying it would be easy to grab a cab, but Brynn would not take no for an answer.

Brynn and I helped Michael down a small flight of stairs to the townhouse. Again, I was perplexed by the tendency for healers to have offices that further challenged people with disabilities. The healer's wife opened the door and greeted us. After I saw Michael settled in the small waiting area, I went into the office to hand over the cash, The healer's wife was efficient, brisk, and bordered on being brash. She had black hair and wore siren red lipstick. On first impression she did not inspire confidence.

When I joined Michael in the waiting room, his eyes told me that he was having the same doubts. Our reservations were immediately dispelled, however, as we entered the treatment room and shook hands with the healer, who appeared as gentle and authentic as his wife seemed fraudulent. He helped Michael onto the treatment table, while I sank deep into an over-stuffed chair a few feet away. As the healer placed his hands on different areas of Michael's body, Michael emitted some sonorous sounds, a cross between laughter and tears. I scrutinized this healer's every movement. There was a heightened sense of reality. Was it my imagination? My wish for a miracle?

The room seemed electrically charged. This was not Michael's usual nasal bleating. I knew he was feeling something different. I knew something unique was happening.

For nearly an hour, the healer moved his hands over Michael's legs, throat, hands—all over his body. The room was silent, except for spurts of Michael's ALS giggling, as if he was a child delighted at being tickled. Often, I found his guttural moans upsetting, but these giggling sounds were enticing. I found myself smiling. This healer caught my eye and we laughed, joining Michael in his glee.

This healer turned to me and asked if I wanted to feel what Michael was feeling. He had helped Michael to a sitting position on the examining table, but Michael was still making irrepressible sounds and smiling. The digitalized Link voice intoned, "That was fun," and we laughed again. Michael's face was relaxed. He looked more like the old Michael than he had in months.

This healer put his hands on my shoulders, as I had seen him do on *The View*. I felt a buzzing vibration. Wherever he moved his hands, I felt the same warm sensation, like friendly, fuzzy bees were swarming beneath my skin. It was altogether a unique feeling. Like Michael said, it was fun.

But was it real? This healer's wife was pushy with a hard "carnie" edge. Did that mean this healer was a fraud? Clearly, she was very protective of him. We had both felt the funny, warm, happy buzzing sensation. Was this healer holding something in his hand? Michael tapped out his assessment on the Link and, over dinner, we analyzed the experience.

"I don't think he could have had anything in his hands," Michael's digitalized voice sounded confident. Best of all, he was hopeful. We ordered our traditional celebratory champagne cocktails and toasted our future.

24

I HAD TO PULL HIM TO ME TIGHTLY

On a temperate night in July, I overheard my parents arguing. Or rather, I heard a mechanical voice quarrelling with the loud shrill voice of my mother. I could tell my dad was frustrated by the occasional slam of his hand on what I could only guess was the dresser. The rattling sound of the brass picture frames gave it away. When their fight got to the point where my dad let out a shrill cry, his only way to express himself, I curiously crept into the doorway of their bedroom. He fumbled awkwardly with his shoelaces, in a desperate attempt to tie them. The picture of him sits clearly in my mind. He was dressed in a gray T-shirt and a pair of green shorts. His black Mephisto sneakers had the clear plastic leg support running up his calf. He sat perilously close to the edge of the bed, and I suppressed the urge to run in and pull his body further onto the bed. Making his way to a standing position, he hovered over his new walking aid—the blue walker that had recently replaced his cane. He stalked out the door the best he could without letting us know where he was going. When my mother and I went to the park with our dog, she told me he needed to think on his own.

A Chinese man raced toward us as we sat in the park, and, out of breath, he blurted out phrases in a sharp accent, motioning for us to follow him. We trailed behind him, running up the block leading to our favorite Chinese restaurant. I heard a crowd of people murmuring at the same time as the resounding sirens. The pieces came together for me as I saw my dad lying on the ground, his blue walker towering over him. I could not look at his face, only the blood pooling at the edge of the sidewalk. Not at that moment, but later on, I came to realize that this incident represented his entire struggle. He, as well as I, wished to the highest degree that he could act out life as he always had. The power of the disease had conquered his body. Until then, the two of us had tried to deny it. Life had to be carried on, even under the worst circumstances. However painful the memory is, I would like to believe that the experience had a positive result. That night, I knew that I had to pull him in to me tightly and, despite the harsh affects of the disease, love him until the end.

—Helena Zaslow, daughter (written at age 14)

As two medics ordered the knot of onlookers to stand back so they could lift him onto a stretcher, Michael gesticulated wildly, making his primitive ALS sounds. The concerned bystanders seemed to understand him perfectly, and, for once, so did I. He did not want to be taken to the hospital! As we ran, I noticed familiar faces from the neighborhood. The crowd, so typical of New Yorkers, was vocal and indignant. Some of them recognized Michael, and they were all siding with him against the medics. Michael had scribbled: "I have ALS. Can't talk," on his yellow notepad. Like most people, the medics didn't have a clue about ALS or its symptoms. They jerked at him roughly, as if he was a drunk, some guy who couldn't even talk right.

He looked fine, except for a nasty cut over his eye, which had already stopped bleeding. The medics said legally they had to take him to the hospital. Michael was livid, and scribbled: "NO, NO, NO!" The medics looked at him like he was crazy.

"He can't speak," I tried to explain. "I'm his wife. We live just around the corner. I'll get him home and call his doctor."

"Lady," one medic said, rolling his eyes like an adolescent. "I got to do my job. He goes to the hospital, and that's it."

"Then I have to come along," I said resolutely. I wanted Helena to take Lily home, but she was clinging to her dad's hand so I asked a man in the crowd whom I then knew only as the "Dad" of a black poodle named Lola if he would deliver Lily to our doorman. Helena and I then climbed into the ambulance next to Michael, who looked at me remorsefully as the siren sounded and we sped off.

Michael had simply gone around the corner for Chinese food. Only nothing was simple anymore. Former certainties had become precarious endeavors, and what was once reasonable and dependable was now unreliable and constantly changing. We spent the next five hours at Roosevelt Hospital where we had to cajole the staff into allowing us to wait with Michael while he lay on a gurney. According to one of the non-medical security people, it was against the law for visitors to wait alongside patients. My explanations that he could not speak and that we needed to be with him were met with suspicion. They zeroed in on Helena. A child, they said, could definitely not be in this area, and besides, we were blocking the way for other doctors and patients.

Helena fired back that it would be easy to move aside if someone had to get through. I had to stop her from mouthing off. Her fighting spirit elicited a thumbs-up from Michael. We were both glad she had come along. She held down the fort and protected her dad while I went into the waiting room to telephone Marika and explain what had happened.

When I returned, Michael was having trouble breathing. They insisted on laying him down flat, and when I requested a pillow, I was told that patients on gurneys didn't get pillows. I explained that ALS patients have difficulty breathing when they lie flat. The workers begrudgingly handed over a thin white pillow. This miserly response further infuriated Helena, who went sneaking around to find pillows whenever the security guards weren't looking.

Two days later, Michael was scheduled to tape an episode of *One Life to Live,* so they revised the script and had Michael's character, David, fall and get a black eye. A week later, when Jamie Gangel of *The Today Show* brought her crew to our apartment, Michael still had the mottled yellow and blue residue from the shiner. During the taped interview, Jamie surprised us by announcing that, due to an unprecedented response, ABC was extending Michael's original, ten-episode contract to an open-ended length of time. Delighted, we yelped and hugged each other.

When Jamie asked Michael how long he believed he could continue acting on television his response, with his distinctive ALS laugh, delivered by the digitalized Link, was characteristic, and proved to be prophetic: "As long as I live—maybe longer."

We had only one day between tapings of *The Today Show* and *The View*. I was exhausted, and could only imagine Michael's fatigue. We never could have managed without the help of an angel, in the form of a pony-tailed young man in a baseball cap. Barry Priest was in charge of Michael's augmented voice computers at the ABC studio, and we both considered him a technological wizard. Predictably, the night before an appearance or an interview, the technology would go berserk. We once lost all of the information we had so painstakingly programmed into the machine. Whenever there was a problem, we would beep Barry, and he would fly to our rescue. On more than one occasion, he worked with us at the apartment until after midnight and then drove home to his extremely tolerant wife in New Jersey.

Our time in Connecticut was limited. We drove up on Friday after taping *The View*, but had to drive back on Sunday for a treatment. Although our first impression of this healer's wife had not changed, we were more convinced than ever that Michael was improving in subtle, not radical, ways. He no longer needed me to dress him, and his right hand was stronger. He proudly demonstrated that he could once again hold a cup with either hand.

Marika and I had gone on a "coming of age" trip to the southern part of Scotland the year she turned thirteen. I had promised Helena we would go away together to mark her thirteenth birthday, as well. Michael insisted that Helena and I have our trip. We decided to explore a different area of Scotland and made plans to fly to Glasgow and drive north into the Highlands, and then down to the Isle of Skye.

Everything was a bag of mixed emotions. I was excited about the trip, but I wanted Michael to share it. What would Brigadoon be without him? He assured me he would not only be fine, but with the help of this healer's treatments, he would be much better when we returned. We arranged for Kristie Miller to come and help us out. The day before we left, Michael came out of our bedroom wearing his old Cheshire cat grin, emitting sounds and pointing to his feet. He had tied his own shoes!

We went crazy, whooping around the living room. He had been unable to tie his own shoes for months! This was tangible evidence that all those costly healing sessions were working. His right hand was stronger. It wasn't our imagination. We sat on the couch and I held my breath, half expecting him to fumble. His fingers moved slowly but decisively, and he pulled the final knot with a flourish. Again and again he untied the lace and retied.

He had given me the best possible going-away present. Helena and I took off in high spirits and, even though I was driving on the left, I got out of the Glasgow airport without a hitch. I maneuvered flawlessly around innumerable roundabouts, all the way to Inverness.

We checked in by telephone every other day. Marika sounded happy to have time alone with her dad. The illness, coupled with Marika's adolescence, had driven a wedge into what had once been a close relationship. Seeing her dad deteriorate was just too painful, and Marika's method of coping was to withdraw. When Michael fell, she would sometimes literally be paralyzed, unable to move. Since Helena compensated by being overly vigilant, and more or less in the middle of everything, her absence gave Michael and Marika the opportunity to recapture their old closeness.

After a week in Scotland, Helena and I took the train to London for two days. For the first time during the trip, I had trouble sleeping. I missed Michael. I wanted to see him, but I was afraid. I realized that part of me just wanted to keep traveling. Later, my guilt would twist itself around, and I would regret that I had left him even for a day.

25

CAUTIOUSLY OPTIMISTIC

People who are faced with this disease don't have the luxury of waiting for some FDA approval for a variety of substances, which are in the pipeline. One of the hopes we have because of Michael Zaslow going public is that more people will become aware of this disease, and we will get more money for research. There have been major advances in research, and it's just a matter of putting pieces of a puzzle together to create a treatment. I am cautiously optimistic.

—*Dr. Jay Lombard, for* The Larry King Show

A week after Helena and I returned, we loaded the Jeep and drove Marika to Brown University, where she and her friend, Phoebe, were enrolled in a summer program. Marika had mixed feelings about going, but Michael thought it would be good for her to get away. As we approached Providence, I was alerted by the dense silence coming from her corner of the backseat.

Moving Marika into the dorm was hard on all of us. It was difficult for me to focus on Marika's needs because I was keeping my eye on Michael. I was afraid he would trip as we lugged all the usual paraphernalia into her room. I kept thinking: this should be fun.

I was aware of how helpless Michael felt leaving the lifting to his three women. He stacked small items into the basket of the blue walker, but we were all on guard, dreading the heart-stopping thud of another fall. The presence of other fathers laughing and effortlessly helping their kids did not escape us.

On the way back to Roxbury, Helena fell asleep in the back seat and Michael, beside me in the passenger seat, slept so soundly that several times I was frightened he had stopped breathing. The day had so exhausted him that he did not wake once during the three-hour drive. Once home, he fell into bed, too tired even to eat.

I was not surprised to get a phone call from Marika the next morning, saying she wanted to come home. Michael was adamant. He wanted her to stay. He insisted that she needed a break from his illness. It was only two weeks. She would manage.

I, on the other hand, saw the writing on the wall. Unlike the other members of our family, Marika chose her battles very carefully. She is one of the most agreeable people I have ever known. Even as a toddler she was tolerant, patient, and reasonable. However, she is as tenacious as a dog with a bone when she takes a stance and from the first phone call the situation did not look good.

Three days later, Marika boarded the train from Providence to New York, loaded down with everything except a lamp and a fan. She had arranged for reimbursement, and said she felt better immediately. For the duration of Michael's illness, and for three years following his death, she could not sleep away from home.

Two days after Marika came home, we were deep into preparations for our appearances on *The Larry King Show*. Michael and I, together with Pat Fili-Krushel of ABC and our neurologist, Jay Lombard, would be Larry's guests for the full hour. Other interviews had not been so lengthy, and even though I would be there to speak on Michael's behalf, we brought along three prerecorded Links and Barry Priest, just in case.

An hour on *The Larry King Show* was an unprecedented opportunity to raise awareness about ALS. In addition, viewers would be able to call a toll-free number to contribute to ALS research. We envisoned Michael's appearance bringing in thousands of dollars.

Once again, we were frustrated by the national association's tepid response. Instead of seizing on this unprecedented opportunity, it fell to Michael and me to constantly prod them. It was left to us to make certain the toll-free number was in place and to do whatever we could to maximize such powerful media exposure. The CNN network could not give us the exact date when our interview would be aired. "Some time in August" was the closest prediction they would give. We needed to have everything in place, because in all likelihood, there would be very little advance notice.

I had always thought of Larry King as a cryptic, controlling guy with snazzy suspenders and a knack for booking interesting guests. Neither Michael nor I were prepared for the sharp, sensitive gentleman who greeted us. The only thing he had in common with the brash Larry King I had seen on TV was his suspenders. Larry was instantly tuned in to the emotional nuances of ALS and the interview flowed not only from the prepared questions, but from his heart. At one point, true to fashion, the Link went off the deep end, sputtering and snarling in its digital equivalent of a temper tantrum. Larry was outraged on Michael's behalf. He immediately grasped the frustration and anger that such inexcusably inadequate technology presented to people with communication disabilities.

When Michael announced that he had put on eight pounds and was gaining some strength, Dr. Jay Lombard let out a hoot of unmitigated excitement. Larry found Jay's emotional outburst refreshingly "unmedical." Of course, Larry wanted to know what was responsible for the improvements. Michael mentioned his physical therapy with Tony and the various nutritional protocols. We also attributed his improvements to this healer's treatments, but we considered it premature to raise the hopes of other ALS patients until we were absolutely sure. I had already received several calls from PALS who had heard on the grapevine that Michael was seeing this healer. We wanted to share any good news we had with other ALS families, but considering the expense and all too aware of how desperate PALS were, we resisted mentioning this healer.

After the taping, Michael, Jay, and I gathered in the show's green room. We were all elated and optimistic about Michael's progress. Jay laughed as Michael devoured a whole plate of chocolate-chip cookies, and said he was impressed, with Michael's swallowing and his appetite! Jay's agile scientific mind immediately propelled the conversation towards other courses of treatment, and Michael and I left the CNN studio in a celebratory mood.

That evening, we went out to dinner with a group of friends, an event that was becoming increasingly rare. Dining out on the spur of the moment was a luxury of the past. It was difficult at best, and often impossible, now that Michael relied totally on the blue walker. Many of our favorite restaurants were off limits because of limited access. I had never given any thought to steps as obstacles, but now I calculated our activities in terms of how many steps would be involved and the steepness of those steps. That particular evening I had help. Three of Michael's close male friends hoisted him up the steps and swept him effortlessly to a table. We laughed and drank wine almost like life was wonderful and we were as free as we had always been.

One evening, we went to a downtown theater to see *How I Learned to Drive*. We parked at a nearby garage, and had a spirited dinner at a restaurant across the street. We were feeling great, until we arrived at the theater and were confronted with a marble staircase as steep as the one in *Gone with the Wind*. I held my breath and trailed Michael as he clung to the banister. He baby-stepped his way to the top, whereupon I dashed back down, collapsed the walker, ran up the stairs, and unfolded the walker so that he could make his way to his seat. I collapsed the walker again and gave it to an usher. During the performance, the only thing I could think about was going back down those steps.

It was always a high point for both of us to get out of the house. Michael never felt better than when he was surrounded by friends. Accordingly, we tried to arrange outings as often as possible. Old friends Roger Newman and Fran Myers, who had, along with Caroline McWilliams appeared with Michael on *The Guiding Light*, were among those who did not recoil from the ravages of ALS. There was also the steadfast company of Ellen Levine, her husband, Ivan Strausz, Ric, Susan, and Tony and Teresa in Connecticut. There were many friends who had the capacity to look straight through ALS and see Michael. It was a blessing when we could drink wine and laugh, as Michael tapped out his messages on his fancy new IBM.

Unfortunately, there were a few people who could not look at Michael, who avoided us, and dropped out of our life. Although I was hurt and angry, I now understand how hard it was for them. As the disease progressed and I was called on to assist in Michael's bathing and personal habits, I would often find myself hardened to what was happening. Almost a form of disassociation, my body would stiffen involuntarily. Sometimes, I was compelled to avert my eyes from his struggle to perform the simplest tasks. At those moments, I felt painfully guilty, selfish, and inadequate. Even I, who loved him with all of my heart, could not always bear to watch. I had to look away into order to keep going.

There was also a third category of people in our lives. Many friends telephoned, offering to help, wanting to see Michael. Because of the logistics and the necessity of preplanning every detail of our lives, some of our dearest friends never had the opportunity to spend time with him. Our days and nights felt like a tape on fast-forward. After Michael returned to *One Life to Live*, we were stretched to the breaking point. To this day, I will dimly recollect a call or message from someone who I am not sure I called back. There was simply not enough time. We lived in a war zone. In times of war, the battle is everything.

Since he could only get around with the walker, climbing Mt. Everest to Gary Null's Healing Center was no longer an option. We were thus on the lookout for another source for the antioxidant IV treatments. After encountering numerous dead ends, we found what we were looking for in our own back yard, Dr. S's office located off the lobby of our building. Dr. T, the Candida expert, was no longer on staff and Michael resumed the IV treatment. Dr. S offered to make things easier by sending a nurse up to our apartment so Michael could rest in his own bed during the two-hour treatment.

It sounded great. In reality, the simple procedure, which was a matter of inserting the IV, allowing two hours for the drip and removing the IV, eluded the staff. Inevitably, Michael would have to wait for someone to simply show up. Sometimes they would come up, but sometimes not. Although I always double-checked and would occasionally watch as they wrote Michael's appointments in their calendar, often they called either to say the antioxidants had not been delivered, or that they were so busy they couldn't send someone. Once, I came home to find that Michael had been attached to the IV for over four hours, unable to get up. Clearly, we needed more help, someone to be on hand when I was not available. Frustrated by Dr. S's amiable but disorganized system, I continued searching for the penultimate IV delivery system.

26

SWEET SYNCHRONICITY

Michael and I worked together four times, either a fluke or a sweet synchronicity. I was also present at the Zaslow-Hufford nuptials, but since moving to Los Angeles, we had mostly lost touch, except for updates from mutual friends. When I heard of his illness, I flew from Los Angeles to visit. Friends had alerted me about his physical condition, but I was completely unprepared for the man who greeted me. Michael was bone thin, and the face that had once expressed his thoughts and feelings with glorious animation was expressionless. There were no words between us, only primitive guttural sounds.

Susan came in to say "Hello," and to help smooth our transition. Soon, we began to reacquaint ourselves. The love between Susan and Michael was evident in every exchange. Her support during the illness was Herculean. What had happened to Michael's physical body was truly horrible, but being with my old friend was not horrible at all. His muscles were abandoning him, but bit by bit, but he was exquisitely graceful.

He asked to see a picture of my son, Sean, and after looking at the picture, he typed on his computer keyboard, "What a punim!" When he heard the dry monotone of the computer's version of the Yiddish word "punim," we laughed. I saw that when something really pleased him, his eyes could still dance.

—Caroline McWilliams, actor, friend

Caroline had not been to our Connecticut home since it was a wee cottage at our wedding. We had seen her only two months earlier in the city. Michael was very moved to hear that she was coming again so soon. We bustled around, Marika making her famous lemon tart, Helena preparing the grill. It was a scorching August Sunday, and at mid-afternoon, Helena and I decided to head to the town pond for a swim. Michael had been sitting on the patio for several hours in the sun. From time to time, I reminded him that the sun was bad for him, referencing the medical expertise of our friend Phillip Prioleau.

"I want to look good when I tape next week," he typed, and the digital voice seemed to growl.

His chest was pink, his face already tanned, and he was perspiring.

"You know the sun isn't good for you," I said, trying to be light and casual. I could see he was digging in his heels.

"Leave me alone," he pecked.

"I talked to Jay...the sun isn't good for people with neurological problems. Please go inside."

"Go for your swim."

Helena and I left. I knew he was angry because he was trapped. He could not hop on his bike and meet us at the pond. He couldn't dive in and swim laps around the old wooden float the way he used to do. I felt guilty as I plunged into the cool water, and I couldn't stop thinking of him stuck at home, all sweaty and hot.

At the same time, I was annoyed by his risky behavior.

When we returned, he had relocated from the lounge to the patio table, where he sat under the large green umbrella, taking his vitamins. He was coughing and when I asked him why he typed that one of the vitamins had gone down the wrong way.

I suggested he stop taking his vitamins but he continued with the same defiant manner, hunching over the little plastic vitamin container, popping them in one at a time, and rinsing them down with water.

Caroline arrived, and he rose to the occasion, playing the gracious host. Over dinner, his coughing grew worse as he struggled to eat. We suggested he go inside and lie down, but he refused. The night was too precious. He wanted to linger with us, and so we lit the lanterns and reminisced about *Boccaccio* and *Cat on a Hot Tin Roof,* shows he and Caroline had performed in together. After another coughing bout during which Michael could not get his breath, we helped him into bed and I telephoned Jay in New York. I wanted to take him to a nearby hospital, but he was refusing. Jay said to monitor him and if the coughing got worse or if he said he was having trouble breathing, to get him to the hospital, regardless.

For the next four hours, I lay next to him in our bed, praying either that he would stop coughing or that he would let me call the hospital. Finally, around 4 AM, he scribbled, "I want to go to the hospital."

In less than ten minutes, five vehicles ground up our driveway, their lights cutting through what little remained of the humid August night. Although I was grateful for there speedy response, it seemed to me there were too many people swarming into our bedroom and too much confusion. The medics carried Michael to the ambulance as the children and Caroline watched from an upstairs window. I followed in our Jeep, and stretched out next to him on the examining table in the emergency room as we waited for the doctor on call.

I stayed until they admitted him and moved him into the intensive care unit. It was mid-morning when I drove back home and Caroline had already headed north to Vermont. She left a note asking me to call, and telling me how resourceful and caring Helena had been, making crepes and carrying on with typical Zaslow hospitality.

Some of the nurses were regular soap followers, and they were thrilled to have "Roger" and "David" in their care. Although force of habit resulted in many of them calling Michael by his character's name, I was comforted knowing they would lavish him with the best of care. The only thing was no one really knew how to handle a person with ALS. Unwittingly, they wrenched his back and hurt his leg as they jostled him around. A vitamin was responsible for triggering the coughing, and when he entered the hospital, I was told he had a very slight case of pneumonia. Generally, pneumonia patients are encouraged to get on their feet as soon as possible but because Michael had ALS, no attempt was made to get him out of bed.

For the next three days, he lay there, growing weaker. I told the staff that he was still able to walk. Because of his diagnosis the medical assumptions were so negative that when I visited Michael on day two of his stay, he was deeply morose. He scribbled that a doctor had come in to schedule a percutaneous endoscopic gastrostomy (PEG), a surgical procedure in which the surgeon places a feeding tube in the stomach. Someone else had approached him about having a tracheostomy performed.

I tried to reassure him, but everything was moving too quickly. Maybe it would be necessary to have this feeding tube inserted, but to jump into it in a country hospital seemed premature. He had been doing better. I stopped myself from reminding him that he had drained himself by sitting out in the sun all day.

I called Jay Lombard as soon as I got home. Only a week before, Jay had laughed at Michael as he chowed down on chocolate-chip cookies. He couldn't believe they were suggesting a feeding tube and a tracheostomy, unless Michael had declined rapidly. What did I think?

I honestly did not believe he had declined. If anything, he seemed stronger, though more prickly in attitude. He had negotiated our steps and walked onto the patio that day with only the help of the walker. The sun had sapped his strength, he had choked. I couldn't help it. I was angry at him.

Jay advised me to get him out of the hospital and back to New York, where he could be checked out. When and if the surgical procedures had to be done they should be performed in the city at a hospital with expertise in ALS.

I drove into the city to work early the following morning, and that afternoon Brynn and I interviewed prospective event organizers for ZazAngels' Broadway Theater Benefit in December. I returned to Connecticut late the same evening to find that Michael had already been put into the surgical schedule for the PEG. Although we had agreed the night before to wait, the surgeon had stopped by later and convinced him that since he would need a PEG eventually, he should have the operation in two days.

Early the next morning, I tracked down the surgeon. He explained he was eager to get the surgery into the schedule because he was going on vacation the following week. I, for the moment, kept my opinion to myself. The physicians at the hospital conveyed negativity and hopelessness. They demeaned the vitamins and nutritional treatments in which Michael and I so strongly believed. They looked at me like I was crazy when I suggested they get him out of bed for physical therapy. I met with social workers and nutritionists. I arranged for oxygen to be delivered, and contacted the Visiting Nurse Association to schedule home visits. With Jay's support, I arranged for Michael's discharge.

To my surprise, our friend Ric Sonder had arranged for a new driveway to be installed, so that Michael would have easier access to our house. I arrived ahead of the ambulance that was transporting Michael back home. Several workers were putting on the finishing touches and replanting shrubs as another friend, Marc Olivieri, completed a wooden walkway over our treacherous gravel path. Not only were they gifts of love that made our lives easier, the new driveway and walk were a lovely, almost Oriental addition to the entrance.

I was so relieved and happy to have Michael safely home that it didn't occur to me that he might have a more complicated reaction. He had gone into the hospital able to walk, feeling that all of his hard work was paying off, and that he was actually getting stronger. He returned, twelve pounds lighter, an invalid on a gurney who had to be lifted into bed, put on oxygen, bathed by a visiting nurse, and transferred to a wheelchair. He was furious. Who could blame him?

Only five days had passed since my husband had choked on the vitamin, but it felt like months. I was exhausted. I had imagined a celebration. I can no longer recall what he found fault with, and I'm sure it had nothing to do with me. Whatever it was, though, I knew that I had not achieved my goal of seeing him smile and of creating a happy homecoming.

I collapsed on the patio, crying, my head on the table, and the sound of carpenters' hammers in my ears. I could not stop sobbing, and I did not care who heard me.

After a while, I stood up and stared westward, toward the Berkshire Hills, through the view Michael had cut in our woods. I felt someone come behind me and put their arms around me. I had no idea who it was, and for several minutes I didn't even care. It was just good to have someone hold me. When I turned, I saw Val, our favorite nurse from the Visiting Nurse Association. With her blond hair and pretty serene face, she could have been an angel.

27

A LOUDER, LARGER VOICE

I have lost my voice, but in the process, I have found a louder, larger one. Thanks to ABC and you in the press, I have found a purpose in my life. All my adult life, I have been an activist for the voiceless, money-less people. Never, never thinking that I would be among the disabled. And there are no underdogs like those who have been given a diagnosis of the dreaded initials ALS. Vanity has to take a back seat to what I am doing. I used to act for pleasure and employment, but now I am acting for life, and it has saved my life.

—*Michael Zaslow, for* The Larry King Show

Before going into the hospital, my husband could move cautiously around the house with the help of his walker. Now, he kept a bell by the side of the bed so he could signal when he needed help. Basically, he needed help for everything. Because our home was constructed on various levels, it took two of us to help him move from one place to another. Getting outside to the patio was a major ordeal. We would wheel him to the first step, and while one of us helped him balance, the other would take the wheelchair down the steps to the patio. Then, both of us would assist him down the steps and into the chair. I had often lamented that I was not a statuesque, long-legged woman, but now I felt truly inadequate. Helena, no taller than I at the time, hefted her dad around with a strength that sprang from the depths of her twelve-year-old heart.

Resolved to restore the weight he had dropped in the hospital, I began every day by making a fresh fruit yogurt smoothie laced with high caloric powder. I also readied vitamins, minerals, green algae, and Ambrotose, a nutritional supplement. Although he no longer needed the oxygen, a nurse, who was paid for by our insurance, came for two hours to dispense medication.

When the insurance no longer covered the nurse, we hired someone from the Visiting Nurse Association. We always tried to get Val if she was available. During that window of time, I would do errands and take Lily to Welton Road for a run. On the days when we did not have help, Michael would insist I go for my run anyway. Although I would usually submit, I had to fight the chronic fear that some disaster would occur in my absence.

Fortunately, Michael was not scheduled to work on *One Life to Live* for several weeks. Except for trips into the city to see this healer, we stayed in the country, which was where we were when CNN notified us that our *Larry King* interview would be aired. With only three days' warning, we were glad we had put everything in place for the toll-free number. Larry had been so diligent about mentioning the number that we were sure we would bring in huge funds for research.

Much to Marika and Helena's dismay, we refused to cave in to their requests to install cable television. Consequently, we made plans to watch the show down the road at Ric and Susan's. The trip was Michael's first outing since coming home from the hospital, and, as we wheeled him down the newly-installed "boardwalk" and bumped along the gravel to the Jeep, there was finally a sense of celebration. After locking the wheelchair in place, Marika eased him into the passengers seat while Helena collapsed the wheelchair and hefted it into our trunk.

Michael was in great spirits. The show was as informative and moving as we had hoped it would be. Larry seized every opportunity to promote ZazAngels fund-raising. We had been told the 800 number would flash on the screen, and throughout the show we kept waiting. I was nervous, figuring the national ALS Association had flubbed. As the show neared the end, we were both annoyed. Something had clearly gone wrong, and we were missing a great opportunity to raise money for research. While it was great that Larry was announcing the 800 number, viewers needed to *see* a number so that they could write it down and make contributions.

As the show concluded and went to station break, a number finally flashed on the screen—it was not our 800 number. It was the number for the BAA.

Again the ugly politics between the BAA and the ALS Association surfaced. All the time and energy we had spent putting together an 800 number was for naught. The ALS Association reported five telephone calls had come in from a show that had had millions of viewers.

The next morning, Michael was sitting in his wheelchair on the patio when the phone rang. We had been receiving calls all morning from friends across the country, so when a certain healer's wife said that they had seen us on *Larry King*, I thought she was calling to congratulate us like everyone else.

She was not. She was livid, lashing out at us for not acknowledging that Michael's progress was due to treatments with her husband! This healer, she hissed, was devastated by our "selfish," ungrateful behavior. He never wanted to see Michael again.

I was speechless. I felt bad that we had hurt this healer, and I said so. I emphasized how much we valued the treatments, explaining that we had no control over what had been cut from the show. While this was true, it was not the reason we had not publicly endorsed this healer.

"Let me speak to him," I said. "I can explain."

"No!" she barked. "He is canceling your session tomorrow."

"Please!" I begged. "I understand how he feels about wanting to be accepted by the medical community. I want that too. So does Michael. I know we can talk this through."

The line went dead. I called back, but no one picked up.

I was in tears. I went outside and told Michael. Although we did not understand how this healer's touch worked, we both believed in the power of his healing. Michael was looking forward to the next treatment; we had even discussed increasing the frequency of the treatments.

My husband shot me a steely look and pounded his reply onto the computer. "He can go to hell. He's a fake, and he's just proved it."

I am not sure this healer was a fake. But I am sure he is not a healer. To deny treatment to a terminally ill patient because of a bruised ego is not compatible with the Hippocratic oath or the rigors of the scientific community whose inclusion he claimed to be seeking. On the other hand, this healer's behavior was not so very different from the highly touted, Dr. D who stopped returning Michael's calls because we pressed him about Lyme disease.

Disappointed that our appearance on *The Larry King Show* had raised almost no money for ALS research, we focused our energy on our three fund-raisers—the first of which took place in Washington, Connecticut, on August 15. Thanks to the generosity of Michael's former tennis pal, Pete Gurney, ZazAngels was designated the recipient of funds raised at a production of *Love Letters*, starring James Earl Jones and his wife, Cici Hart.

The gala evening was also Michael's first public appearance in a wheelchair. *Love Letters* had a special meaning for us because we had performed it together on several occasions. Michael was nervous about sitting in the audience; afraid he would have a coughing fit and disrupt the show; afraid he would weep uncontrollably. We waited in the wings with the actors until the lights went out, then I wheeled him to the side of the front row so that, if he began to cough, I could wheel him out.

I can only imagine what he was feeling, afraid of coughing, repeating the lines he had once spoken inside his head. Intermission presented another first. We learned something that was the rule rather than the exception: there are no toilets for disabled people backstage at the theater.

We managed. The second act was easier, James Earl Jones and Cici Hart were fabulous, and, by the time we gathered on the terrace for a champagne reception organized by our friends Teresa Hargrave and Ric and Susan, Michael was in top form. I watched him greet people with his augmented voice computer. He was a natural politician, never more alive than when he was connecting with people. I was invigorated too. There was so much we would be able to accomplish for people with ALS—for people with disabilities. How often does life present one with such an opportunity?

As always, enthusiasm and support strengthened our resolve to win. I think if Michael could have gone to parties every night, he would have had an easier time battling depression. While I was not the social creature he was, I was improving. That warm summer night, everything again seemed possible.

Brynn was back in Los Angeles orchestrating SOS 4 ALS, the first ever ALS event held at Yankee Stadium. Michael and I focused on ZazAngels' Broadway Theater Benefit. We had the good fortune of hiring a tireless, dedicated event planner, Barbi Zakin, and began soliciting corporations for donations. Several other fund-raising opportunities cropped up. Through Michael's friend and colleague Ron Raines, a dinner and auction were scheduled for November 15 at the Reception House in the New York area. The Coria family, who owned the Reception House, donated and organized everything. In addition, the Connecticut contingent of ZazAngels was sponsoring a fund-raiser at the home of Rose and William Styron in early December. We were definitely moving forward.

*   *   *

I feel myself slipping every day. It is very hard, in the face of evidence, that my body is at war with itself, and the skirmish is relentless. I am drooling uncontrollably. Handkerchiefs are no longer enough. S went to William Sonoma and brought me a stack of colorful dishtowels. When I laugh spittle flies. I know that this is unseemly, but that is what this most devastating, humiliating disease is all about. It lays waste to dignity, and it's a constant struggle to fight to hold on to at least that.

I drooled all over Marika's computer keyboard. I felt so bad. She said something that made me laugh, and the spittle flew. She felt embarrassed for me, I know.

*   *   *

Since the spring of 1997 when Michael lost his job, I had joked about the metaphysical challenge of so much laundry. With mountains of Michael's soiled clothes, I had the opportunity for speedy enlightenment. Because of his drooling, we sometimes went through six or more outfits a day. We had a washer and dryer in Connecticut, and it was easy to toss clothes in the washer while listening to Mendelsohn or Bach. Michael was amused when I opined that doing the laundry (as opposed to sending it out or shelling out two dollars a load in our New York building) was keeping us financially solvent. I realized there was a cognitive distortion there somewhere, but we never drove to Connecticut without bulging bags stuffed between Marika and Helena and Willy, Lily, and Lucky. Once Michael returned to work and our economic situation was not as dire, I continued the laundry bit because it always got a laugh from him since I am not known for proficiency in the domestic area.

Another surefire way to get a laugh was when I peeled off a dirty shirt—as I did many times a day. I would violently wad up the dirty article and hurl it ferociously into the hamper as if it were a bomb that would blast ALS off the earth. Laughter, rare as it was, was our link to love and sanity.

We were determined that he would regain his strength and walk. But until that happened, we decided to purchase a motorized wheelchair so he could be more independent. The board of our New York co-op installed a ramp on the steep steps that led from the street to the lobby. While it was not ideal in that we had to call ahead every time Michael wanted to go outside, it was the only solution, and it did, finally, afford him some degree of autonomy. For the first time since going back to work, Michael could travel to the studio on his own.

Because of Michael's trip to the hospital, Marika and I had postponed our trip to Ohio to clean out my Dad's house. Knowing the ordeal was hanging over my head, Brynn offered to fly out and stay with Michael and Helena. We carted clothes to the Salvation Army and crates of books to the Lebanon Public Library. We worked like Trojans, but there was something cathartic in emptying closets and drawers, and, for all the hard work, we had a good time.

As always, returning home to Michael was jarring. It was as if I developed amnesia when I was away from him, forgetting that he was not that man anymore. When Marika and I walked in to our apartment, he was sitting on the couch next to Brynn. I had been looking forward to seeing him, but his gaunt face and fierce, unblinking stare threw me off kilter. I was shocked. How could I have forgotten in such a short time?

My body stiffened involuntarily and I girded myself. I answered his computerized "Welcome home," with a flat, cold reply that mortified me. I saw hurt in his eyes and disbelief in Brynn's. I felt sick inside, weak and inadequate. I needed a magician in my life.

I headed for our bedroom noticing that the French doors in the hallway had been removed. They had become a major obstacle to Michael, now that he was using the motorized wheelchair. I had known the doors were in the way but had been unable to face the reality. Brynn had arranged for them to be taken down and stored. Their absence evoked a sense of irrevocable despair. I thanked Brynn for doing what I could not bring myself to do, but the sick, ineffectual feeling struck me every time I walked down the hall where our beautiful doors had been.

Communication between Michael and me was kept to a minimum of necessities. Anything beyond that required too much effort. Because of the demands of work and the time-consuming medical treatments, sometimes I learned more about what was going on inside his head when I listened to a computerized recording laid down for an interview such as this, which was made for *Soap Opera Weekly.*

I am blessed to be working with the gifted head writer, Pam Long, who in addition to her manifold accomplishments, has written speeches for Stephen Hawking. So there is a serendipitous authenticity in the portrayal of my character.

A recent episode chronicled an event similar to one that actually happened to me at the rude hands of an employee at a neighborhood deli. Even though I had programmed my computer to begin with a statement that I was speech impaired and using a speech device on which I must type, I was hung up on three times, and the third time I was called a "yutz," which I believe is Yiddish for "dummy." I have also programmed in an instant message that I can hear perfectly well, given that many people assume that because I cannot speak, I must be either deaf or mentally challenged—or both—and shout at me, gesturing wildly at the same time.

We never know what fate has in store for us. What's made the biggest impression on me is the reaction of friends. It seems they all expected I would respond the way I have. Admittedly, a good portion, if not all, of my apparent bravery, stems from my belief and intention that I am going to beat ALS. I told a therapist that I had always wanted to be the center of attention, to which she replied, "But not like this." I responded, through my tears, that I didn't know. Who among us knows his shadowy motives? Be careful what you wish for.

*　　　*　　　*

Following Brynn's lead, I hired someone to rearrange our bedroom furniture and move the bed inside the door so Michael could ride in on his scooter, swing alongside, and, with Herculean effort, roll onto the bed himself. The preferred procedure, of course, was to ring for help, but my husband was not one to relinquish his independence without a battle.

We tried to view the motorized chair not as the end of Michael's mobility, but as a temporary aid. Five days in the hospital had set him back, but he and Tony Hearns were more determined than ever to get him walking. The great advantage to the chair was that we no longer lived in constant fear of the heart-stopping crashes that signified another fall.

One evening in late summer, I was in the kitchen tidying up when a crash fractured the peaceful silence. I dropped everything and ran.

By the time I reached our bedroom, Helena was kneeling beside her dad who was sprawled on the floor. He had tried to get out of bed on his own and had fallen, hitting his head on the edge of the bureau. There was no blood, but he was rubbing his head with a silly grin on his face.

I placed my hand on the huge knot that had already formed. He shook his head, looking bemused, then confused. He motioned for the ubiquitous, yellow legal pad and wrote, "Why can't I speak?"

Marika appeared in the doorway. We all gaped at him. He looked happy, his face so completely relaxed that he seemed like his old non-ALS self. Panicked, I ran to the kitchen and telephoned Jay who told me to measure exactly where the lump was in order to determine if there was brain damage.

When I returned, Helena had helped her dad into a sitting position, holding him steady so that he would not flop over. He was still smiling as I bent over him, and I placed two fingers between the lump and his ear as Jay had directed. I ran back to the phone and reported the results to Jay. I could hear the relief in his voice. The lump was not in a critical area. He reassured me that Michael's memory would be restored within the hour.

Helena and I helped him back into bed. He looked quizzically at the motorized wheelchair and then at me. His looked implied, "What the heck is that doing here?" He clearly recognized us because he smiled happily as we plumped his pillows. A very large part of me wished he could stay just as he was in that moment.

28

MAKING EGGS WITH MY DAD

Making eggs with my dad was my Sunday morning ritual in Connecticut. Ever since Dad got sick, we didn't do nearly as many activities together, like reading, sports, or making eggs. Making eggs may seem like a very random thing to do, but it was a morning activity for us. My dad, not the best chef, made the best eggs: eggs of all different kinds, scrambled, fried, soft-boiled, hard-boiled, and so on and so forth. But once sick, he stopped making those eggs of his, and it was never brought up.

My mother and my sister had to go into the city one evening when the air was disgustingly humid, and the roses on the trellis were still blooming. I have a vivid memory of that night, walking down the path to wave goodbye and walking back into the house where my father was waiting for me in the breezeway in his wheelchair. "Wheel me into the living room, please," he scribbled on the notepad in his lap. I groaned.

"Why?" I whined. He shrugged and bent over the pad again.

"Because I want to spend some time with you," was his written reply. I nodded and wheeled his chair up the ramp into the living room, adjoining the kitchen. I swerved the chair around facing the couch and plopped down as he started to write something again.

"Are you hungry? Do you want something?" he wrote.

"No." I paused. "Actually, could we make eggs?"

A smile appeared on his face, which said the answer was a definite yes. I prepared everything in the kitchen, and then I wheeled him out. A feeling of sadness flooded through me because I thought of the old times when we could make our eggs without going through the hassle of setting the wheelchair up so that it was lined up to the stove the right way. Or making sure he was propped up enough, and then checking to see if he was all right every now and then. But that feeling faded away, and the feeling that

191

replaced it was happiness. I was happy that we were doing something important to him, and to me—something that I had thought had been forgotten forever.

I had thought things could never be the same, but suddenly the atmosphere changed from a deep hole of sickness and death to a loving atmosphere, where everything felt like home. We both felt it. As much as this sounds crazy, making those eggs meant a lot to both of us.

—Helena Hufford-Zaslow, daughter (12)

Michael worried constantly about the effect his illness was having on the children. Helena was going into seventh grade and Marika would be in tenth grade, which was known to be an academic killer at Trinity School. We hoped that returning to school and to friends would provide them with some respite from the war zone that was our home.

The new boardwalk made access to the house easier, but watching Marika and Helena wheel him out, it was hard to imagine coming to Roxbury once bad weather set in. As the three of us maneuvered him from the chair into the car, I knew he was thinking the same thing. When would he see his beloved home again?

The only way I could deal with the future was by juggling my obsessive focus on domestic details with my denial. When did Helena see the orthodontist? When was Michael's next checkup at Johns Hopkins? Had I given Lily the heartworm pill last month? Did I possibly give her two? I lost track, or thought I did, when I counted out Michael's vitamins and pills for the week. Sometimes I recounted them several times. There were so many balls in the air, and my mind was scattered in so many different directions that it was hard to convince myself I knew what I was doing, so I would recount the pills and vitamins again, to be sure.

The logistics of travel, of disassembling the motorized wheelchair, of rounding up Willy, Lily, and Lucky, of loading medical equipment, including the Shealy glasses, meditation tapes, children's gear, computers, violins, leftover food, vitamins, and pills was daunting. And it all had to be repeated at the other end.

Our cat, Lucky, a decent chap until someone tried to comb him, was a matted mess of a silver Persian. Huge clumps of hair, some as large as a baby kitten, hung off his body, pulling painfully at his pink skin. He would not even let Marika, who could do anything to him, go near him with the comb. Predictably, when he saw the car being packed up, as we were almost ready, Lucky vanished.

Under normal circumstances this was annoying, but, with everyone crammed in to the Jeep, Lucky's wayward behavior pushed us all closer to the edge.

Michael typed an irate digital command. "Leave the ingrate!"

Marika began to cry, "You can't just leave him!"

Helena added fuel, "Dad's right. He deserves it."

"He's my cat!" cried Marika.

"He's not your cat!" Helena screamed. "He's both of our cat."

"Oh shut up, Helena. You don't even like him."

"I do so!" Helena added her own tears to the melodrama.

I tuned out the rising hysteria. My stomach tightened in anticipation of lugging the contents out of the Jeep once we got back to the city. It made sense to order out Chinese food so the children could maybe get to bed at a decent hour.

"*Stop!*" Michael had turned the volume up on the computer. Lily looked terrified, as she always did when there was conflict. She rolled her spaniel eyes at me, plagued by her highly evolved sense of responsibility. If only she had done something, could this family crisis have been averted?

Willy, our elderly silver sage was curled up in the driver's seat patiently waiting for me to get in the car so he could go to sleep on my lap, which is where he rode. Will had seen everything in his nineteen years with us, and he conveyed utter confidence in me as he gazed up. "You know how Lucky is. Don't worry. It'll all work out. Let's get going so I can start my nap and get home for supper."

I ran around the house calling for Lucky while Marika went inside, looked under beds, got a can of cat food, and began clanging on it with a spoon. I knew perfectly well he was not going to show up. I promised Marika I would drive up the next day and pick him up and then went in the house and telephoned Ric who said he would come up around dark and put Lucky inside. In all likelihood, he would surface as soon as he saw the car drive down the driveway. Someone leaned on the car horn, but I took an extra minute to make one last phone call to Zoom and Groom and schedule Lucky to be shaved.

I couldn't figure out how I was going to squeeze in a trip to Roxbury the next day, since the following day, September 9, Michael had to be in Washington for the 17th Annual Communication Awards and the day after that Helena had to be up and ready for seventh grade orientation. We had not even written his speech, let alone programmed it into his computer. Ric would have to leave three days worth of food for Lucky, and I would drive up Thursday after Helena got off to school. A resentful silence permeated the car, but at least it was quiet and I could play out various moves in what felt like a diabolical chess game. I thought of how we used to drive into the city singing. Now none of us wanted to be where we were, except Willy, who snored peacefully on my lap the whole way.

I succumbed to Marika's pleas to bring *poor* Lucky home and drove to Roxbury the next morning. It was a splendid day. I was grateful to the errant rascal for affording me the gift of an unexpected walk on Welton Road with Lily and an hour stretched out on our patio.

When I arrived home, Michael was working on his speech with the help of Barry and Iris. By one that night, we were in bed, and then I was up at 6 AM to drive Helena to an orthodontist appointment before school. Michael had physical therapy with Tony at noon, and at 3 PM a car picked us up to take us to the airport for a 5 PM shuttle flight to Washington. The Communication Awards began at 7:30, and we knew we were cutting it short.

Everything ran smoothly; the flight arrived on time at Reagan Airport, and our car was waiting. Michael was transferred from the airline wheelchair into the car, and we weaved seamlessly through rush hour traffic to The John F. Kennedy Center for the Performing Arts.

We were sprung for a night and looking forward to time alone. It was a gorgeous warm evening, and, after the awards, we had only to go next door to the Watergate Hotel where we were meeting our good friends, Byron Kennard and Glenn Pindar, as well as Michael's godsister's son, Mark Hodge. I knew by his easy smile that Michael was anticipating our brief vacation as much as I was. We had fond memories of the Kennedy Center. Earlier in our relationship, Michael had appeared here in *Cat on a Hot Tin Roof* with Elizabeth Ashley. When Marika was three, he returned to play one of his favorite roles, Shostakovich in *The Master Class.*

I got out of the car and looked for the person who was supposed to be waiting with another wheelchair. The esplanade surrounding the colonnaded edifice was deserted. I sat down in the backseat next to Michael and waited a few minutes, hoping I would not have to go jogging around in my high heels to find our escort.

"What time is it?" Michael's computer voice asked.

"I better go find someone!" I replied. The minutes ticked by as I sprinted around the monolithic structure trying to find the stage door. When I finally found it, it was locked. I charged back toward the car, aware that I was perspiring and that our leeway was shrinking. As I reached the car, someone finally appeared with a wheelchair. Now we really were in a rush.

Our tardy wheelchair driver went to find the person assigned to help Michael. When he was out of earshot, Michael's digital voice said, "I have to find a bathroom."

There then ensued the most unbelievable odyssey, a search for a handicapped toilet in a public building of our nation's capitol. Hadn't they put together that since Michael needed a wheelchair, he could not walk? The grandmotherly lady assigned to help us had no idea if there was a toilet for disabled people and went off to ask someone else. Michael and I looked at each other. He did not need to type a message on the computer. This was urgent.

I scooted around opening doors and found two options, both of which were inaccessible with the wheelchair. As a flustered contingent, commandeered by our grandmotherly helper, ran toward us, a voice over the public address system announced that the curtain was going up. Michael looked panicked and absolutely livid.

Amidst heartfelt apologies, we were shown to a bathroom. I bit my tongue as I wheeled him to a narrow door smack off the congested hall. Someone held the door open as I maneuvered the wheelchair inside a miniscule cubicle. There was scarcely room for one person. I shoved the wheelchair against the toilet and climbed over Michael to help him. For once, my small size was an asset, and I wriggled and squeezed so that I would have leverage to lift him. People could be heard scuttling up and down the hall; every conversation was as distinct as if they were all in the cubicle with us. I whispered. If I could hear them, they could certainly hear us. Michael was in a state of impatient agony, and we were mad as hornets. But what could we do? We managed.

I opened the door a discreet crack and slipped out to give him a slim measure of privacy. I scowled at everyone as I stood guard, waiting for him to signal me. The incident was absurd, but par for the course. The oversight, albeit human, was especially alarming since the evening was sponsored by people who were devoted to those with special needs. If *they* were oblivious to such basics, how blind was the rest of the world?

An amazing lightness swept over us as I wheeled Michael, following behind our grandmotherly guide who led us backstage where we could view the show. Michael was to receive the Annie Glenn Award, presented to an individual who has a communication problem and who serves as an inspiration to others. His was the final award, in what promised to be a very long evening.

Standing in the dark and hushed theater wings, I suddenly felt safe, as if I had come home. Released from not having to speak, I relaxed into just being. As theater professionals, we accepted that talking backstage was not only rude to fellow actors, but virtually sacrilegious. Except for a few whispers and occasional cues by the stage manager, we were enveloped in a familiar shadowy silence. I was transported back to earlier days in *Fiddler on the Roof* at New York's Broadway Theater. I'm certain Michael felt as liberated, as protected, as I did. In silence we were equal. Eventually, he pulled me onto his lap, and I sat with his arms wrapped around me. The simplicity of our past was reborn. Words were really not necessary. There had always been something more, and there still was.

Brynn's SOS 4 ALS at Yankee Stadium was slated for September 12, 1998, and, as soon as we returned from Washington, she began prepping us. We had been so focused on work, press, and the early December Broadway Theater benefit, that we had not realized what a Cecil B. deMille extravaganza she and her intrepid assistant, Kristie Miller, had created.

"You will need to get plenty of rest," Brynn alerted Michael. "It's going to be a long day!" And that was just the beginning.

"A van equipped to transport you, your family, and the electric chair will pick you up at 9 AM. I've hired a terrific guy, Paul Donevan. His mother had ALS. He'll be with you from start to finish. You need anything—ask Paul. After the game, you'll be driven back home. You'll have three hours to rest before being picked up for the party at the All State Café with press and the Yankees!"

According to Brynn's specifications, the day dawned September crisp and perfect. Paul appeared at our apartment at the appointed time and helped disassemble and reassemble the electric wheelchair and load other paraphernalia onto the van. I felt pounds lighter with Paul baring the brunt of the labor and blessed Brynn for putting this particular piece in place. Marika and Helena were excited; we were all off duty, at liberty to enjoy the day with Michael.

We climbed into a large, well-worn van driven by an ample, jolly angel, Darryl, who owned the vehicle. Our first stop was the pre-game brunch, which was held at an elegant midtown French restaurant off of Fifth Avenue. As the van pulled up, Brynn, in a blue and white striped SOS 4 ALS Yankees shirt, flew towards us as if she had sprouted wings.

A cheer went up as Michael wheeled into the restaurant. We were totally flabbergasted. The place was packed, wall to wall with friends and colleagues from *All My Children, Another World, As the World Turns, Guiding Light* and, of course, *One Life to Live*. Wearing SOS 4 ALS Yankee shirts, they pounded ball gloves, raring to go. Michael Park, Grant Aleksander, Beth Ehlers, Rebecca Budig, Michael O'Leary, Robin Strasser, Bob Wood, Nathan Purdee, Gina Tognoni, Michael Lowry, Kelly Ripa, and, of course, our dear Krim, were but a few of the fifty stars who donated, not only their time to raising ALS awareness but their hearts as well.

If we could have bottled the vitality and optimism in that room, I think we could have found the cure that day. I had to nudge Michael away from socializing with friends he had not seen in a long while so he could enjoy the sumptuous buffet. Once he dug in, I filled his plate three times, and he didn't choke once.

Michael was a baseball lover. His team was the Brooklyn Dodgers. One evening, years earlier, we attended some large Hollywood function where he glimpsed Duke Snyder. Jumpy with adolescent excitement, he dragged me through the crowd to shake the former Dodger's hand. He told me later it was a dream come true. Being honored at Yankee Stadium in the first ALS event since Lou Gehrig's day must have been beyond thrilling for him.

As a prelude to the SOS 4 ALS pre-game, our family, together with PALS Chris Prendergast and Mark Reyman, were driven around the outfield. The stadium stretched upwards; fans, friends, everyone else seemed to exist in some other distant world. The cart was electric, and there was a calm silence as we glided around the razor flat green turf past colorful billboards, on what seemed to be a surreal, timeless journey. I was glad that I was wearing sunglasses. It was the first of many moments in this long day that my eyes filled with tears. Lou Gehrig. Chris Prendergast. Mark Ryman. Pat Pepper. Judy Wilson. Michael Zaslow. Catfish Hunter. How long would it be till we discovered a cure for this damned ugly disease?

We sat in the dugout cheering the daytime players as they fielded and batted. By the time the pre-game was over, the stadium was filled to capacity, and the crowd was wild with Yankee mania.

The omnipotent voice, familiar to baseball fans, boomed out over the public address system about the significance of SOS 4 ALS and acknowledged Michael for bringing more awareness to ALS than anyone since Lou Gehrig. Together with Dorine Gordon and John Ernst of the ALS Association of Greater New York, Michael motored onto the field to accept a $40,000 check for ALS research, contributed by ABC. The commanding voice directed our attention to the giant screen above the field. I had been aware that Brynn was collaborating with a filmmaker in LA on a five-minute film depicting

Michael's struggle, but neither of us knew it would be shown at Yankee Stadium.

Despite the clamoring for the game to start, thousands of Yankee fans watched in rapt silence, bearing witness to Michael's physical decline, his humor, courage, and determination to win the battle against ALS. The stadium erupted in a loud cheer, and, a few moments later, with the cheering for Michael at its peak, the winning Yankee team ran onto the field.

My husband had been assigned the honor of throwing out the first ball. Sensitive to the disabilities of PALS, word came back that Derek Jeter would help Michael throw out the ball. Michael shook his head adamantly, waving his good arm, groaning in protest. He was a leftie, and his left hand still worked. There was no way he was not going to throw out the ball himself.

Marika and Helena and I were sitting with him on the cart, and I watched the faces of the Yankees as Michael mustered all of his remaining strength. Derrick Jeter moved closer to make it easier. Michael waved him back. He threw the ball hard, harder than anybody expected.

The three hours Brynn had allotted for rest was barely enough for an IV drip, a nutrient-packed smoothie, and a passel of vitamins. Everything always took longer than expected, and, by the time Michael was combed and dressed, we were running an hour behind. It was nearly nine o'clock when Darryl's van let us out in front of the All Star Café. We were all exhausted, but the minute Michael got inside and the crowd—which included a table full of Yankees—began to cheer, he rallied. At the top of his form, he gave a vigorous thumbs-up to the photographers. The fatigue vanished; he was smiling and laughing his ALS laugh, typing like crazy on his voice machine and having a marvelous time.

Less than a week later, we were off to Philadelphia for another public appearance. Even though Michael had a doctor's appointment the same day, he told Ellyn Phillips, who headed the Philly ALS Chapter, he would come if she would provide us with a car and driver.

It was another long day, but somehow the long days, with the two of us, were the easiest. Just as the shadowy hush backstage insulated us from the inevitable terrifying thoughts about the future, so too the cushiony back seat of the limousine absorbed our fear. Suspended between here and there, we were remarkably happy—reading, writing notes, listening to music, and munching on this and that.

Ellyn Phillips, whose husband died of ALS, and Dorine Gordon, who lost her mother to the disease, greeted us as the limousine pulled up to the high-tech movie theater complex. We shifted Michael into his wheelchair, and the place, which was packed with fans, erupted at the sight of him. There was a carnival atmosphere, and everyone was eating hot dogs. His mind was never far from the next meal, and, being especially fond of hot dogs, his digital voice made a ravenous request the minute we were inside. Dorine returned with a mustard and sauerkraut slathered hot dog, and Michael grabbed it with his good left hand and took a bite. Immediately he began choking and coughing. My heart went to my throat, and both Ellyn and Dorine looked stricken, remembering all too well the terror of choking.

"What can we do?" Ellyn's helpless question mirrored my own. "I can't remember what to do!"

I saw the panic in Michael's eyes as the coughing continued.

Where would it lead? Another trip to another hospital? Everyone with ALS lived in dread of choking.

But this time, the moment passed. After several minutes, the coughing subsided enough so that he was able to sip some water with a straw. Ellyn, Dorine, and I were shaky, Michael probably was too, but he pecked out a message on the computer that he was ready to go meet his fans.

For the next three hours, we met and talked with fans and PALS. I met an African-American woman, only nineteen years old, who was still able to speak but who had been wheelchair bound for almost a year. So much for ALS being a disease of late middle age. My eyes told me that younger people were getting sick. Her family was with her, and they all wore the same, hopeful smile that I was wearing. Without words, we all knew each other intimately.

Despite the choking, when it came time to leave, Michael was lobbying for the next meal. I loaded up on food, and Ellyn made sure we had an open bottle of wine, which we enjoyed on the ride back to New York.

The following week was less hectic, just the usual IV therapies, doctor's appointments, and physical therapy sessions with Tony. Michael complained constantly about fatigue, but why wouldn't he be tired, considering our pace for the past month? After choking several more times, Jay ordered a blood gas test, which would reveal exactly how much oxygen Michael was able to take in. Lack of oxygen would account for the increased fatigue, and, if that were the case, Jay would put him on a BiPAP machine to increase his oxygen levels.

He was more irritable than usual and forgot to tell me, or I had neglected to hear, that PBS was coming to our apartment for an interview. I was fed up with invasions, and I was concerned that he was pushing himself far beyond his limit. Paul worked part time, but he was not on duty the day of the PBS interview, and I had appointments in my office. I changed my appointments and helped Michael dress for the interview, but I was in a foul mood.

It felt like no matter how much I chanted, I could not contain my anger and resentment. I especially could not tolerate the happiness and *joie de vivre* of certain couples. Friends, people I truly liked, felt close to, and shared fun with, suddenly appeared arrogant, blind, insensitive, and selfish. On occasion they became targets of my rage. I was all too aware that insulting people who were trying to support us was not helpful, but the jibes spilled out anyway. My Buddha nature was critically challenged; I mostly lived in the world of anger.

29

BEFORE THE REAL FLOOD

Before the real flood comes
I want to take you on board my ark.
See the sights-
Hidden caves beneath the rocky surface
Where we used to dwell
Safe among stalactites
Walls rich with Paleolithic paintings
Calm pools where we would swim
And breathe
Our laughter ringing beneath the sea.
I do not know if the ark will stand against the tide.
If Noah can be resurrected in time.
I do not know if my feet will touch the floor
When I climb down from my perch in the morning
Or if there are enough animals
To populate a new world, a new beginning.
Before the real flood comes
I want to take you on board my ark
I want to rescue you from the silence,
And myself too.
I want to return to the water cave beneath the sea
Where we were safe among stalactites
Walls rich with Paleolithic paintings,
Calm pools where we could swim
And breathe
Our laughter ringing beneath the sea.

—S. Hufford

The balls I juggled felt more like meteors. When I woke Michael each
morning, I saw the agony in his eyes. I could not know precisely what he was
thinking—how deep and far his fear ran. Sometimes I would come into our

201

bedroom with the morning nutritional smoothie to find him on his side, grasping the far side of the bed with his good left hand, his face red from straining as he exerted every ounce of will and strength to roll over. Turning over by himself became a major accomplishment. We had put Marika in the middle of the same bed when she was five months old, waiting breathlessly to witness her newly acquired skill, which, until then, she had only managed in the privacy of her crib. How we cheered when we finally saw her roll over. What an accomplishment that was.

On September 24, our Marika turned sixteen, and, the following Sunday, our home was full of guests of all ages to celebrate. Even as a toddler, Marika befriended adults as often as children, so our apartment was bursting with her friends from Trinity and grownups, family friends, teachers from Trinity, and, to our great delight, her violin teacher, Louise Behrend. Ric and Susan drove in from Connecticut; Steve Yates arrived with one-year-old Madison who was Michael's goddaughter. And, of course, the crowd included our next-door neighbors, Diane Lesser and Richard Pollen and their daughters, Julia and Rachel, who were, and still are, like sisters to Marika and Helena. It was a joyous celebration in all ways but one. I was no longer terrified of hearing a crash signifying Michael had fallen. Instead, I was hearing a new silence. There wasn't a moment that I was not aware of the unfathomable silence that engulfed him, even when he was engaged and wearing his ALS smile. Wherever his electric motor chair took him, this silence moved with him. I could feel it even if I wasn't looking.

We have received many blessings in our life, and many of them have come in the form of people Michael worked with and befriended with his warmth and generosity. Sherry Stringfield, one of several actresses who played his—Roger's—daughter on *Guiding Light* and later went on to star in *ER* was and is one of those blessings. Fresh out of college when she joined the cast, Michael appointed himself a stand-in for Sherry's father who lives in Texas. Despite her active social and professional life, Sherry became a part of our family and even found time to baby-sit for Marika, who adored her.

A few months earlier, Sherry had telephoned to say she had found the one! She and Larry Josephs, who received Michael's thumbs up the moment they met, were to be married on October 17, and they wanted Marika to be one of two bridesmaids. In the midst of so much sadness, Marika was elevated into a state of bliss. A sixteen-year-old bridesmaid! Who wouldn't be excited? Michael wept with happiness at the news.

As Sherry's wedding day approached, we continued our search for an apartment that would accommodate Michael's disability and allow our lives to run more smoothly. Enormous effort was required to get Michael dressed, into the electric chair, down the ramp, and finally out onto the street. Having at last achieved a degree of independence he would then shoot full speed ahead in the direction of our destination as I ran to catch up. But he remained game, and, when we saw a large elegant space only two blocks down the street from our building he typed, "Let's go for it!" The place required a major renovation before we could move in. I vacillated between excitement at having a fabulous home with enough room for everyone and a flat lobby so Michael could come and go as he wished and trepidation about how I could fit one more thing into my life. Looking back, I think I was out of touch with reality to even consider such a move. Still, I had to believe we could create an easier life, and I wanted to believe, and did believe, that we had time, that our life would improve once we figured out how to live with ALS.

I was more relieved than disappointed when our lawyer notified us she had found a "not insurmountable but costly" legal detail. We decided not to go forward but immediately saw another apartment in the same flat-lobbied building. Michael loved it even more. Again our lawyer moved toward a closing. I stretched my schedule to meet with contractors and poured over their bids. The numbers were scary. Michael, as always, was confident.

For weeks we researched electric wheelchairs and finally decided on a fire engine red Amiga. The chair was delivered in time for Sherry's wedding. The nuptials were to take place at the historical St. Joseph's Church in Greenwich Village—unfortunately for us—at ten-thirty in the morning.

Mornings were the worst. There was the inevitable depression upon waking, followed by the arduous tasks of eating, dressing, and getting underway. As a member of the wedding party, Marika left early, so Helena and I worked together to get Michael ready. Helena was far more deft than me. She knew exactly how to pull his socks on, how to balance his body, and how to ease him into the wheelchair, and, unlike me with my dyslexia, she was a whiz at taking the electric chair battery out and collapsing the chair so it would fit in the trunk of our Jeep. However, for this special occasion, we had wisely opted not to drive and had hired Darryl to deliver us to the church and pick us up later.

Regrettably, I was not wise enough to engage Paul to help. Michael was more on edge than usual; he groaned in disapproval when Helena held up the mirror so he could brush his hair. He was angry at me for not helping him brush his teeth. I had forgotten. How could I forget? Didn't I know even with

ALS he had to brush his teeth? There was a spot on his jacket; he wasn't sure the battery to the electric chair was charged, and it took him longer to take his vitamins. We arrived outside the church to find the steps were so steep that there was no way we could get inside.

Sherry's mother, amazingly composed under the circumstances—the organ was playing another chorus of something—located the custodian and showed us to a tiny rickety freight elevator. It was another tight squeeze for the chair, but we made it, entering the sanctuary from the nave, minutes before the priest walked out. Michael parked, and Helena and I sat behind him in the front row. He always had a knack for getting the best seat in the house.

He looked amazingly handsome and relaxed now that we had finally made it. I wished I were sitting next to him so I could take his hand and make up for my many oversights. Tears are an expected addition to the joys of a wedding, and I myself was prepared to shed a few. When Marika walked down the aisle holding her bridesmaid's bouquet, I teared up.

Michael let out a deep plaintive moan. At first I was worried that people would be upset, frightened by such a primitive outburst. Helena stiffened as another sound erupted from her dad.

I knew he was mortified about doing anything that might mar Sherry's wedding, but I knew he couldn't help it. Sherry appeared on her dad's arm at the top of the aisle, and Michael emitted another sound and then another. Sherry looked straight at him with her biggest Sherry grin, and I knew that it was all right. It was more than all right. Michael was a musician who could no longer sing or play the piano. His soulful interludes continued throughout the ceremony, accenting Sherry and Larry's beautiful wedding.

30

"HELLO BEAUTIFUL!"

The phone would ring, and, when I picked up, there would be a pause, then a click before a digital voice said, "Hello Beautiful! What are you doing tonight? Want to go on the town?" And I would say... "Wait a minute, who is this?" There would be another pause as he programmed the computer. I could almost feel him laughing.

—*Susan Monseurd, friend, Connecticut neighbor*

Leaving the church was even more daunting than getting inside, and the short walk down narrow cobblestone streets to the wedding brunch at the Waverly Inn was grueling in the hot sun. Not only was the new chair a bit too wide for the sidewalks, demanding an expertise in steering that was impossible, but there was traffic and each intersection presented a terrifying moment as Michael bumped down off of the curb. The rest of the wedding party had gone ahead, and, at every crossing, I held my breath, praying the Amiga would not tip over. Michael thought I was exaggerating the danger, but he could not see how the chair wobbled. Finally, I couldn't stand seeing him bump down another curb, and, for the rest of the way, I walked down the center of the street, waving my arms to fend off oncoming cars with Michael motoring ahead of me.

We arrived hot, sweaty, and thirsty. The champagne was flowing, and, after puzzling out the logistics of getting Michael and the chair inside, we relaxed into the festivities. We were actually enjoying ourselves like regular people! I was reminded how much fun we had together, relishing simple pleasures—a gorgeous day, a breeze, great Italian food, good people. It occurred to me that maybe we had made the wrong decision devoting all of our time and energies to ALS. Sitting at an outside café was something at which we had always excelled.

Our bid on the second apartment was accepted, and, once again, the night before we were to sign the contract, I got cold feet. Michael was furious with me. *He* needed more space! It wasn't just about me. He accused me of taking advantage of him, making unilateral decisions, and ignoring his wishes. I was selfish and cold and did not understand!

Arguing was more of a challenge now that he could no longer write legibly. He scrawled large unwieldy letters on the yellow pads, sometimes no more than two words per page. I felt weak and ridiculous for going to the wire with yet another real estate deal. I said I was sorry, but I just couldn't bring myself to take it on.

Then why had I dragged him around looking at apartments? I was again the enemy, and, to my deep regret, I could not take it even though I understood where it was coming from. I flared, saying that he was using his disability as a weapon. It was insulting and untrue to be accused of not taking him into consideration when my entire life revolved around trying to make things better. I sobbed, and he pounded out a message that I was playing the martyr. I countered that martyrs suffered in silence, and I was a loud, complaining bitch and said what was on my mind. I was definitely not a martyr!

Martyr, I looked it up in the dictionary. Shoving the book in front of him I read: "*Martyr*, one who voluntarily suffers death rather than renounce one's religion or principles."

It was true, I was voluntarily taking on suffering, but did that make me a martyr? Under the circumstances, how could I not suffer? When I wheeled him into the bathroom and helped him, how could I not suffer? I hated the idea of being a martyr—the label had a pejorative connotation that I couldn't abide. His saying it made me determined to prove him wrong.

People with ALS get left, I told him. It was true. In many cases the disease was so demanding and exasperating that marriages broke, families were shattered, and PALS were left. This was particularly the case when the PAL was a woman.

Confrontations such as this made me sick with guilt, exacerbating all my feelings of inadequacy. I should have been able to make things right—if not perfect—at least easier than they were.

That night he fell again as he was getting into bed. I was alone and could not lift him. I rang for our elevator operator, Dan, a strong sensitive young man from Romania who had picked Michael up on several occasions. I watched how effortlessly he lifted Michael and laid him gently on our bed, wishing I could do the same.

When Dan left, I put the Breath Right tape across the bridge of his nose and adjusted his pillows so he was not lying flat. Of course he was angry. He was almost totally dependent on me.

Several days later, he announced via the computer that he needed to buy a new watch. He had seen one in a store window on Columbus Avenue as he wheeled to the studio. There was no one to go with him, and he fumed. He seemed obsessed with buying this particular watch at this particular moment.

It finally dawned on me that while he was devoted to physical therapy and IV treatments, he was no longer seeing anyone for psychotherapy. With so much going on, I had lost track. When I suggested that his increased negativity and depression might be helped by therapy, he ignored me and said if there wasn't anyone to go with him to buy the watch, he would go alone.

He continued seeing Penney, who came to the house. I was grateful for that because he seemed lighter when she left, but it was not enough. The days that he worked were always more positive, but they were few and far between.

Michael too was weighted with guilt. The illness was taking a toll on everyone, taking up more and more time. Bedtime was a prolonged demanding ordeal, and Marika and Helena had to be enlisted to help. Rarely did anyone get to bed before one or one-thirty. A close friend, sensitive and smart, someone I trusted, made a suggestion that took my breath away. Seeing the stress in our lives, he recommended we hire a full-time nurse and move Michael down the street in a separate apartment. Had anyone else made this suggestion, I would have exploded, but, coming from him, I began to glimpse how desperate our situation was. I felt dizzy and replied there was no way I would ever do that. My angry threats about leaving came from the same source as Michael's threats.

We were in Connecticut the Saturday before Michael's birthday on November 1. There was a birthday celebration at Ric and Susan's and Marika and Helena had gone ahead to help cook. I was to call when we were ready, and Tony would drive up to help me get Michael and the chair into the car. Since he was using the electric chair pretty much all the time, I have no recollection of how it happened, but I have a vivid memory of what followed. Somehow, he fell. He lay next to the couch looking almost bemused. After making sure he wasn't hurt, I stretched out next to him. Over the past two weeks, he had gained strength in his legs. For the first time since being in the hospital, he could stand without support. On one occasion during a treatment with Tony in New York, I walked in and saw him. We were all ecstatic, and Tony and I began trying to figure out how we could strap Michael onto an exercise bike so that he could build up his leg muscles and get a cardiovascular workout.

As we lay on our beautiful cherry floor in Roxbury, I told him we would always remember this moment because this would be the last time he fell. He was getting stronger. I had seen it with my own eyes. He would walk again. It was only a question of time.

31

YOUR LAUGH

You throw back your head and laugh. I love that. You can give bear hugs with both arms, even though that's hard now.

—*Teresa Hargrave, Connecticut friend*

The birthday celebration was fun for everyone but particularly for Michael, who devoured his piled-high plate without once choking. After dinner we played a game where everyone wrote on a piece of paper what we most loved about Michael. The papers were put in a round wood box, which we took home later. Many of the comments centered on Michael's laugh.

Brown and Brownie were my special nicknames for Michael, and I wrote, "Dear Brown, I love most your laugh and where it comes from. So even though it is not the "old" sound—the source, the place it comes from, is there and the source is endless. Also, you are the most competitive person I have ever met, so I am sure you will *always* keep competing until you *win!*"

Thanks to Ron Raines, who played Michael's old nemesis, Alan Spaulding, another fund-raiser was held on November 15. The Supper Benefit and Auction would feature stars from the daytime community. Michael was wired. For the first time in over a year since he had been "let go," he would see colleagues from the show—and they would see him.

As the stars arrived, I waited with Michael in a tiny paper strewn office. Although he had pulled himself out of his last bout of depression, he was pale, his mouth gaped involuntarily, and he swatted at it with one of the many handkerchiefs I had stuffed in his jacket pocket. He was nervous and wanted a mirror to see if his hair was combed. Finally, someone tapped on the door, and, as the band played a fanfare, he shot forth in his red wheelchair. Ron, Maureen Garrett, and a few others had seen him recently, but most people had not laid eyes on him since April 1997, and they were shocked by his gaunt fragility. It was a joyous but tearful reunion as former cast mates stood in line to embrace him. He did not bother to use the talking computer. He held each person, with his eyes speaking with an eloquence that infused the evening with a feeling of gratitude. I especially remember how he held Kim Zimmer in his unwavering gaze, and, although I could not interpret his unspoken communication to her, I am certain she understood every nuance. Thanks to the love and generosity of his friends in daytime, over thirty thousand dollars was raised for ALS research. More important, the evening raised Michael's spirits. When I left with Marika and Helena, who had school the next day, he was still going strong. He held forth until midnight and probably would have stayed longer if Krim and Robin hadn't prevailed.

Partly due to Pat Pepper's enthusiasm for Lyme disease specialist Dr. Joseph Bouriscano, and partly because I had never totally given up on the possibility that there was a Lyme connection to the illness, Michael and I drove to East Hampton for an appointment on November 19. Michael munched on the lunch I had packed and handed me a sandwich to nibble on. With Lily in the backseat, we were on the road again and when we were on the road, life was always good.

Dr. Bouriscano was intrigued by the course of the disease. Blood was taken for tests, and, after a thorough examination, he found Michael's heart strong and the strength on his left side still holding. We spoke with Dr. Bouriscano for over an hour. He was particularly interested in the chills that arrived without fail in the late afternoon. He sent us home with lengthy instructions and charts on which to record Michael's temperatures throughout the day. While he did not give us false hope, he believed there was a chance he could be helpful. We both judged him to be a creative, intelligent physician who was committed to his work on Lyme disease.

It was already dark when we got back into the car. Despite the tiring day and the prospects of a long drive, our spirits were high. Lily had waited patiently all day in the car, so, even though we had to be back in time to attend opening night of Marika's school musical, we drove to a deserted beach. I let Lily out and breathed in the salty autumnal air. Michael watched from the car as Lily cavorted on the deserted moonlit beach, chasing wildly in ecstatic, canine circles.

The following week was Thanksgiving. We had invited Michael's physical therapist, Tony Hearn, and his fiancée, Susan Reardon, to spend the weekend with us in Roxbury. Our friends Ric and Susan were joining us and I was looking forward to what has always been my favorite holiday. Kindly overlooking my militaristic hysteria when I called to practically demand that he build ramps to make Michael's access easier, Marc Olivieri had installed classy ramps into our bedroom and living room. Michael's access was no longer a dreaded chore. He could once again move freely around his own home.

I was optimistic because Michael's temperature readings followed a pattern, which Dr. Bouriscano said would support further investigation into Lyme disease and more prolonged antibiotic treatment. Despite everything, I was feeling thankful.

Michael was feeling something else, and it was not thankful. The weather was November dreary, and he coughed a few times and began fretting about coughing more. This was more than understandable, given the disastrous coughing episode in August, but nothing could lighten his mood. He scarcely acknowledged the existence of the ramps. Even Tony's Irish humor did not have its usual effect. I stayed up late after dinner, preparing for tomorrow's feast, and finally slipped into bed around one o'clock. He was still wearing his Shealy glasses, and, since they had stopped emitting their electronic blinks, I got up and removed them carefully. He seemed to be sleeping peacefully, but every time I would fall asleep he would groan.

Finally, I moved to the loft above our bed, stuffed earplugs in my ears, and put the pillow over my head. Sleep was impossible, and I was already sleep deprived. The groans were erratic—just when I would think they had stopped and was finally drifting off, a grim moan would jolt me awake. In addition, I had a low-pressure headache from the weather and far too much wine.

I got up and loaded up on aspirin. Back in bed, I chanted inside my head and did relaxation exercises, but his groaning jabbed at my nervous system until I thought I would start screaming and never be able to stop. Around dawn, I relocated again and crawled into bed with Helena. My head was pounding, and I had to put the twenty-pound turkey in the oven in three hours.

Thanksgiving dinner is a meal I love to cook; I'm good at it and normally don't even get flustered when the gravy lumps and the turkey slides off the platter. But I was jittery and flustered all day. Michael was in a black mood. At one point, I heard his computerized voice say that it was too hard for him to eat.

The next week, Jay ordered the BiPAP machine, and a medical aide arrived at the apartment to show us how fit the straps over Michael's head and adjust the mouth piece and controls to release the proper amount of oxygen. The aide fumbled with the straps, and I thought that if he couldn't get it right, how could I with my dyslexia manage to without hurting Michael?

And sure enough, every time I tried to strap Michael in, my dyslexia would take over, the tapes would get mangled, and we would both be frustrated. For the next week, we tried to get the BiPAP routine down. Occasionally it was funny, and we would have a much-needed laugh. I felt inept, a total klutz. Finally, Michael decided it wasn't worth the hassle. He was totally convinced that the BiPAP was not helping, and he called to have someone pick it up. It is a decision I deeply regret, and one that haunts me to this day.

I had been putting off my own medical checkups because of time constraints, but mostly because I was nervous. What if something was wrong with me? Always edgy before the annual gynecological exam/mammogram, I was even more anxious. How would we function if I had a problem? I girded myself and was hugely relieved when I got a clean bill of health.

I couldn't wait to get home and tell Michael, who was familiar with my anxiety in this area. He was parked in front of the window in his red electric chair when I burst in. I couldn't wait to raise his spirits by sharing my good news.

He shoved his response, scrawled in pencil on the yellow tablet. I can still see the shape of the letters in my mind. "I'm a goner."

32

GOING MAD AGAIN

I took the over-the-counter sleep material, but it stimulated me and my mind raced all night until it seemed I was going mad again. I had intended to sleep to help restore my flagging spirits. My desk is piled high. I keep thinking about Ohio and what to do with my dad's car and Love Letters *and Marika and Helena and you and IVs. I'm sorry. I want you back so desperately. I'm sorry.*

—*Susan Hufford*

The *g* in goner was larger than the other letters, taking up most of the yellow page. I was furious.

"Aren't you glad I'm okay?" I blurted. "This is good news! I don't have another ovarian cyst; there is not a lump in my breast! We can't stand any more bad news! Can't you be happy for me?"

He willed his paralyzed head to move in a motion of defiance and stabbed the pencil at what he had written.

"Is there something new? Something you haven't told me? You told me what a great session you had with Tony…that you could stand without assistance? What about all the positive information you put out to your fans, all the publicity, is it all lies?"

"Yes." He stabbed at his communication again, this time ripping the page. "All lies."

I was relieved that the house wasn't filled with people as it usually was. The children were not yet home from school, and I threw myself in front of my Buddhist altar and began chanting through my sobs. I had nothing left—on every level I was depleted. The word *goner* loomed above everything.

Immediately I felt his left hand on my shoulder and heard the digital voice intone. "I'm sorry."

I knew how sorry he was. He knew I was. I cried as he pecked out a lengthy message. "I am glad you are all right. I am just feeling so low. But I am going to do better."

Where could I have gone in that moment to make it easier for him? Did he want me to say, "Yes, you are going to die"? I couldn't. There was nowhere to go with it, so we began making calls about the Broadway Benefit. Corporate money was hard to come by, and we were rank amateurs, always naïvely believing that if we just let the money people know how bad it was, they would sign over hundreds of thousands of dollars. Our goals had always been on the far side of reality. That was the way we were, both of us.

The December schedule was packed, which was the way Michael liked it. He had more work days at ABC and our Connecticut friends, Susan Monseurd, Teresa Hargrave, and Pete Gurney were mounting a fund-raising evening at the home of Rose and Bill Styron's on Saturday, December 12. We were both indebted to our computer angel, Barry Priest, and when Barry's wife asked Michael give a "talk" at Rutger's University on December 2, he was more than happy to say yes.

Thanksgiving and the week that followed had been so grueling that when I woke Saturday morning to a spring-like day, I decided to drive to Connecticut with Lily for the day. Michael urged me to take some time for myself and stay overnight. I wasn't sure I could handle being away overnight, but I said I'd consider it and check in with him later.

Lily and I had just returned from our walk on Welton Road and were sunning ourselves on the patio when the phone rang. It was Steve. He began by saying not to be alarmed, but Michael was in Roosevelt Hospital.

Somehow we got cut off, and, for the next twenty minutes, I tried to find someone at Roosevelt Hospital who could tell me what was going on. I was totally beside myself and about to get in the car and drive back when Steve called again. Michael had been short of breath and had called him to go to the hospital to get checked out. Steve assured me Michael was fine; in fact, Steve was chuckling because Michael had driven himself to the hospital on his red electric chair and had driven himself home. He relayed that Michael said there was no reason for me to be worried. Another blood gas test showed his oxygen level was normal.

I got in the car and drove back to the city.

Three days later, I came home from my office to find Paul exasperated and worried. Michael was stretched out resting on our bed. Paul whispered that he had "blacked out" while Paul was helping him in the bathroom. He had not fallen and had recovered almost instantly. When Paul said he was going to call the hospital, Michael ordered him not to. There was no way he was going to the hospital. He just needed to rest so he'd be in shape to go Rutgers that evening.

After Paul left, I crept into our bedroom and stood next to him. He seemed deep asleep. I watched his chest move evenly, and, after a few moments, I telephoned Dr. B downstairs, relaying what had happened. I asked him if he would come upstairs and check Michael. He told me to get Michael to the hospital.

I sat on the side of the bed next to him trying to decide what to do. He did not want to go to the hospital. I began to chant softly for his happiness. I would not go against his wishes.

I stayed there chanting for about twenty minutes. He woke up smiling. I gently wondered if he shouldn't be checked out at the hospital, but he insisted he felt fine and was ready to drive out to New Jersey for his appearance at Rutgers University.

I laughed with relief and the predictability of his response. I kissed him and told him he was crazy if he thought I was going to go along with an evening in New Jersey after what had happened. I had telephoned Barry to say we would have to reschedule.

Michael started to protest. He was perfectly up to sticking to the plan. When told him that rescheduling was no problem, he relented and even seemed relieved that I had imposed my "authority."

The next day was one of those amazing early December days where the birds are singing and spring is in the air. Michael and Tony had had an especially productive physical therapy session. Michael had taken several steps without support, and, to celebrate, he and Tony went into Riverside Park with the massage table and finished the three-hour workout there.

On top of that good news, Jay Lombard had received a telephone call from a scientist in California who had read an article about Michael and gleaned Jay's name from that. After a lengthy conversation, he faxed Jay a report on his successful stem cell treatments with AIDS patients. Jay was impressed with Dr. Z's science and his candor. Although he acknowledged modest success with several Parkinson's patients he volunteered that he had treated only one person with ALS and the benefits had been very limited and short-term.

Still, Jay thought it was worth looking into, so I called Dr. Z who promptly faxed hundreds of pages of research, which Michael devoured in one sitting. Of course it was a gamble, but according to Jay, the only downside was money. The stem cell treatments themselves were not dangerous. The cost for consecutive treatments over three days was high but not prohibitive. When compared with this healer's thousand-dollar-a-crack fee, it even seemed reasonable.

Dr. Z did not have access to the stem cells he needed in the United States and only performed the treatments in the Bahamas or Romania. He offered us an appointment in the Bahamas for the following Tuesday, December 8, and we grabbed it.

Always eager to get the best buy and make a deal, Michael told me to see if Dr. Z would reduce his fee. In turn, Michael would make Dr Z famous by acknowledging him at the ZazAngels' Broadway Theater Benefit. Dr. Z responded that, far from seeking fame or publicity, he would do anything to avoid it. He was frightened. As a scientist devoted to his work with stem cells he had to be vigilant.

I liked Dr. Z's honesty, which I later learned proved to be authentic. He told me that Pat Pepper and another ALS patient, Bill Barvin, were also going to the Bahamas. He openly discussed his reservations about treating ALS patients, acknowledging that the main hurdle with stem cells was the method of delivery and precisely where the injections should be made.

That Saturday evening I tucked Michael into bed, adjusting his pillow, placing the Breathe Right tape over his nose. We were excited about the stem cell treatment, and we were both laughing because I successfully slam-dunked a pile of dirty shirts into the hamper.

For the past week, I had been sleeping in the back room in Helena's loft bed because Michael's coughing and groaning had left me shaky with sleep deprivation. I longed to return to my place next to him, and tonight I was sure that would happen. Not only was he going to have a treatment with stem cells, but we were going to get away for a few days.

I leaned down to kiss him, and he took my hand squeezing it meaningfully. "This is the last night I'm sleeping in Helena's room," I teased. "I miss you. I'm coming back to our bed."

He bobbed his head the best he could.

"Tomorrow night," I promised.

I booked our flight for Tuesday, but, as we were eating breakfast the next morning Michael, still in high spirits, scribbled, "Call Donna at American

Airlines Special Services and see if we can get an upgrade. If we can't, let's use our miles."

I laughed. Some things didn't change. I made a note to call Donna and one to call Pat Pepper to see what hotel we should book. Michael was enjoying the eggs and sausage that we had ordered from Pier 72 across the street. I had ordered waffles with strawberries. My upbeat mood vanished and I was suddenly and inordinately irritated to find they had not included the strawberries. Michael was relishing his eggs. I whined and fumed, and he stopped eating to type something to the effect that I was ruining a beautiful day and why didn't I just call them so they could correct their error and send over some strawberries?

Maybe I continued griping because the list I was writing was getting out of hand and I felt overwhelmed by the complexities a trip to the Bahamas would entail. In any case, I continued fussing like a two year old until he got rightly pissed at me.

I *was* excited about the stem cell treatment. From all I had read, I believed that stem cells, and not necessarily fetal stem cells, were the medical miracle wave of the future. But my mind was reeling with everything that had to be done before we left.

I flew around the house so Helena and I could get out in time for her violin recital. I knew this was a painful moment for Michael, who would have given anything to be present when Helena played *La Folia*.

Recital days were always hectic, but with the Bahamas, and fund-raising, and trying to figure out a good plan for Marika and Helena in our absence, I was a spinning top. Paul Donevan had taken a full-time job, so Michael had asked me to call Kofi, the young man who had cared for his dad, to stay with him while we were out. Kofi came in as we were in the final stages of mania and about to leave.

As I gathered up Helena's violin, Michael turned up the volume of his computer. "Get me the checkbook."

I was literally out the door. "I'll get it when I come back."

"Get the checkbook!" boomed the digital voice. I grimaced, but part of me was once again amused at how the mechanical voice could take on his emotional state.

Checkbook? I searched my mind for where it might be. Why hadn't he asked me before I was on my way out? I dumped the contents of my purse onto the sofa, feeling his critical gaze on me. I wasn't good with checkbooks.

He was. I rummaged through the top drawer of my desk as he thrust an angry note at me.

"I was going to balance the checkbook. You have ruined my day."

How many things in my life do I have to be deeply thankful for? What follows is the one I am *most* thankful for. I had behaved like a jackass at breakfast. He was furious with me, and it would have been just like me to retaliate. For some reason a buoyancy came over me and I felt only love. I was in that moment, the way I have so often wished I had been able to be. My hand fell on the checkbook, and I put it on the table in front of him.

"Here it is. Don't be mad at me," I said. I put my arms around him and kissed the top of his head. When I returned from the violin recital two hours later his heart had stopped beating.

33

THE EASTER BUTTERFLY

"When a butterfly flutters its wings in one part of the world, it can eventually cause a hurricane in another..."

—*Chaos Theory*

The first "message from Michael" came the day of his memorial service at Riverside Chapel. Was it really a message? Did I make it up? Was the message an unconscious wish? Is there *proof*? I can only offer questions, without which there can be no answers.

Why was there something so familiar about the face of ALS?

Throughout my life, I have held a sweet memory of a tall, crippled boy who drooled and could not speak clearly like the rest of the children. I was barely three, the youngest and the smallest child in the half-day nursery school program my mother sent me to. Bobby King was the oldest and the biggest, and I loved him with all my heart. I clearly recall that I especially loved his drooling. I remember my mother laughing at me for prattling on and on about how great his drooling was. I gave drooling performances to make sure she got the picture.

Bobby was unique, and I was fascinated. He had trouble walking, and I led him around, protecting him from the innocent slander of other kids. Whenever possible, I invited him to our house after nursery school. My mother told me how much Bobby's parents appreciated my kindness. I didn't understand why. As far as I was concerned, Bobby King was the most special boy I had ever known—until I met Michael Zaslow.

The only other person I have known who drooled so proficiently was my husband. When Michael's drooling started, I was reminded of Bobby King, of the intensity and depth of my feelings for him. I loved him with a purity that was beyond words. It was the same inexplicable, magical, childlike love I felt for Michael.

My husband, the perfectionist, was far more attentive to details than I am. When I began the arduous task of wading through our financial affairs, one of the first things I did was call about a life insurance policy. He had taken out this particular policy on impulse only months before he had any symptoms of ALS—and felt extremely lucky to have done so. When I was told that the policy had been cancelled because of a missed payment, I did not even panic because I knew it could not be so. As chaotic as our life was in those last months, Michael would never have neglected such a detail. Also, I was sure we had never received the required notice of cancellation. The policy was for a very significant sum. Understandably, the insurance company would not pay without proof.

There was no proof. One of my theories was that since Michael received so much publicity, the company knew he had a terminal illness and that they would eventually have to pay. Perhaps they did not send a notice for the missing payment? It seemed highly unlikely that we would overlook both the notice for payment and the two cancellation notices, which are required prior to termination. Over the next year, I consulted lawyers, made numerous written appeals, solicited help from friends, and chanted for a positive outcome. Insurance companies are not known for flexibility and there was *no proof*, only my word that we had not received any notification of termination.

I struggled with depression, some days were better than others, but no day was without pain. Then, one morning, after about a week of severe depression, I woke up feeling not so bad. When one has been depressed, "not so bad" is a major improvement. As I left our building to take Lily to the park, I realized that I not only felt "not so bad," I felt good. As we headed down 73rd Street toward Riverside Park, I had the sense that Michael was hopping around, teasing me, and singing a song from *West Side Story*.

"Something's coming I don't know what it is but it is…going to be great!"

The sensation persisted. In my mind's eye, whatever that is, I saw him up ahead. He was dancing backwards so that he faced Lily and me as we walked. There was such a grin on his face, and the whole thing was so preposterous, that I laughed out loud and joined in singing.

It made no sense. Yesterday I had been miserable. Now I felt like dancing myself, like celebrating. I had not felt this good in so long, so I decided not to question the feeling but to see if I could make it last longer. After walking Lily, I bought a *Times* and took myself out to breakfast at Pier 72, something I almost never do. I indulged in a waffle with strawberries, and, when I returned home still chuckling over Michael's performance, there was a message on the answering machine. The insurance company had mailed out the check, and I would be receiving it in a few days.

Messages also arrived in the time-honored tactic of those communicating from the "other side"—flickering lights. The first flamboyant electrical display occurred six months after Michael's death in my dad's 1990 Oldsmobile as Marika and Helena and I were en route to Nantucket Island. It was our first vacation without Michael. Suddenly the radio came on and the lights blinked. We were all stunned, thinking the same thing, even Helena, who tends to be dubious about this sort of thing. The radio in my dad's car had never worked before—and has never worked since.

Invariably the lamp above our bed would flicker when I was in a particularly vulnerable state. Why did the lamp flicker sometimes but not consistently? I checked the wires. One night, the flickering developed into a game. I was weeping—morose—when the light literally went out for several seconds then came back on. This was the first time the light had remained off, not just flickering. I stopped crying. He had my attention. Just as I put my hand out to switch the light on again, it came on. Now I was overcome with emotion, his presence was palpable, but a damn light was not good enough. I wanted him. The light flickered. I glared at it. I waited and dared it to flicker again, pathetically testing the validity. Nothing.

"Go ahead," I said, feeling fairly ridiculous. The lamp glowed impassively. Disgruntled I got up to go to the bathroom. The moment my feet hit the floor the light flickered. I burst out laughing.

Another "light show" took place on the first Mother's Day after Michael's death. We were visiting Michael's friend Steve at Steve and Carrie's new home in Chappaqua. We were sitting at the dining room table, two-year-old Madison, Michael's goddaughter, was sitting to my right in the high chair that both Marika and Helena had used. Suddenly, all the lights in the kitchen went out. Steve laughed and said "Michael's here." Then, as if on cue, Madison leaned over and whispered in my ear, "Susan, I love you."

"What is it?" Carrie caught the look of amazement on my face. We all knew Madison and I got along great, but her declaration of love was something neither Steve nor Carrie had seen before.

In May of 1999, just one year after Michael and I had met with Speaker of the House Gingrich as part of ALS Advocacy Day, I decided to make the trip to Washington. Although Michael had been walking at the time, he had reluctantly agreed to use a wheelchair. I had the idea that the ALS Association could dramatize the sense of urgency if I appeared pushing an empty wheelchair.

As Advocacy Day drew closer, I began having second thoughts. Did I really want to put myself through such agony? I was still raw inside. Considering how I had felt last year facing a room filled with PALS, how could I deal with it now? I called Dorine Gordon and told her I had reconsidered. She understood.

Then I got a message. *"You have to go."* Here was Michael inside my head badgering me just as he had done before the Memorial service. I was having a hard enough time getting through each day, let alone pushing an empty wheelchair. I was not a masochist.

"You have to go to Washington." His voice yammered away inside my head.

I tried to ignore it. In addition to the emotional pain it would cost me, there were a dozen of other good reasons, having to do with work and children why I should not go. Whenever I would let my guard down, he would start in, *"You have to go. You have to go. You have to go."* Two days before Advocacy Day he played his trump card.

"You have to go to Washington because you will see me there."

I knew I was living on very shaky emotional ground, and I did not find this particular message amusing. I had a difficult enough time accepting thoughts as messages, and now I was going to "see" him. If I was making this up, I was in trouble. Of course I was not going to "see" him. I wasn't crazy.

"Yeah, yeah, yeah. You have to go. I promise, you will see me. Keep your eyes open. You have to go. I'll be there!"

The teasing, nagging style was definitely his, and, as usual, I eventually caved in. I took the train to D.C. with our good friend and godmother to Marika and Helena, Liz Perry. I confided in Liz, adding that I thought I might be losing my mind.

We were met at Union Station by someone from the local ALS chapter who had secured a wheelchair for me to push, and we headed toward the Capitol steps where the first press conference was scheduled. For the second year

PALS from all across the country had travelled to our nation's capitol to lobby their representation on behalf of ALS. I recognized PALS in wheelchairs and PALS on respirators who had been present the year before. Michael had appeared so much stronger, and yet the disease had claimed him first. Why?

Senator Robert Torricelli who sponsored this year's Bill spoke, as did various other dignitaries. I kept looking around for Michael, all the while reminding myself that there was no way I would see him. The Capitol steps were in the distance. I imagined him doing a tap number down the steps, but it was only my imagination. After the press conference, I wheeled the empty wheelchair behind the throng of ALS advocates, still alert to a "sighting."

Liz and I spent the night with friends, and I fell asleep easily for once. The next morning I attended a breakfast briefing, which was held prior to breaking up into lobbying delegations. Michael's super fan, Teresa Brown, had made the trip, and, although she was from West Virginia, she joined our New York delegation so we could catch up.

I had stopped keeping my eye out for Michael and was chatting with Teresa when Dorine Gordon signaled that our delegation was about to begin the trek to the Senate. As we started out, I caught my breath. Included in our delegation was a tall, lean, dark-haired man with a wide, friendly grin. While he was not as drop-dead handsome as Michael, he emanated the same boyish charisma that drew people to my husband.

This was the Bill Barvin we would have met had Michael lived to go to the Bahamas. According to Bill and his wife Lynn Casaritti, Bill had shown significant improvement in his speech immediately after the stem cell treatment. Unfortunately, his speech had then deteriorated. Dr. Z had refunded their money!

I recognized in Bill Barvin the same intrepid, playful spirit that had drawn me to Michael. Throughout the day of lobbying, thanks to his understanding wife, Lynn, I walked at Bill's side. Bill's long strides reminded me of Michael, as did his humor and his politics—the way he walked into a room and made himself at home. I felt as if I was quite miraculously spending the day with Michael.

I seemed to know Bill and Lynn, and, as the relationships continued after that initial meeting, each detail I learned about their lives felt more like a rediscovery, something I had already known. Bill was a joy, he loved to eat, and he loved to dance; he was a free spirit, a man with his arms open wide to life. Like Michael, he was larger than life. I was honored to have Bill by my side on the stage of the Richard Rodgers Theater in 2000 for our second

ZazAngels Theater Benefit, *Tuesdays with Morrie*. By then, less than a year after our first meeting, he had had a tracheotomy and was in a wheelchair. Lynn was backstage suctioning him before we went out. Because he could no longer speak, I read his message to the audience, a message of hope and determination.

The connection I felt for Bill and Lynn strengthened my commitment to finding a cure for ALS. It also confirmed the growing conviction that there was a deeper meaning to Michael's life and his death. I should add, a deeper meaning to everyone's life and death. Messages from Michael were everywhere, and I was more inclined to accept them since meeting Bill.

My friend Liz had told me about James Van Praagh, a psychic who she had seen contacting people "on the other side" during *The Larry King Show*. I called *The Larry King Show* and ordered a copy of the tape. From the day the tape arrived, every plan I made to watch it was somehow foiled. I would bring the tape to Connecticut where ostensibly I had time to watch it on the weekend, but then "something" would happen. I would invariably leave the tape behind, so that when I had a window of opportunity in New York, the tape would be in the country or vice versa. This went on for over a year. I had lugged the thing around for so long, several times I lost track of where it was. It got to be funny. The message seemed to be: It's not the right time to see the James Van Praagh tape.

In July 2000 with Helena away at camp and Marika working in the city, I had an opportunity to go to Connecticut by myself. As I was packing, my hand fell on the tape. Obviously, I had overlooked it since it was in a desk drawer I had gone through countless times. Nevertheless, I took this as "a message" and tucked it safely in my purse. This was finally the right time.

When I arrived in Connecticut, there was a message waiting from Dorine Gordon of the ALS Association. I did not have to call her back to know why she had called. Instinctively I knew. Bill had died. He had passed as soundlessly and unexpectedly as Michael had.

It seemed entirely fitting that after over a year I finally viewed the elusive tape on July 6, the evening of Bill's death. The format of the show consisted of viewers calling in. Giving only their name and location Van Praagh would intuit whom they wished to contact. Most often he referred to the spirit by name followed by a rapid-fire, dazzling display of identifying information, including when and how the "the spirit" had died. The message I had been waiting for came from the third caller, a woman devastated and filled with guilt over the untimely death of her husband. Van Praagh responded that the "decision to leave" came from her husband who could no longer communicate or move about "on this plane." After offering several highly specific identifying details, he promised the woman that her husband was finally free and able now to work on behalf of those who suffered from the same paralyzing disease that had claimed him in the "prime of his life."

"He wants you to know that he is happy. You could not do any more than you did." Van Praagh's words became a litany and at first they were a balm that eased the predictable eruptions of regret. As time passed I became immune to their healing power. I hungered for another message.

At dusk one evening later that summer, Lily and I were walking on a deserted Welton Road. As much as I loved being in the country, I was often lonely. I was virtually cutoff from people who had been our steady social community. I had thought many times of selling the house, but I loved it as Michael had, and the children loved it. The rage erupted. I knew my life would never be as wonderful as it had been with Michael. Michael was cheated out of his life. Marika and Helena cheated out of their dad. We had been cheated out of almost half of our life together.

"Why?" I cried out loud "Why did our life end like this?"

The answer was swift and unequivocal. "This time. Our life ended like this…this time. This time. It was *only* this time." The message was clear: we had been together before, we would again.

I was, as recovery parlance goes, "doing better." Doing better meant that by 2002, more minutes or hours could go by without the sickening ache of loss. Attacks of despair were less frequent, and I was grateful that time was working its reputed wonders. But though they were not as frequent, when an attack came, it could occur with the same violent, crushing ferocity that followed Michael's death. The whims of time were unpredictable and uncanny.

On Good Friday of 2002, I knew that I would not be able to continue living with such pain. There appeared to be no end to it. Loss was not something to outgrow. Someone commented: "You mean your husband died four years ago and you're still not over it?" It's because I'm weak, I sometimes thought, because I'm neurotic and always have been, because I'm prone to existential obsessing and depression, because my serotonin is sketchy.

That the attacks were less frequent was a cruel deceit, I thought as I trudged along Welton Road with Lily galloping ahead. I could be seized at any moment with the horrible finality of never hearing him laugh, never seeing him walking towards me, touching, tasting, or arguing with me. What did it matter if there were good moments; it always came back to the same dark, malignant hole. I was exhausted from clawing my way out.

April 13, Good Friday, there was misty rain and I could scarcely see out of my rain streaked, teary glasses. Off to my left, a butterfly was bopping along. There are no butterflies in Connecticut in April. I took off my glasses and found a dry corner of my sweatshirt. The butterfly was a few feet ahead of me. I was healed—shot with joy. This was the most amazing message. I forgot the malignant, black hole and quickened my pace to keep up with the undulating butterfly. I walked all the way to the end of Welton Road and back to where the car was. Sometimes the butterfly would disappear into the woods, but then it would flutter out at me.

Despite feeling that this was something of a miracle, I was greedy for more. I challenged the message from Michael. If this was to be taken seriously, I thought, there is one more test. If I go further into the woods, where I have never in twenty years seen a butterfly, and I see a butterfly when I come out of the woods, I will have *proof*.

Lily and I continued deep into the woods. For about fifteen minutes, I threw sticks into the stream for her to fetch. When we came out of the woods into the parking area, I was feeling ashamed for making the test so impossible, for my lack of faith and gratitude.

I looked down. There in front of me was the butterfly. It was not fluttering. It was standing still on the road and it did not move. I went closer. Lily was zipping all around, but the butterfly did not move. I knelt down, not believing that this was really happening. I had never been so close to a still butterfly. Only inches away I could see his eyes. We stayed there on the muddy road for several minutes looking at each other.

On Monday after the Easter weekend, we were back in New York City. Mid-morning, as I usually did, I went out into the hall to pick up my mail. Gazing at me from a window in a large envelope was a butterfly with the quote: "When a butterfly flutters its wings in one part of the world, it can eventually cause a hurricane in another." The envelope was addressed to Michael Zaslow.

There are other butterfly stories and messages too numerous to mention. How many, I wonder, would it take, to constitute unshakable *proof*?

I was in Connecticut, quite near the completion of the book. I had targeted June 7, our wedding anniversary, as my goal for completion, but I was not going to make it. I wasn't feeling bad because of that; I knew I would soon be finished. I was just feeling desperate and sad—back in the malignant hole.

There had been upsetting problems with Helena, and I was missing Michael even more. I was so wishing he could be in Helena's life to ease the pain of adolescence, academic pressures, and the challenges she faced with ADD and recently diagnosed bi-polar disorder. I was wishing he could hear Marika laughing for the first time in so many years and see how strong and politically fearless she had become as a Sarah Lawrence student. I woke with the thought: I'm depressed.

I lay in bed, considering. There were reasons for my depression on this rainy morning. I enumerated them, to reassure myself. "Don't worry," I told myself. "You can take care of these problems. They are real enough problems, but you will manage, just as you have."

The words I gave to myself steadied me somewhat, but the ache and emptiness did not shift until I heard other words inside my head.

"Don't worry, S. It will be fine. You have friends in high places."

I laughed out loud as my feet hit the floor.

ABOUT THE AUTHORS

Susan Hufford, M.A., C.S.W., is the author of over twenty books, including *Miracles* for EP Dutton. She appeared on television and on Broadway where she met her husband, Michael Zaslow in *Fiddler On The Roof*. She is also a practicing psychotherapist with a private clinical practice in Manhattan. She serves as a Trustee on the National Board of the ALS Association. As president of Michael Zaslow's ZazAngels she has produced five Broadway Theater benefits, raising funds for ALS research.

Emmy Award winning actor Michael Zaslow created daytime television's ultimate villain, Roger Thorpe, on *Guiding Light* and the romantic conductor, David Renaldi, on ABC's *One Life to Live*. Michael appeared in numerous films and Broadway shows including *Fiddler on the Roof* and *Cat on a Hot Tin Roof*. After his diagnosis of ALS he formed Michael Zaslow's ZazAngels to raise awareness and funds for ALS research. For more information please go to www.michaelzaslow.com.

ACKNOWLEDGMENTS

It is with great pleasure and profound respect that I acknowledge the National ALS Association. Since Michael and I were first involved with ALSA in 1997, the organization has transformed itself into an efficient, creative, innovative, tirelessly energetic and compassion entity which, as President, Gary A. Leo likes to say: "….is working to go out of business. To Allen Finklestein, Alan R. Griffith, Dorine Gordon, Diane Winokur, and all those who serve on the National Board of Trustees, as well as on the board of the ALS Association Greater New York Chapter, I am deeply honored to be down in the trenches with the likes of you! Andy, I love you so much, and Chris and Adele, you are my heroes. Dear Amy, you are beyond magic, the best of bodhisattvas. Lynda, Mimi, Ann, Nancy, Susan, Teresa and Teresa, Kelly, MaryLou, Nanette, CCCMcW, Judith, Richard, Marti…how did I manage to have such loving and faithful friends?

I thank Barbi Zakin for always going the extra miles. I thank Ellen Levine for years of friendship and the editorial insight to see how this book could fall into place. Our next door neighbors, Richard, Diane, Julia, and Rachel, for being with us through so much.

Finally, I could not have survived without Nam Myoho Renge Kyo, without the encouragement of my Buddhist friends in the (SGI) Soka Gakki International, without the absolute promise from Nichiren Daishonin that "To conceive of life and death as separate realities is to be caught in the illusion of birth and death. It is deluded and inverted thinking. When we examine the nature of life with perfect enlightenment, we find there is no beginning marking birth, and, therefore, no end signifying death." I am grateful to SGI President, Daisaku Ikeda for devoting his life to world peace, for introducing this Buddhist practice to people in 189 countries and for reminding us of our inter-connectedness with this earth and with all people and that boundless joy comes from compassion and reaching out to others.

231

"When a tree has been transplanted, though fierce winds may blow, it will not topple if it has a firm stake to hold it up. But even a tree that has grown up in place may fall over if its roots are weak. Even a feeble person will not stumble if those supporting him are strong, but a person of considerable strength, when alone, may fall down on an uneven path."

—The Writings of Nichiren Daishonin

ALS RESOURCES

Michael Zaslow was diagnosed with ALS in 1997, the same year the ALS Association's Advocacy office was established in Washington, D.C. Since then, federal funding for ALS research has increased by almost 300 percent, from about $15.1 million to about 44 million. This is remarkable for an orphan disease like ALS and it is a tribute to the ALS Association, Steve Gibson and his Washington staff, and to the tireless energy of PALS (People with ALS) and their families.

ALSA (ALS Association) has helped to establish a special funding mechanism in the Department of the Defense that will shed more light on the environmental factors of the disease. The Peer Reviewed Medical Program at the Department of Defense has awarded a total of $3.8 million for ALS research over the past two years. Because of these efforts, ALS is one of two diseases for which the Medicare twenty-four-month waiting period has been eliminated.

Today, drugs can slow the progression of some symptoms and there is real hope that the more than one hundred research projects under way right now will bring not only more treatments, but means of prevention...and a cure.

ALSA is the only national not-for-profit voluntary health organization dedicated solely to the fight against ALS. ALSA's mission is to find a cure for ALS and to improve the lives of those living with the disease.

Through the national office and its growing network of chapters and support groups throughout the country, ALSA wages battle against ALS through four primary programs:

- Patient and Community Services

- Education and Awareness

- Advocacy

- Research

WHAT IS ALS?

Amyotrophic lateral sclerosis (ALS), also known as "Lou Gehrig's disease," is a progressive, fatal neuro-degenerative disease that attacks the nerve cells and pathways in the brain and spinal cord that control voluntary muscle movement. When these nerve cells die, the brain's ability to initiate and control muscle movement dies with them. With all voluntary muscle movement affected, patients in the later stages of ALS are totally paralyzed. Yet, through it all, the mental faculties of most patients are not affected. The mind remains sharp despite the progressive degeneration of the body. Other important facts about ALS are the following:

- ALS occurs throughout the world with no racial, ethnic or socioeconomic boundaries.

- ALS is not contagious.

- More people die every year of ALS than of multiple sclerosis (MS).

- Approximately 5,600 people in the U.S. are newly diagnosed with ALS each year.

- It is estimated that as many as 30,000 Americans may have the disease at any given time.

- Every 90 minutes another person dies from ALS.

- Most who develop ALS are between the ages of 40 and 70, although there have been numerous cases of the disease attacking persons in their twenties and thirties. Men and women are affected in nearly equal numbers.

- There are two types of ALS, **sporadic** and **familial** (inherited).

  – Sporadic ALS is the most common type. It may affect anyone, anywhere.

  – Up to 10% of ALS is familial, occurring more than once in a family lineage.

- No single test or procedure exists to conclusively establish a diagnosis of ALS. It is only through a clinical examination and series of diagnostic tests, that rule out other diseases that mimic ALS, that a diagnosis can be established.

- The onset of ALS is insidious, with muscle weakness or stiffness as early symptoms. These symptoms are followed by inevitable wasting and paralysis of the muscles of the limbs and trunk as well as those that control vital functions such as speech, swallowing and even breathing. When the muscles that support breathing are affected, ALS patients need permanent ventilator support to survive.

- The life expectancy of an ALS patient averages two to five years from the time of diagnosis. Half of those with ALS live three years or more, 20% live five years or more, and up to 10% survive more than ten years.

- The cause, cure or means of prevention of ALS is unknown.

Current treatment is aimed at symptomatic relief, prevention of complications, and maintenance of maximum optimal function and quality of life. In advanced stages of the disease, round-the-clock management is required by nurses and family members for patients who are functionally quadriplegic and bedridden.

The financial cost to families of persons with ALS is exceedingly high. In the advanced stages, ALS care can cost up to $200,000 a year. A family's life savings can be quickly depleted due to the extraordinary cost involved in the care of the ALS patient.

CERTIFIED ALSA CENTERS

The following clinical facilities have been certified by the ALS Association (ALSA) as having met rigorous standards of quality care for ALS patients. Each has a multidisciplinary team approach to provide a continuum of care and an appropriate diagnostic standard of quality care regardless of race, creed, or color.

To locate the center nearest you please go to the ALSA website: www.alsa.org.

ARIZONA

Mayo Clinic Scottsdale

13400 E. Shea Blvd.
Scottsdale, AZ 85259-5404
Phone: (480) 301-8000
Fax (480) 301-8451
E. Peter Bosch, MD - Medical Director

Mayo Clinic Scottsdale

13400 E. Shea Blvd.
Scottsdale, AZ 85259-5404
Phone: (480) 301-8000
Fax (480) 301-8451
Mark A. Ross, M.D. - Medical Director

CALIFORNIA

Forbes Norris ALS Research Center
California Pacific Medical Center

2324 Sacramento Street
San Francisco, CA 94115
Phone: (415) 923-3604
Fax (415) 673-5184
Deborah Gelinas, MD - Medical Director

The ALS Center at the University of California, San Francisco

350 Parnassus Avenue, Suite 500
San Francisco, CA 94117
Phone: (415) 476-7581
Fax (415) 502-4868
Richard K. Olney, MD - Medical Director
http://www.ucsf.edu/brain/als/

CONNECTICUT

Motor Neuron Disease Clinic of Connecticut

University of Connecticut Health Center
263 Farmington Avenue
Farmington, CT 06030
Phone: (860) 679-4888
Fax (860) 679-1042
Kevin Felice, DO - Medical Director

DISTRICT OF COLUMBIA

George Washington University

Department of Neurology-ALS & MS Centers
2150 Pennsylvania Ave., NW, 7-401
Washington, DC 20037
Phone: (202) 741-2700
Fax (202) 741-2721
Raul N. Mandler, MD - Medical Director
http://gwdocs.com/p1725.html

NEW MEXICO

University of New Mexico
School of Medicine
Department of Neurology
915 Camino de Salud, N.E.
Albuquerque, NM 87131-5821
Phone: (505) 272-3342
Fax (505) 272-6692
John E. Chapin, MD - Medical Director
http://hsc.unm.edu/neuro/gordon.html

NEW YORK

Beth Israel Medical Center
Phillips Ambulatory Care Center

10 Union Square East
New York, NY 10003
Phone: (212) 720-3050
Fax (212) 844-8481
Daniel J. MacGowan, MD - Medical Director
http://ALS-NY.org

Beth Israel Medical Center
Phillips Ambulatory Care Center

10 Union Square East
New York, NY 10003
Phone: (212) 720-3050
Fax (212) 844-8481
Stephen Scelsa, MD - Medical Director
http://ALS-NY.org

NORTH CAROLINA

Wake Forest Baptist Medical Center
ALS Center
Department of Neurology
3rd Floor, Meads Hall
Medical Center Boulevard
Winston-Salem, NC 27157-1078
Phone: (336) 716-9056
Fax (336) 716-9489
Peter D. Donofrio, MD - Medical Director

OHIO

Center for ALS and Related Disorders
Department of Neurology
The Cleveland Clinic Foundation
9500 Euclid Avenue
Cleveland, OH 44195
Phone: (216) 444-5559
Fax (216) 445-4653
Erik P. Pioro, MD, PhD, FRCP - Medical Director
http://www.clevelandclinic.org/neurology/treat/als.htm

PENNSYLVANIA

The ALS Center at The Penn Neurological
Institute of The University of Pennsylvania

330 S. Ninth Street
Philadelphia, PA 19107
Phone: (215) 829-3053
Fax (215) 829-6606
Leo McCluskey, MD - Medical Director

The ALS Clinic at Penn State Milton S. Hershey
Medical Center

Division of Neurology
500 University Drive
Hershey, PA 17033
Phone: (717) 531-1802
Fax (717) 531-4694
Zachary Simmons, MD - Medical Director
http://www.als-phila.org/services/hershey.htm

TEXAS

UTHSCSA- Department of Neurology
South Texas ALS Clinic

7703 Floyd Curl Drive
San Antonio, TX 78284-7883
Phone: (210) 567-1945
Fax (210) 567-1948
Carlayne E. Jackson, MD - Medical Director
http://www.alsa-south-tx.org

VERMONT

ALS Clinical Department of Neurology
University of Vermont College of Medicine

C225A Given Building
89 Beaumont Avenue
Burlington, VT 05404
Phone: (802) 847-1613
Fax   (802) 847-4190
Rup Tandan, MD, FRCP, MRCP - Medical Director

Chapters

ALSA chapters located throughout 21 states help to carry out the mission and activities of ALSA a local level. Subject to their agreements with the ALS Association, ALSA chapters are tartered as autonomous with their own accountability. As such, chapters develop independent and raising and membership campaigns to support patient service and public education rograms and the nationally directed research program.

ALSA Chapter Locations

Arizona
- Valley of the Sun Chapter
  Phoenix, Arizona
- Southern Arizona Chapter
  Tucson, Arizona

California
- Orange County Chapter
  Huntington Beach, California
- Greater Los Angeles Chapter
  Los Angeles, California
- Greater Sacramento Chapter
  Sacramento, California
- Bay Area Chapter
  San Francisco, California

Colorado
- Rocky Mountain Chapter
  Denver, Colorado

Connecticut
- Connecticut Chapter
  Westport, Connecticut

District of Columbia
- National Capital Area Chapter
  Washington, D.C.

Florida
- Southern Florida Chapter
  Margate, Florida
- Tampa Bay Chapter
  Tampa, Florida

Georgia
- Georgia Chapter
  Marietta, Georgia

Indiana
- Indiana, Chapter in Organization
  Indianapolis, Indiana

Kansas
- Keith Worthington Center
  Kansas City, Kansas/Missouri

Massachusetts
- Massachusetts Chapter
  Wakefield (Boston), Massachusetts

Michigan
- ALS of Michigan, Inc.
  Detroit, Michigan
- West Michigan Chapter
  Grand Rapids, Michigan

Minnesota
- Minnesota Chapter
  Minneapolis, Minnesota

Missouri
- Greater St. Louis Chapter
  St. Louis, Missouri

New York
- Greater New York Chapter
  New York, New York

North Carolina
- North Carolina Chapter
  Raleigh-Durham, North Carolina

Ohio
- Northeast Ohio Chapter
  Canton (Cleveland), Ohio
- Western Ohio Chapter
  Columbus, Ohio

Pennsylvania
- Greater Philadelphia Chapter
  Philadelphia, Pennsylvania
- Western Pennsylvania Chapter
  Pittsburgh, Pennsylvania

Rhode Island
- Rhode Island Chapter
  Warwick, Rhode Island

Tennessee
- Central Tennessee Chapter
  Columbia, Tennessee

Texas
- Dallas/Fort Worth, Chapter in Organization
  Arlington, Texas
- South Texas Chapter
  San Antonio, Texas

Wisconsin
- Southeast Wisconsin Chapter
  Milwaukee, Wisconsin

Freestanding Support Groups

. addition to ALSA chapters, the following freestanding support groups provide a local link to :rsons with ALS:

Alabama
- Central Alabama Support Group
  Birmingham, Alabama
- North Alabama Support Group
  Elkmont, Alabama

California
- San Joaquin Support Group
  Modesto, California
- Santa Barbara Support Group
  Santa Barbara, California
- Central Coast Support Group
  Santa Maria, California
- Santa Rosa Support Group
  Santa Rosa, California
- Santa Ynez/Solvang Support Group
  Santa Ynez, California
- San Bernadino County Support Group
  Victorville, California

Connecticut
- Southeast Connecticut Support Group
  Uncesville, Connecticut

Florida
- Orlando Support Group
  Casselberry, Florida
- Northwest Florida Support Group
  Crestview, Florida
- Ocala/Marion County Support Group
  Ocala, Florida
- Palm Beach Support Group
  Palm Beach, Florida
- Tallahassee Support Group
  Tallahassee, Florida
- Brevard/Indian River Counties Support Group
  Vero Beach, Florida

Illinois
- South Chicago Support Group
  Chicago, Illinois
- Quad Cities/Easter Seal Support Group
  Moline, Illinois
- Springfield Support Group
  Springfield, Illinois

Iowa
- Southeast Iowa/West Central Illinois Support Group
  Burlington, Iowa

Nebraska
- Nebraska Support Group
  Lincoln, Nebraska

New Mexico
- Greater Albuquerque Support Group
  Albuquerque, New Mexico

New York
- Upstate New York Support Group
  Albany, New York
- Buffalo New York Support Group
  Williamsville, New York

North Dakota
- North Dakota Region VI Support Group
  Jamestown, North Dakota

Oklahoma
- Northeast Oklahoma Support Group
  Broken Arrow, Oklahoma
- Southwest Oklahoma Support Group
  Cement, Oklahoma

Oregon
- Southwest Oregon Support Group
  Medford, Oregon

Puerto Rico
- Puerto Rico Support Group
  San Juan, Puerto Rico

South Carolina
- South Carolina Midlands Support Group
  Columbia, South Carolina
- Upstate South Carolina Support Group
  Taylor, South Carolina

Tennessee
- Volunteer State Support Group
  Friendsville, Tennessee

Texas
- San Angelo Support Group
  San Angelo, Texas

Utah
- Northern Utah Support Group
  Roy, Utah

Vermont
- Vermont Support Group
  Burlington, Vermont

Virginia
- Blue Ridge Support Group
  Palmyra, Virginia
- Richmond Support Group
  Richmond, Virginia

Washington
- Western Washington Support Group
  Kent, Washington
- Kitsap County Support Group
  Silverdale, Washington

Wisconsin
- Northwest Wisconsin Support Group
  Chippewa Falls, Wisconsin

For more information contact: The ALS Association National Office

27001 Agoura Road, Suite 150

Calabasas Hills, CA

91301-5104

1-800-782-4747

(818)-880-9007

Information and Referral: (800) 782-4747

Website: www.alsa.org

978-0-595-34050-7
0-595-34050-4

Printed in the United States
55849LVS00004B/256-270

9 780595 340507